Dad,   Ch

from Richard

REMEMBERING HENRY

REMEMBERING HENRY

edited by
Stephen Lock and Heather Windle

Published by the British Medical Association
Tavistock Square, London WC1H 9JR

Preface

"Why, man, he doth bestride the narrow world
Like a Colossus; and we petty men
Walk under his huge legs, and peep about
To find ourselves dishonourable graves."

Julius Caesar

I met Henry Miller properly only once, at a garden party in Sydney. There, gazing down through the trees where the sails of Utzon's opera house were beginning to rise, was a glum, but unmistakable, figure. The glumness turned out to be jet-lag, and disappeared as soon as I introduced the topical subject of large versus small hospitals of the future. His reaction was even brisker when I told him of the then Health Minister's reply to my question: "Why not try building one city hospital and see what happens?" "It seems an expensive way of proving Professor Miller wrong," Kenneth Robinson had said. Next day, at the Australian Medical Conference, there was no glumness, real or apparent. Henry Miller gave a sparkling performance, in a lecture on "How many doctors?" with wit, learning, and style.

What was the secret of the man? He himself would have been the first to admit that his contributions to academic neurology were relatively modest; his influence on the Newcastle Medical School limited; and his effect on the university restricted by his illness and early death. Yet thousands of doctors and laymen knew him as a magical figure and a great man.

The answer does not lie merely in Henry Miller's undoubted solid achievements—his deep love of patients, the Newcastle department of neurology, the teaching, the writing, the talks. It lies principally in style. The British are suspicious of intellectuals and conceptual arguments; but they love a clown. Henry Miller used his wit and keen intelligence to put over new ideas and to get them accepted: judged merely by the absence of student unrest at Newcastle University, his achievements were remarkable.

The obvious comparison that springs to mind—a man greatly admired by Henry himself, and mentioned by several contributors to this anthology—is Sir Thomas Beecham, and it is no accident that this book closely resembles *Beecham Remembered*, the tribute published last year. Like Henry Miller, Beecham wore his learning lightly, in subjects other than his own as well. Like him, too, he had style and swagger. I remember arriving at Waverley Station early one summer morning in the bleak weather which often goes with the Edinburgh Festival. There

vii

on the adjacent platform outside a line of sleeping cars was Sir Thomas, clad in a silk dressing gown, smoking a long cigar, and talking to the assembled reporters of the iniquities of Covent Garden, with which he was then having a feud. The next night I sat behind the orchestra for *Harold in Italy*. During the long pianissimo in the second movement the second trumpet dropped his mute and leant down to pick it up. "Leave that bloody thing alone," hissed Sir Thomas in a voice that could be heard at the back of the Usher Hall. I know few people who could have got away with holding a press conference at 7.30 am or destroying the magic of Berlioz in that way, but Beecham and Henry Miller certainly could.

Readers will get a fuller idea of the breadth, character, and greatness of the man from the contributions we have assembled here, and Heather Windle and I thank them all for their time and trouble, as well as the Editors of the *Lancet* and the *British Journal of Hospital Medicine* for permission to reprint two articles. We have tried to get a cross-section of friends and colleagues, but the choice was so large that to our great regret we have had to leave many uninvited.

In particular, Eileen Miller and John Walton helped greatly in planning this book, which we hope is a fitting tribute to a great man and lovable character—though what he would have said about the project would have filled another book.

Stephen Lock
Editor, *British Medical Journal*

June 1977

Contents

Henry George Miller 1913–1976

3 December 1913   Born at Chesterfield, Derbyshire.
At school he studied English, French, and History in the sixth form but switched to medicine and was a medical student at the Newcastle College of Medicine (University of Durham) from 1931.

1937–war   Graduated, held house appointments at the Royal Victoria Infirmary, Newcastle upon Tyne, and went for a year to Johns Hopkins Department of Pathology in Baltimore. Then did six months as house physician at the Hospital for Sick Children, Great Ormond Street.

1940–2   Proceeded MD and MRCP. Working under Professor F J Nattrass became particularly interested in neurology.

1942 and war   Married Eileen Cathcart Baird, MRCOG. They had two sons and two daughters. Served in the RAFVR, first as general duties medical officer with Bomber Command, and then as a neurological specialist. Acquired DPM in 1943.

Postwar   Further training at the National Hospital, Queen Square, and the Hammersmith Hospital. In 1947 returned to the Royal Victoria Infirmary, Newcastle upon Tyne, in Professor Nattrass's department and further developed his interest in neurology.

1953   Elected FRCP.

1961   Appointed Reader in Neurology.

1962   Clinical sub-dean and instrumental in launching a new medical curriculum at the university.

1963   Sir Edwin Tooth visiting Professor of Medicine in Brisbane General Hospital, University of Queensland.

1963–6   On establishment of University of Newcastle upon Tyne became its first Public Orator.

1964	Visiting Professor of Neurology in San Francisco. Made Professor of Neurology of University of Newcastle upon Tyne. At this time he was described as a "highly unsuccessful fisherman and an almost excessively humane shot and his hobbies were collection of pictures, motor cars, restaurants, opera performances, and a cosmopolitan staff (*University of Newcastle upon Tyne Medical Gazette*, December 1964).
1965	Secretary-General-Treasurer of the World Federation of Neurology.
1966	Appointed Dean of Medicine at University of Newcastle upon Tyne.
1967	Director/Chairman of BMA Planning Unit until 1970. Chairman of Medical Panel of the Multiple Sclerosis Society of Great Britain and Northern Ireland.
1968	Appointed Vice-Chancellor of University of Newcastle upon Tyne. He was consultant neurologist to the Ministry of Social Security and a member of the Medical Appeal and Mental Health Tribunals, the GMC, Association of Physicians of Great Britain, and Association of British Neurologists. An Honorary Foreign Member of the American and French Neurological Societies, he was also Honorary Clinical Adviser to the Demyelinating Diseases Research Unit of the MRC.
1971	Visiting professorship in Canada.
1974	John Rowan Wilson award for medical journalism and, in particular, *Medicine in Society*.
25 August 1976	Died in Newcastle upon Tyne at the age of 62.

Compiled by Heather Windle

Introduction

I first met Henry Miller when, on my return to Newcastle from
Army service in 1949, I was appointed to a medical registrarship in the
Royal Victoria Infirmary and found myself working in that capacity
with him (as assistant physician) and with Dr A G Ogilvie. Life was full
of excitement in those days, not least because of the remarkable attributes
of both men, so totally different in personality and style and yet so
effective and inspiring to an eager young doctor, anxious to learn. We
worked hard because both chiefs set high standards and expected much
of their juniors in very different ways; but there was also, between times,
a great deal of fun to be derived from the friendly and endless repartee
between Henry and "The Og." Thus Dr Ogilvie, witnessing an attractive young blonde in one of his female beds, remarked that this must be
one of Dr Miller's patients and moved on. And on yet another occasion,
being aware of Henry's openly-professed left-wing leanings, he said,
"Ah Miller, I saw a patient yesterday who was complaining of walking
to the right; I would have sent him to you but I thought you were only
interested in those who walked to the left."

This was an era when Henry, active in clinical work, in teaching,
writing, and in clinical research, was also engaged in building up an
immense private practice. Known locally in his own registrar days just
before the war, because of his elegance, as Henry "Gorgeous" Miller,
even in 1950 he often dressed in black jacket, grey waistcoat, and striped
trousers with a carnation in the buttonhole, and, as he taught a class of
students at the bedside, the "Geordie" in the next bed was heard to
say, "What a toff, I wonder what he wears on Sundays?"

Now that he is no longer with us, memories come crowding in,
tinged with affection, with respect, and with deep regret that we shall
not again be able to enjoy his lively company, to benefit from his
wisdom and his inspiration. The knowledge that my own career was
largely moulded by him; that I forsook my earlier intention to become
a paediatrician as a consequence of his influence; and that I followed
him first into consultant work in neurology, then into a personal chair,
and later became dean of medicine constantly reminds me of the debt I
owe him and of the way in which he shaped my career. It is, therefore,
a signal honour to have been invited to introduce this volume of
reminiscences of a great man. Perhaps I may be forgiven for quoting

I

Introduction

verbatim the obituary notice which I wrote for the *British Medical Journal* soon after his untimely death, as reproduced and slightly expanded, with the kind permission of the editor and publishers, in the *Journal of the Neurological Sciences*:

"Henry Miller was a dedicated North-Easterner throughout his life and was one of the most distinguished graduates of the Newcastle upon Tyne College of Medicine in the University of Durham. After house officer posts in Newcastle and a period of training in pathology in the Johns Hopkins Hospital in Baltimore and following a brief flirtation with paediatrics under the influence of the late Sir James Spence, who was inevitably attracted by his energy, high intelligence, and ebullient personality, he embarked upon a career in clinical medicine and neurology on the advice of Prof F J Nattrass. During his service as a neuropsychiatrist in the RAF, a period of fruitful training and experience in which he was greatly influenced by Sir Charles Symonds, having already acquired the MD and MRCP, he went on to acquire a Diploma in Psychological Medicine, a qualification which after many verbal brushes with colleagues in psychological medicine, he subsequently suppressed, even though he had a deep interest in psychiatry, which he regarded as 'neurology without physical signs'. After demobilisation he underwent further training at Hammersmith and at the National Hospital, Queen Square, before being appointed Assistant Physician to the Royal Victoria Infirmary, Newcastle upon Tyne, in 1947. Following this return to his beloved North-East, new distinctions followed rapidly. For several years he prospered as a busy and much sought after consultant in part-time private practice. His forthright handling of some difficult patients occasionally caused offence but more often proved almost miraculously effective. Generations of medical students and house staff owe much to his inspired teaching and example, and even senior colleagues never ceased to marvel that, being so quick, he was nevertheless so often right. Later he established a new department of neurology, firmly based in both clinical work and research, which grew rapidly and acquired an international reputation. His own research on multiple sclerosis, on accident neurosis and on many diverse neurological topics won him wide renown and his review articles, many published in the *BMJ*, were widely read and quoted, as were his outspoken criticisms of deficiencies in the National Health Service. He was appointed to a personal chair of neurology in 1964, became Dean of Medicine in 1966 and Vice-Chancellor of the University of Newcastle upon Tyne in 1968, an appointment which he still occupied at the moment of his untimely death.

"How can one possibly find words to do justice to this remarkable man? His energy, his drive, his remarkable intuitive clinical ability, his

abounding flow of language, spiked with barbs of (at times) slightly
wounding wit, but above all his limitless generosity to friends, colleagues
and junior staff were extraordinary. Books could be (and probably will
be) filled with quotations from his tongue and from his fertile pen,
some few of which were hallowed for posterity as 'Henry Millerisms'
in a popular medical journal. Who can forget such comments as: 'The
best instrument for obtaining the plantar response is the ignition key
of a Bentley'; or, 'Hemiplegic multiple sclerosis is a rarity and is to be
diagnosed only by me'? And there are many more such which we shall
all remember with sadness but with gratitude. If not always popular with
his peers who frequently misunderstood (and more often misinter-
preted) his roguish wit, he was loved and respected by his juniors and
contemporaries, especially by those who worked closely with him and
knew him best and readily forgave his at times outrageous but impish
comments; above all he will be mourned by his students whose adula-
tion came little short of worship. Foreign and national honours were
showered upon him: visiting professor in many universities overseas,
honorary member of many national neurological associations, Secretary-
General of the World Federation of Neurology, Chairman of the BMA
Planning Unit, President of the Association of Physicians of Great
Britain and Ireland, these and many more distinctions came his way.
His years of office in the World Federation of Neurology, during Dr
Macdonald Critchley's presidency, brought his conspicuous talents to
the attention of a world-wide audience of neurologists to whom he was
invariably an impressive figure; and when he was there the meetings
were never dull. Clinical neurology was his first love, writing his second;
not only will his textbooks and scientific papers be a lasting memorial
to this man of stature, but so will his perspicacious monograph on
Medicine and Society and his wickedly provocative but thoughtful
articles in the *Listener*. Always a bon viveur and lover of the Arts, a
man of wide culture despite his outward buffoonery, he strode through
life with an aura owing something to Max Beerbohm and perhaps also
to Rabelais.

"When the new Newcastle undergraduate medical curriculum was
introduced in 1962, Henry was one of its most outspoken critics and
was heard to say that 'Curriculum review is an occupational disease of
Deans which simply results in the same subjects being taught in a
different order'. But when he himself became Dean he also became a
firm convert to the new order and one of its staunchest advocates. He
had many critics, especially among those who were the recipients of his
verbal onslaughts, but he loved a spirited riposte and was never reluctant
to admit either that he was wrong or that he had been bested in an
argument. As Vice-Chancellor his skill in handling the student body
was matchless and all will agree that there never was or will be another

3

Introduction

Vice-Chancellor like 'Henry'. Whether with senior academics, students, porters, clerks, or visitors, however distinguished, he was superbly unpredictable, original and always irreverently cheerful. Medicine, neurology and the academic world will be much the poorer for his passing; the reader will forgive the cliché, as he certainly would not, he was an unforgettable character. He will be remembered not as a phenocopy of some or several great men of yesteryear but as the one and only Henry Miller. He is survived by his loyal, charming and vigorous wife Eileen and two sons and two daughters; we would wish them to know that it was a privilege to have known and worked with him."

Stephen Lock's decision to publish this book under the imprint of the *BMJ* is, I am sure, a happy inspiration which will be welcomed by Henry's friends and admirers the world over. As one sponsor of the Henry Miller Memorial Appeal launched by the University of Newcastle upon Tyne Development Trust in order to establish some lasting memorial to this great man in the City and University to which he devoted the enormous energies of his professional and academic life, I must express the sincere gratitude of the trustees for the recommendation that any profits deriving from this publication will be donated to that appeal. We hope to be able to establish a research post in neurology in perpetuo in the university; to support an annual concert or recital in his memory; and perhaps, if funds allow, to promote some aspect of student welfare. No doubt if Henry had been able to read this book, parts of it would have infuriated him, parts would embarrass, and parts would amuse; but we hope that it would leave him in no doubt of the affection and regard we all felt for him.

John Walton is Dean of Medicine and Professor of Neurology, University of Newcastle upon Tyne.

Contributors

Hugh Bannerman

Although Henry must have been a medical student when I was still working in the Royal Victoria Infirmary in Newcastle, the first time I ever met him was, I think, in 1942, when Flight-Lieutenant Miller came to RAF Bassingbourn, an operational training unit in Cambridgeshire, whose group headquarters was at Abingdon where I was senior medical officer. These units, of which there were 10 (spread out between Cornwall and the Moray Firth), were the last stage of training of bomber crews. The crew was usually trained in the aircraft it would fly on operations. There were two airfields for each station, and flying went on on each more or less round the clock.

Because of his neurological brilliance and high qualifications, Henry had come into the RAF as a flight-lieutenant, passed on, as it were, from Nattrass in Newcastle to Symonds in the RAF. Whittingham, himself as good a pathologist as he proved an administrator—and who had recently become Director General of Medical Services—had made an admirable rule whereby whizz kid specialists like Henry who came into the RAF should always start off with a spell on an RAF station to see what it was all about before getting buried in their specialty; and, incidentally, quite a headache some of them were while they were doing this. Not so Henry. He was a natural. His keen intelligence quickly mastered Service procedure and bureaucracy and all ranks fell for this slim handsome charmer (as he then was). For some reason, which I forget, shortly after his arrival the senior medical officer disappeared and Henry was left in charge of the station and two aerodromes. He was so good that the station commander asked me if I could not arrange to leave him in charge. As I had had the same idea myself I said I would see what I could do, and I managed to persuade the fellow in Air Ministry who did medical postings to leave Henry there and supply a flying officer to replace the squadron leader.

My warrant officer at Group HQ said this was a disgraceful piece of Geordie nepotism, but later he, too, became converted, and the Bassingbourn Station Commander told my Air Officer Commanding, who had been highly amused when he heard of this backstairs lobbying, what an excellent SMO I was. Everybody was happy.

Contributors

Shortly after Henry's arrival we held a conference of station senior medical officers at Abingdon. The chief object of this was really to get the station medical officers to know their headquarters and each other. In the evening there was some party at which most of them stayed. They were all distinctly hand-picked specimens—one of them, George Gunn, later became Director General of Medical Services—and they were all charmed and impressed by Henry and congratulated me on my find.

One of the things we discussed at this conference was the trade testing of nursing orderlies. Before the war this had all been done by the Medical Training Establishment, but the RAF had got too big for this. Our problem was to get a fair and uniform standard throughout the scattered group. Henry suggested that we divided the group into five pairs of stations; that I should circulate specimen questions; that each SMO should arrange his own training; and that his opposite number should come over to do the examination. This scheme, suggested by a young man who had only been a month or two in uniform, was adopted, proved a great success, and, I believe, was copied elsewhere.

A new operational training unit was being formed. Shortly after this conference I appeared before Henry, like Satan to Jesus in the wilderness, and offered him, while hardly the Kingdoms of the World, at any rate an extra 10/– a day and a half ribbon on his sleeve to go there as senior medical officer. The posting would have to have been made by Air Ministry, but I think I could have fixed it. I gave him a week to think it over.

Sadly, he turned it down and spent the rest of the war under the Symonds's umbrella. The RAF's loss was probably neurology's gain, but several times after the war he told me he wondered whether he had made the right decision. Our last communication was a letter telling me he had had a coronary thrombosis and saying that he thought his time at Bassingbourn had been one of the happiest in his life. He added that one of the many crosses his secretary had to bear was listening to his reminiscences from this period. I question this, for he was a superb raconteur and it was this faculty—as well as always having something to say—that enabled him to hold large audiences spellbound, hanging on his every word. I have twice heard him do this for over an hour with no pauses, no hesitation, and no notes. A unique, attractive, and very human genius.

A sad sequel to this Abingdon conference is that, to my knowledge, three of the ten present have since died from coronary thrombosis. An interesting theme here for an address by Henry?

Hugh Bannerman was a Wing-Commander in the RAF Medical Branch.

E M Bettenson

My first recollection of Henry dates back to the early 1950s, when he only vaguely knew who I was. I was walking northwards on the main road through Low Fell as Henry drove an open car south. Seeing me, he stood up, took one hand off the steering wheel, waved, and shouted a greeting. The action was unexpected, flamboyant, and dangerous and, though it shocked some onlookers, it cheered up the neighbourhood. It was in all respects characteristic of Henry as he was then and as he was when vice-chancellor.

He was an improbable choice for that office and general university opinion had not considered him: hence his appointment to the selection committee. In practice, the committee found discussion of the candidates with Henry more stimulating and enjoyable than discussion of the job with the candidates and it drew the logical conclusion.

Although he had already experimented with administration as dean of medicine, he had not seriously ventured outside the realms of medicine and the vice-cancellarial world was new to him. His reaction to it was consistent with his whole career, whether as medical consultant, public orator, or concertgoer: he stayed Henry Miller. Although he could adapt his manner to an occasion, the adaptation was usually minimal and the normal Henry was always recognisably present.

It followed that since he was, by universal consent, an unusual man, he was an unusual administrator. He did not need to be deliberately controversial because controversy was as natural to him as the upward flight of sparks. In his new surroundings he had much to learn and he did not like a good deal of what he learnt, for he regarded it as academic pedantry and pretentiousness. He did not take for granted many of the conventions of academic life and, until persuaded of their point, was apt to ignore both them and the consequences of ignoring them. Strong in his beliefs—and even stronger, by his own confession, in his pre-judices—he longed to "do" things and was galled by the slow progress of business in a university. He was particularly infuriated by the difficulty of stopping an activity once started. There was sometimes a danger that he might use vice-cancellarial authority to stop something less because he wanted to than to show that it could be stopped. He believed intensely in the value of vocation and education going together and was always good for several rounds of drawn battle over the consequences of pushing this belief to its extremes. He could clearly have excelled in any branch of learning he had chosen, but having chosen medicine he was reluctant to admit equal merit to any other branch—except perhaps law and architecture. He was genuinely worried by the number of students in English and history and was never really

7

satisfied by any of the answers given to his question "What are they going to do?"

This made him, in some ways, an uncomfortable head of a multi-disciplinary institution. Contrary to the views of many people, however, he did not allow his preference for medicine to affect his attitude to the distribution of university resources. Here medicine had to make its case with the rest and the vice-chancellor was only one voice and one vote. On the other hand, his dislike, whether justified or not, of certain subjects affected both his speech and his vote. Quite apart from any early engrained prejudices, such as those engendered in many people by compulsory Latin or real intellectual doubts, he could not help distrusting a subject not associated with cheerful and entertaining colleagues.

Examples of behaviour to prove the justice of this reading are almost impossible: he was so consistent that nothing stood out. All discussions were conducted in a mode of flippancy designed to veil, but not necessarily to obscure, the serious issues. The most characteristic "mot" I can remember was an aside in senate, "This man could bore for England" (senate would on that occasion probably have nominated the speaker for a UK team). But his complaint that he could never persuade senate to agree with him on anything (not even on dress for the annual senate dinner, for which he favoured lounge suits and senate favoured dinner jackets) simply meant that he did not like compromise when he thought he was right. His imperfect sympathy with the intellectual interests of many of his colleagues did not mean any animosity in most cases, and what there was usually arose from misunderstanding. Not everybody realised that he liked being attacked almost as much as he liked attacking. A good opponent was a pleasure to him and, though he detested all the views of Mr Powell that he understood, and distrusted all those he did not understand, he could not withhold respect from a man who in public debate had held his own with him. He himself both in debate and on paper had a trenchant style and he abominated long-windedness.

His insistence on being himself necessarily made him unconventional and this was the more obvious because his sense of humour like his approach to many problems was straightforward to the point of simplicity. The result was sometimes memorable because Henry's personality, voice, and manner invested his remarks with an authority that could be impressively incongruous. He would refer to the registrar of the unversity as "the head clerk," or "buggerlugs," and did not restrict these expressions to informal occasions. He would shout cheerful insults at colleagues down office corridors, drop in for a chat with the registrar's personal assistant regardless of her pressure of business, or appeal to any passerby in the office—whether academic staff, junior clerk, or bemused commercial traveller—for protection against an obviously imaginary physical attack by his secretary who was telling him to do something.

When he was a member of the Newcastle delegation to the annual Northern Universities Conference he was always top of the bill, and the discussions in which he took part were usually the liveliest. In the course of day-to-day business he would affect to confuse the identities of members of staff or address them as if they were people in the public eye preferably for unedifying reasons. "Morning, Archbishop" he would say to a senior officer during the crisis in Cyprus, to which the correct rely was "Morning, Mr Denktash." "Give these biscuits to Miss Blank," he said on another occasion when he weighed well over 15 stone, "and tell her she too can have a body like mine." A caller accidentally connected to the Vice-Chancellor's outside telephone line would be told with great seriousness, "No, Madam, this is the Chinese steam laundry. I'm afraid we can't help you."

It was natural for him to treat students on equal terms and I believe that this was one reason why the more intelligent and responsible students recognised the real difference that his age and experience represented. Students were absolutely essential to his idea of a university, and students instinctively knew that he would never forget them. Consequently his relations with them whether in the medical school or in the university as a whole were consistently happy.

He was not, perhaps, so successful with the academic staff, for whom he was less willing to make allowances, but he could in a difficult interview be endlessly patient. His natural sympathy for a rebel often turned into sympathy for an underdog and made his surprisingly emollient in many personal matters. He could also be disconcerting. A long and ostensibly idealistic harangue by one academic politician at a public meeting was pithily and accurately summarised—to the general amusement of the audience—"You mean that power should be transferred from me to you." He was, moreover, accessible. It was a great merit that he was not given to long or frequent absences from the university. No problem ever grew worse because the vice-chancellor was not available. Indeed, he used to gird at the amount of public money that had to be spent in transporting vice-chancellors to their monthly committee meetings. Problems that were referred to him got prompt, even if sometimes unwilling, attention.

Although he could in practice be an impartial chairman, his manner was always his own and new members of, for example, the Senate Development Committee (the nearest thing to a general purposes committee that Newcastle has) were apt to spend their first meeting in a daze ("I have paid for less entertainment," said one of them). He could and did convulse one university committee with a description

Contributors

of an inspection of his grand pianos by an expert from Steinway's (I forget what the committee was discussing but it was certainly not Steinway pianos). He was exemplary in allowing full debate and, though he might not have liked or even understood the papers for a meeting, he had usually read them sufficiently well to note any awkward points he could make to keep his old enemies on their toes.

It would be easy to underestimate Henry as a vice-chancellor. He will not be associated with any dramatic developments but he took office when economic, political, and intellectual conditions rendered such developments impossible at a long-established but poorly endowed university such as Newcastle. He did, in fact, see some positive gains (two of personal interest to him were the chairs of music and clinical pharmacology) but his major achievement was that in troubled times he was vice-chancellor at a peaceful university. The controversies he engaged in were subjects for civilised difference of opinion—I can recollect only two occasions when an Old Testament prophet would have deprecated the intensity of his emotion: once when it was suggested that R D Laing should be invited to give an official lecture, and once when he referred to a medical man's misuse of the Health Service to make money. And he never lost touch with reality. Thus, at the end of 1973, when the economic blizzard was beginning, he was probably the first British vice-chancellor to introduce effective economies as distinct from bewailing the necessity for having to do so.

His consistency was in being himself but like every other human being he was a bundle of contradictions, and if he was more so than usual that was because he was more of everything. It is not possible to sum up Henry as vice-chancellor in a single sentence but perhaps the most striking feature of his term was the style he brought to the office. It may not have been to everybody's taste but it was unmistakable; it was intensely personal; it was genuine; and most people felt more cheerful as a result of it. Too many Henrys would undoubtedly spoil a good deal of broth, but every university should have one, though no university can now have the original model.

E M Bettenson was Registrar of the Federal University of Durham, of which Newcastle formed the larger part.

Dianne Boyle

The first time I met Henry Miller I thought he was the rudest man I had ever come across—and, four years later, I had no doubt that he was.

Contributors

But by then I had also decided his was the most brilliant, colourful, volatile, and witty personality I was ever likely to encounter. He could, in a few acid words, lash the most hideous and cutting insult on a senior university lecturer—and almost instantly match it with the most witty and charming aside, leaving the man—and all in earshot—bemused, and roaring with laughter. One minute he could look half asleep as university committee members battled it out across the polished oak surfaces: then, like an eagle swooping on its prey, he would dramatically cut into the row with sarcastic, logical, or just plain funny comments.

Either way Henry Miller was always winning—and that's how I remember him most clearly. It was no mere coincidence that Newcastle University students were tagged "moderates" by the new universities caught up in conflict after conflict with lecturers, officials, and their own vice-chancellors. It wasn't that students flocking to the North-East were any different, and it wasn't that the idealism of the day was any less: it was because Dr Henry Miller was too clever for them. He had a knack of bursting the balloon before it was even half blown up—and he loved every minute of it.

The first time I saw Henry's brilliant speechmaking at work was at a freshers' rally in the ABC cinema in the Haymarket. I vaguely remember the student president and other officials talking about poor grants and the need to reorganise the university's accommodation service. Then Henry took the rostrum—and the militancy of his speech made the student officers look like amateurs. He slammed his students for their conservatism and, I remember so clearly, said that the trouble with Newcastle's student leaders was they were always so much to the right-wing. It was an incredible thing to hear from a vice-chancellor. But it was Henry at his best, and it illustrates the way he always handled problems. I don't believe for a minute this man really wanted to see a hot bed of revolution in his campus but, by turning the tables, he was making very sure he wouldn't get it. Students always felt that Henry was their ally—and most of the time he was. Because, I really believe, Dr Miller had a lot of time for students. I remember the day that I bid my farewells to him at the end of my presidential year and he said: "I often think students have much more sense, and speak it, than the staff—and even if they don't, at least you know they're going in a year or two."

And, once, I asked Henry Miller what it was like to be a vice-chancellor. He retorted without a flicker: "Just like a headmaster, only no one does as they're told." Another day with this amazing man sticks clearly in my mind. It was a cold, windy, and rainswept day and I, along with the union secretary Paul Lynchy, had been asked to take part in some shooting for a local film on Dr Miller called *My City*. Paul and I were sitting in Henry's chauffeur-driven car waiting for the film crew to get themselves organised. We were parked outside the university arches and, as always, a constant stream of students poured out of of adjoining buildings. "Why is it," Henry remarked, "that you lot always look so happy?" Well, they didn't look particularly happy to me but perhaps Henry saw something I didn't. And I remember feeling that day Henry's genuine warmth for young people.

At the beginning of every academic year Dr Miller and his wife invited student officers to a cocktail party at their home. The party for my presidential year will always haunt me. I gingerly lingered in the magnificent hall as the butler took my coat—and I wondered if I should pick up a duster and pretend I had been sent to help the maid. I was shown into the party and caught the rather tense atmosphere which told me that I wasn't the only one feeling nervous. It was, I decided, going to be a distinctly strained night—but I couldn't have been more wrong. I hadn't counted on Henry and Mrs Miller's personalities and within less than half an hour students were sitting on the deep, deep carpet floor and next to myself squatted Henry himself. The wine flowed, the delicious eats kept coming, and the party was a roaring success. Henry ended the evening seated at his piano playing a duet with a student, who, if I remember, left with a sample of Henry's operatic record collection.

For all his charm, wit, and sparkle Henry Miller could, however, be ruthless in argument. He was dry, to the point, and bitterly scathing. There were few lecturers or professors I saw ever even match him as a sparring partner. Students never did. Someone remarked to me quite recently that Henry Miller made a point of never destroying students over the committee room table, or in debate. I don't think that was true. The fact was I and, I'm sure, my predecessors knew just how far to go with the V-C. No one likes to be made a fool of in public, and Henry was capable of doing more than that—and it only took a few words. But, for all that, Henry, more than most, was the one who took the student line. His attitude more often that not was, "why not?" And time after time it was he who, after listening to both sides, spoke up and clinched the deal. Henry believed in the students' union and its role in university life. It was often he who made the oldest of student traditions the best—and, more important, enabled them to take place.

The year I was elected president probably saw the start of the financial cutbacks that were later to claw so deeply into university life. In my husband's era, a few years before, the union presidency had been a year of wine, women, and song—with a bit of admin thrown in for good measure. In 1973 we were all aware that things were changing and it wasn't any longer the done thing to throw sumptuous parties, travel all over the country for debates and dinner, or do too much entertaining in the union. But there was one tradition dying very hard in Newcastle University Union—and that was the President's Spring Ball. Year after year it lost money, but year after year the union voted for it to go ahead. And, always, Henry offered to help out financially. He had a special fund for "this kind of thing" he told me when my turn came. It was a gloriously formal affair steeped in university tradition—and always held on the eve of FA Cup Final. My president's ball fell on the eve of the 1974 Cup Final, when Newcastle United were preparing to battle it out with Liverpool. As ever, Henry Miller was to join the list of after-dinner speakers—but when he arrived it was his wife who stole the show. For her chic and stylish outfit that night was in United's colours—black and white from head to toe. When the speeches were made, it was Henry Miller who toasted "the lads" and, as ever, brought the house down.

Henry had charisma, sparkle, and a sharp wit, but, though he was outrageously funny and forthright in his insults, they always came with a twinkle of the eye and a hearty chuckle. And I, anyway, never did know when Henry Miller was serious or just having fun. One day I was invited back to the students' union for a jubilee celebration—and who should suddenly catch my eye, or at least my ears, but Henry. "Well Miss Nelmes," he said in a booming voice from the other side of the room, "I know these things bore you, but did you have to come out in your pyjamas!" He was referring to a particularly voluminous trouser suit I was wearing—but before I could even blush he was striding up, a broad grin on his face, and shaking my hand.

And that was Henry Miller in sparkling form. As a vice-chancellor Dr Miller was nothing if not himself, and I always felt he cared not one jot for convention. My husband, Frank, recalls a president's ball before my time when a friend of ours—well known then for his debating talents—was asked to propose a toast. His speech brought everyone to their feet and was full of pointed and witty knocks at Henry. At the end of the speech Henry turned sardonically to my husband and said: "That bastard will go a long way." He was right.

But then Henry usually was. He was a unique vice-chancellor. There cannot be a student officer who does not remember this brilliant man for his wit, charm, and cynicism. A daunting figure he could be, but his door was always open—and there was always a laugh and a gin and tonic waiting on the other side.

Dianne Boyle, née Nelmes, was President of the Newcastle Students' Union 1973-4.

Jack Brymer

I was one of the unlucky ones. I knew Henry only briefly personally, though I had certainly not been unaware of his work and his influence for quite a long time before we met. When we did meet, it was in very crowded circumstances—the sort of occasion when even the most telling personality might fail to make an impression. It was at a reception preceding a congregation at his university. Henry didn't fail. Within minutes I was aware of a very strong personal influence which seemed to dominate the proceedings, and I looked forward very much to knowing more about this remarkable man.

Subsequent meetings were in no way a letdown. There was the delightful occasion when he quizzed me about a recording he possessed —which I should have known, and did. The catch was that, although I knew conductor, soloist, orchestra, and date, I also knew that it had never been recorded. It had, of course—and that was typical of the sort of odd slant Henry could bring to music. Of his life as a medical man I know nothing at all, other than hearing him air some very good sense from time to time on the BBC. What I feel sure about, deep in my bones, was that he was a man capable of an extension of this good sense into any sphere of life he graced with his presence. His death came as a shock to me. He had been in touch a very short time before, with an appreciation of something of mine he had heard. I knew he was far from well; but before I could even reply to his message he was dead, and it seemed as impossible then as it does now. To say he will be missed is a ridiculous understatement. He certainly cannot be replaced. We tend to need the Henrys of this life.

Jack Brymer is principal clarinettist with the London Symphony Orchestra.

Richard Cave

When it fell to my lot to be the founder of the Multiple Sclerosis Society of Great Britain and Northern Ireland way back in 1953 my knowledge of the medical profession was confined virtually to my parents' family GP. During the winter season he was always away shooting on a Thursday, with the result that illness, accident, or death was known to be banned on that day of the week.

Had I been asked in '53 how I visualised a neurologist, I think I would have replied in some such words as: "A dedicated medical scientist peering at laboratory specimens, more interested in their inter-action than in the human beings to whom they related." I learnt very soon how wrong I was. I learnt that neurologists came in all shapes and sizes and that, whatever else they might lack, they certainly were not lacking a warm, human interest in their patients. Even so, I was not fully prepared for the quite exceptional and engaging personality that emerged from Newcastle upon Tyne.

The first time I met Henry Miller was when, as the Chairman of the Multiple Sclerosis Society, I went by train to Newcastle on the society's business. I was met at the station by Henry, who levered him-self into the most sumptuous Jaguar in which it has ever been my good fortune to be driven.

During the short journey across Newcastle, Henry told me that his wife also had a Jaguar. When I asked whether Women's Lib had progressed so far that Mrs Miller drove the same model car as her husband, Henry replied "Good God no, my wife's Jaguar has only one carburettor."

A vivid memory of Henry is of him at a meeting in Vienna of the World Federation of Neurology. Some 1000 neurologists of many nationalities streamed into the Hofburg each morning, to be viewed with indifference and detachment by the green-uniformed attendants on duty there. Indifference, that is to say, until the arrival of Professor Henry Miller (United Kingdom). For him the attendants sprang to attention, saluted, and growled "Guten morgen, Herr Professor." What it was in Henry's hormones that triggered off this reaction on the part of the attendants I must leave it to a medical man to explain. It was at this same conference that Henry Miller deflated in five minutes flat the claim of those who were urging the latest so called "cure" for multiple sclerosis.

On four occasions Henry was the guest speaker at annual meetings of the MS Society. It is a glimpse of the obvious to record that on each occasion he gave a masterly account of the state of medical research into multiple sclerosis and related demyelinating diseases. What is equally worth recording is his flair for putting this highly technical subject across to the members of a lay audience, his ability to hold their attention, to establish a rapport with them, and to step down into the lay arena without lessening his medical authority. And how he endeared himself to his audience when he pronounced with some emphasis: "If a diet makes you feel miserable, drop it."

In 1963 Henry Miller succeeded Dr Douglas McAlpine as Chairman of the MS Society's Medical Research Advisory Committee. He held that post for $4\frac{1}{2}$ years. I give away no secrets when I say that Henry's penetrating analyses of the numerous applications for research grants, combined with his flair for achieving agreement among his medical

Contributors

colleagues, contributed in no small measure to the presentday success of the MS Society.

Richard Cave is the founder and President of the Multiple Sclerosis Society of Great Britain and Northern Ireland.

Cohen of Birkenhead

In relating these random recollections of Henry I might well appear to have run counter to the injunction of the first editor of the *Dictionary of National Biography*, who wrote to his contributors on notepaper which bore the printed maxim, "no flowers, by request." But for this I make no apology. For a man to become an institution and a legend in his lifetime special and remarkable gifts are needed. Henry was such a man. He had the presence which reminded one of Benjamin Jowett's saying that "there are some men whom it does one good even to look at." His sheer intellectual brilliance was manifest in a vigorous, lucid, and precise style in speech and writing. He had the quality of strength, and the courage of his opinions—opinions which have not at all times been equally acceptable to all persons. A remarkable knowledge of man and affairs eased him out of a high place among neurologists into the more exacting life of a medical dean, and later of a vice-chancellor. But, above all, he had a genius for friendship.

We first met shortly after his appointment to Newcastle, when, with him, I saw a patient suffering from dermatomyositis. This and similar consultations led to my inviting him to become an external examiner in medicine in the University of Liverpool. When he became dean of the Newcastle Medical School, he was appointed to the General Medical Council during my presidency, though his election later as vice-chancellor led to his resignation after only three years' membership. I knew him also as a most tolerant editor, for I contributed to some of his published works.

But, apart from what might be termed these official meetings, we met frequently in London either at the Athenaeum or Garrick clubs, for, like Boswell, Henry was "a clubable man." Over dinner with ministers of the Crown, judges, doctors, actors, musicians, and others, who were all attracted by Henry's geniality and wit, we had long discussions on medical, educational and general matters, whose later conclusions often found expression in his writings, which fortunately provide a more permanent record of his ideas and work. In these, and his various text-

16

books and lectures, we all treasure our favourite recollections of Henry's aphorisms:

> Jewels five words long
> That on the stretched forefinger of all time
> Sparkle for ever.

I suspect that he modelled his writing on Sir Francis Walshe—if not the enfant terrible of neurology, certainly its homme terrible; but Henry's strength lay in his being able without asperity and acerbity to achieve the same devastating effects as Walshe. Although he had himself gained the Diploma in Psychological Medicine, for example, he shared Walshe's view that psychoanalysis is an ineffective instrument, though Henry recognised its domination in clinical psychiatry in the United States. Of this, he wrote, it "need not surprise us after 50 years of passionate concentration on laboratory medicine, the psychiatrist is often the only person who can spare the time to take the patient's history." For many years, Henry would have echoed Nabokov's view that Freud was a Viennese quack, but with the passage of time he somewhat mollified this view. In *Freud* (1972), a compilation edited by his namesake, Jonathan Miller, Henry wrote on psychoanalysis—clinical perspective—"To the clinician the contribution of Freud and psychoanalysis to psychiatry is a limited one with something on each side of the balance sheet."

He had a deep and continuing interest in medical education and his lecture on *Fifty Years after Flexner* embodies his mature views, and many of his most quotable epigrams. But he did not swallow Flexner's solutions without question, especially the thesis (Flexner was not a qualified doctor) which suggested that the physician should not act unless all the necessary data were available. In this, Henry was at one with Sherrington, who wrote, "Science, nobly, declines as truth anything but complete proof; but commonsense, pressed for time, accepts and acts on acceptance."

Henry was an avid reader. During one of our meetings he told me how helped he had been by Sir Henry Taylor's *The Statesman*, first published in 1836, but republished in 1957. It dealt with the training and place of the administrator in the formulation of policy in terms which are akin to those of Stephen Potter in his various publications on gamesmanship, and the low cunning which is necessary to achieve one's ends. It is not surprising that another book which delighted Henry was Pullar-Strecker's *Proverbs for Pleasure* (1954), which includes such distilled wisdom as, "Always take the fee while the tear is in the eye."

Whenever he came to Liverpool, a visit to the Playhouse was one of the high spots, for he loved the theatre. In examinations he put students at their ease, for they soon appreciated that he was concerned to learn

Contributors

what they knew rather than to expose the area of their ignorance, and a student never felt that he or she had not passed easily.

Music was another of his relaxations. We enjoyed many concerts in each other's company, and there was the occasional visit to Covent Garden. I remember well during an international conference being with him at a performance of *Aida*, for it was the only occasion in my presence that he uttered a pun. Radames was not only a bad actor but his singing was flat, and as we left he turned to me and said, "his singing was *unverdi* of Aida."

He knew of my interest in medical history and often attacked it. He suggested that doctors turned to medical history when they were too old or too tired to keep abreast of advances in medicine. But as he grew older he recognised with Santayana that those who neglect the lessons of history are compelled to relive them. I recall that at a meeting of the section of the history of medicine at the Royal Society of Medicine, which I chaired about a decade ago, Henry presented a paper on "Three Great Neurologists"; his opening was characteristic:

> Neurologist are, of course, great ancestor worshippers never happier than when they are insisting on the superiority of the 1892/3 edition of Sir William Gowers's *Diseases of the Nervous System* to any puny contemporary successors, visiting tombs or ceremonially unveiling plaques in honour of their distinguished predecessors on Yorkshire farmhouses or in obscure villages in the Midi.

Henry's interest in medicopolitics came somewhat later. His testament remains in *Medicine and Society*. It was Beatrice Webb who wrote of politics reflecting the war of the As and the Bs—the anarchists, and the bureaucrats—and certainly Henry railed against the bureaucrats, not as an anarchist, but as an articulate and accomplished amateur who offered constructive ideas towards the solution of current problems. For many years he believed that what was needed to revitalise the National Health Service was simply an injection of more money— another five hundred million pounds, he said in 1967. But he later recognised that money alone would not of itself suffice: there was needed a greater devotion on the part of the medical profession to the aims of the Service.

His disillusionment with the role of the royal colleges was seldom veiled. He tended to regard them as ancient monuments, redolent of an extinct culture. In referring to the United States he wrote, "It is evidently possible for a country to lead the world in medicine without a galaxy of royal colleges and a plethora of postgraduate diplomas." He had, however, given the Milroy Lectureship at the RCP in 1961, on "Accident Neurosis" (he had to apply for this). When these were published in the *British Medical Journal* I recalled a collection of papers which I possessed in book form on "The effects of injury on the nervous system" written, 50 years earlier, by Dr W B Warrington, a distinguished neurologist, and a former pupil and colleague of Sherrington in Liverpool, so I sent the book to him. He acknowledged this saying he found the book "fascinating and most intriguing in its own right," and added, characteristically, "I am glad I hadn't seen it earlier otherwise my plagiarism would have been indubitable."

Some thought that Henry often took a contrary view out of sheer perverseness for the delight he derived from argument. I did not find this. Indeed, he often opposed current doctrine by sound argument which later gained the approval of the majority. Let me quote but two examples.

For long the concept of positive health held sway. Henry's observation was, "I will not labour my own conviction that the normal state of most people is to feel faintly tired, harassed, and under the weather—and that my clinical observations lead me to believe that an abounding sensation of positive health usually presages either a cardiac infarction or incipient hypomania." Again, many years ago, Max Rosenheim, Henry, and I were lunching at University College Hospital, London. Max was expounding a view he had earlier expressed that more energy be devoted to the application of scientific research to medicine, and that it would benefit medicine and society if a moratorium were pronounced on research for two or more years. Henry countered this with a direct denial in words which as nearly as I can recall are replicated in Henry's *Medicine and Science*.

"Of course, a moratorium wouldn't work, even if it operated through a selective Rothschild-type diversion of resources to establishment-authenticated activities. Since the Spanish Inquisition failed to quench scientific curiosity, it seems unlikely that the British Civil Service would be more successful. As for the philosophical pessimist, however, he faces the awkward dilemma that the investigator can never envisage the ultimate social implications of his discoveries, whether for good or ill."

His general philosophy led many people to seek his support for euthanasia. But he stated categorically that he had never knowingly terminated a patient's life nor did he feel it right to do so. In any case, he wrote, "the involvement of physicians in euthanasia is surely inadvisable; any step that leaves the patient in doubt as to whether his doctor has come to administer treatment or a quietus would irreparably damage the doctor/patient relationship. It might be more appropriate for an enthusiastic prelate to conduct the patient to the Elysian fields."

My last letter to Henry arrived at his home within 24 hours of his death. I had long felt that academic recognition of his gifts had for too long been withheld. The opportunity to remedy this came when the University of Hull agreed to confer the honorary degree of Doctor of

Contributors

Science on him at the official opening of the Wolfson Research Laboratory in March last. As chancellor of the university, I wrote telling him of this. Two days later his wife, Eileen, wrote of his delight on receiving the news. But alas! in the early hours of the morning following the receipt of my letter he died.

Many of us feel, to our infinite sorrow, that we were deprived of his friendship and counsel in the prime of life and at the zenith of his powers. To some Theocritus's famous epigram—"whom the Gods love dies young"—plausibly suggests that those whom Heaven favours pass on prematurely. But with Henry the true meaning becomes clear: it is that fortunate persons are still young in spirit when they die.

I must end by expressing that my words reflect only faintly the admiration and affection in which I held him, and the very personal debt of gratitude I owe to him for his friendship.

> Yes, I believe that there lived,
> Others like thee in the past,
> . . . Souls tempered with fire
> Fervent, heroic and good
> Helpers and friends of mankind.
>
> (*Matthew Arnold*)

Lord Cohen of Birkenhead, CH, is former President of the General Medical Council and now Chancellor of the University of Hull.

(Lord Cohen died on 7th August 1977, after his contribution had been printed).

Nancy Deegan

Henry Miller was my third dean—and certainly the most remarkable—and my contribution to this book comes from my having been his secretary from January 1966 until October 1968, when he became vice-chancellor. He was Professor Miller when I knew him, though strangely enough he attached little importance to the title (but he did, of course, accept it)—he always said that the Americans never used it—and, in fact, when he became vice-chancellor he reverted to being Dr Miller. When Henry Miller first arrived in the Dean of Medicine's office I was buried under an avalanche of reprints. He had written hundreds of papers in his time, his colleagues said. Thank God he didn't bring them all with him; as it was, it took me several weeks to sort them all out and catalogue them for future reference—because even old ones seemed still to be in demand.

My submission consists of no more than a series of anecdotes, each being a short narrative, often entirely personal and written in conversational terms—a few unconnected stories.

Contributors

I recall that after a particularly bruising encounter with members of a laboratory medicine department he observed how he could not understand why it was that some people who worked in these departments should sometimes be so difficult when they should, in his opinion, have few problems in connection with their work compared with those in clinical departments who dealt with sick people. He thought that many of them seemed to spend most of their time peering down their microscopes while thinking up ways and means of doing one another down.

Although he had a bell at his side he always preferred to whistle as he passed my door to summon me to "the presence" to start the day's work.

It was a laugh a day working for Professor Miller, but you had to be on top of the world all the time, never flagging. He was a gregarious character and liked to have cheerful people around him. He saw the funny side of most things, except on those rare occasions when he was depressed—and those were the days when you had to watch your step. He was described by one journalist in a newspaper article as "this jolly, cigar-smoking dean."

He disliked the telephone and used it as little as possible, preferring face-to-face discussions with people.

Once one of his daughters told him that there had been a telephone call from Buckingham Palace, but he thought it must be some kind of a hoax (and didn't take much notice of it) until he received an official invitation to one of the Queen's informal luncheon parties. He was very excited and thrilled by this, and, when he came back, told us all about what they'd had to eat, how charming and informal the Queen had been, how pleasant the whole atmosphere was, and how much he'd enjoyed himself.

He was very well organised and cleared his desk every day. He was a genius at dictation because he was a clear thinker and knew precisely what he wanted to say. He had a great facility with words (he certainly taught me a lot of new ones) and two of his favourite were turgid and tedious. These he applied freely to prose that offended him, or to people he did not like.

He was a prolific writer and a hard worker, but I fancy he played off one secretary against another to get the maximum effort all round— he had three secretaries in all.

He thought holidays a complete waste of time, particularly bank holidays, when he could not pick up his mail, and he frequently complained loud and long about this inconvenience. He would leave innumerable notes about this state of affairs ending up on one occasion saying, "what a way to run a railway."

He was a good talker and delighted in creating controversy. He was much in demand as a lecturer and after-dinner speaker and in this capacity travelled extensively both in this country and abroad. While he was dean he visited Malta on behalf of the General Medical Council to inspect their medical educational facilities and their hospitals.

He liked comfortable surroundings and had the dean's office refurbished when he took over. He said the previous furniture and decor was like that of a third-class waiting room.

He was a convinced atheist and attributed everything to science—which conflicted oddly with his appreciation of great music and the theatre.

He seemed to be a man of simple tastes and liked nothing better than a nice cup of tea, though that was not all that he drank.

He dressed well and liked having his photograph taken. He kept a postcard in his wallet and for future reference, used to jot down any jokes he heard.

Whenever he wrote a letter by hand he always addressed the envelope first.

These are just a few reminiscences about an ebullient personality who spent a short part of his remarkable life in the office of the Dean of Medicine in Newcastle.

Nancy Deegan is secretary to the Dean of Medicine at the University of Newcastle upon Tyne.

Shirley Fallaw

I "inherited" Henry in 1968 when he became Vice-Chancellor and I was the "sitting" vice-chancellor's secretary. He was not sympathetic towards colleagues who complained about having to inherit staff: he had had to put up with me, he said, and what could be worse than that? One of my first problems was how to address him: it did not seem right to call him plain Dr Miller, when he had been Professor Miller until the time of his appointment to the vice-chancellorship. Nevertheless, he usually used to refer to himself as Dr Miller—for example, when announcing himself on the telephone (although he would occasionally answer the office telephone by saying "Miss Fallaw's butler here"). But he made an exception when travelling by sleeper, and would use the name Professor Miller, because it was longer and easier to pick out on the passenger lists—this was in the days when the lists of sleeping car passengers were posted up on the platform, and you had to find your name in order to ascertain the number of your sleeping compartment; he used to describe himself as the only "British Rail professor" in the country. He strongly objected to my calling him vice-chancellor; perhaps this smacked too much of pomposity for his liking. He seemed to like plain speaking. I remember him saying that he would like to be told straight out if any of us in the office felt that he was behaving like a fool (or words to that effect). At first, I think, I was a bit nervous of him; his face could look deceptively stern in repose, and he would sometimes bellow "Don't keep going away," as I withdrew (discreetly as I thought) to allow him to take a telephone call. In fact, he very rarely got annoyed and had the great ability of being able to keep a sense of proportion and to appear calm and unruffled.

For his part, he had his own distinctive way of addressing people. "You miserable old cow," or "you old bag," or "keep on taking the tablets" (together with one or two unprintable variations) were fairly standard greetings for first thing on a Monday morning—a time not regarded by others in the office as his secretary's shining hour. He used to remind me that people had remarked to him that I had livened up since working for him; at home they said I had coarsened. "You'll go far—and soon, I hope," was fairly appreciative and reserved for special occasions. Even rarer, when my expression indicated perhaps that he had been particularly exasperating, was "Now, now, remember you are working for a great man" (quoting a remark made of him by a television producer who had come to pick his brains—he was always much in demand for television and radio programmes). He used to tease me about looking fierce from time to time, and one morning he hung on my office door a very smart little enamelled plaque with the inscription "Beware of the ferocious dog."

In addition, he had his own special nicknames for various institutions. In the university we had our departments of "adulterous education" and "pubic health engineering," and meetings of the "academic bawd"; the Newcastle General Hospital was always "the Genereal." He had his own industrial relations at Scunthorpe, and described his job as Vice-Chancellor as a professional weeping-post. He referred to the *Daily Torygraph* or *Daily Smellygraph*, and *The Grauniad*, and the "terror-vision." He like to manipulate words, and journalism was something that he very much enjoyed; he would do several drafts of book reviews, articles, and so on before being satisfied with the final manuscript, and would assure us that they were queuing up in India for the latest edition of his medical textbook.

He enjoyed being provocative, and was particularly so about any form of physical exercise. Whenever I returned with a glowing suntan after a weekend's walking ("in those thick hairy stockings") he would inquire how I had acquired my rash. Two years after he became Vice-Chancellor I developed tennis elbow ("one of the few conditions that is not neurotic in origin"), and he wrote to a consultant: "I am most

23

grateful to you for seeing Miss Fallaw and to your secretary for so kindly arranging it without delay. She is my principal secretary here, and invaluable. Unfortunately she is rather a rough type of girl who goes in for energetic sports (outdoor) and appears to have given herself a tennis elbow. I wonder if you would be so kind as to have a look at it and if you think fit give her a cortisone injection, in order that she can keep working for me." Other colleagues in the office recall with gratitude similar good offices on their behalf and Dr Miller's ready willingness to help with medical problems by making sure that they (or their relatives) were referred in the right direction for advice or treatment.

Working in the office was never dull. The vice-chancellor and the registrar (who has contributed to this book) worked in offices adjacent to each other, and they shared a fondness for words (written and spoken), and they both liked an audience. They were a splendid foil for one another (like a sort of Morecambe-and-Wise type of comedy act on occasions), and from time to time sounds of much hilarity from one or other of their offices used to resound along the corridor. One day they both demonstrated to me some remedial floor exercises for backache. Meetings chaired by the vice-chancellor were enlivened by his presence, and an unexpected peal of laughter would suddenly be heard issuing from a committee room: he could always find the apt retort or witticism.

Taking dictation from him was often a diverting experience—he had a unique style and turn of phrase. Writing to thank a local consultant urologist for his reprint on bladder dysfunction, he said that he had read it with great interest and enjoyment "despite a minor attack of giggling incontinence." He was also very observant and rarely failed to make some kind of remark (favourable or unfavourable) about a new outfit; one day I appeared for the first time in a black trouser suit, and he asked if I was an advertisement for "keep death off the roads."

After his coronary thrombosis in 1972, which he described as "almost obligatory for the middle-aged neurotic," he wrote to a university colleague: "I am glad to say that evil has triumphed and I am well on the way to recovery—despite medical treatment." He often used to tell people that he was a convert from intensive coronary care to what he called "the Lord Cohen routine" of morphine, whisky, television, and a comfortable bed at home.

It seems very fitting that this should be a book of reminiscences, since the subject of them was himself great addicted to reminiscing—about his early training in Newcastle, London, and the United States; about his time in the Royal Air Force; and about trips to foreign countries (and especially their restaurants and eating places). Sometimes during a slackish period, when he had finished dictating and had a clear desk (having shifted the paperwork from his desk on to mine), he would lean back and talk for a while. He was an endless source of information on a wide range of topics (including food, wine, and music). If asked for his advice about the programme being presented by a visiting opera company, he would gladly make suggestions about which opera to see and would hum or intone selected excerpts. He was a skilled raconteur and much in demand as an after-dinner speaker; speaking in public was no effort to him. He was a lecturer of international reputation and experience, but admitted that "there's no thrill like crossing the Tyne in the train, seeing all those marvellous bridges, and knowing I've come home."

In fact, although he enjoyed most foreign parts, and especially Australia, Canada, and the USA, the first time I heard him complain of feeling unwell was after a visit to Israel about a year before his actual coronary attack. He had been consulted by a paediatric neurologist working in Jerusalem about a patient, a 3-year-old boy, whose parents wished to bring the boy to England to see Dr Miller; he felt, however, that it would be cheaper for the parents and less traumatic for the patient if he himself flew to Israel to see the child. After seeing the boy in hospital, and a day's strenuous sightseeing in Jerusalem in the July heat, he returned to Newcastle complaining of breathlessness. Subsequently he followed the child's progress with great interest and saw him three years later in London; a patient was always a top priority. Another visit abroad which gave him much pleasure was a fairly strenuous medical research fund-raising tour of Australia, which lasted three weeks and which he undertook three years after his coronary—"with some trepidation, but my ashes can always be scattered for the sharks in Sydney Harbour." His final visit overseas was to America about two months before his death and included several days' appearances in court on behalf of a patient engaged in litigation.

Many will testify to similar generous gestures—and to his sense of fun. During his last winter he presented the office with a large volume of *Beachcomber—the Works of J B Morton*, and cast us in the roles of the various characters in the book. I was Lady Cabstanleigh, and others in the office were identified as Captain Foulenough, Prodnose, Miss Boubou Flaring, Dr Strabismus, Big White Carstairs, and the Filthistan Trio.

No one would disagree that working for such a character was a stimulating experience; with his departure many have echoed the sentiment expressed in the students' newspaper headline—END OF AN ERA.

Shirley Fallaw is secretary to the Vice-Chancellor of the University of Newcastle upon Tyne.

Contributors
J B Foster

It is difficult to be dispassionate about a 33-year association with a man who has had such a profound influence on one's personal career and lifestyle as had Henry. In an obituary in the *British Medical Journal*, I commented on the three phases of Henry's postgraduate life, knowing little except from hearsay and anecdote of his student days or of those immediately following his qualification.

As a medical student, I first met him in the clinical years in the middle of his first phase, and was immediately impressed and influenced by the power of his personality. The clinical ward rounds with the junior students were both hilarious and challenging, for here was a general physician in his prime willing to expound upon medicine or any other aspect of life (depending on the mood and the day), and yet at the same time quite prepared to extract the maximum value from the embarrassment, naïveté, and general lack of urbanity of his pupils. His extravagant behaviour was, nevertheless, endearing and we recognised that we were being taught by an astute, impressive, and inordinately successful part-time clinician. He always dressed in the uniform of the time—black jacket and striped trousers—and carried a gold cigarette case. The latter was subsequently discarded, and was replaced by castigation of those who had failed to follow his example by giving up smoking; indeed, he once declared that any doctor who smoked should be struck off the *Medical Register*.

During this first period he led life to the full, wrote many serious articles, and just as many pot boilers, and at the same time brought out several editions of *Progress in Clinical Medicine*. His interest in neurology stemmed from the influence of Sir Charles Symonds and the time spent as a supernumerary registrar at Queen Square immediately after his Service career. His interest was essentially clinical, and he never failed to goad the academic research worker of the time—and in particular the research neurophysiologist—a penchant he never lost during his career. It was a curiously persistent misjudgment which blunted the enthusiasm of many of his admirers in his later life, and at times in public caused amused embarrassment to his closest supporters. I recall a famous dinner of the Association of British Neurologists held at, of all places, a mediaeval banquet in Seaton Delaval Hall, Northumberland, which had been preceded by champagne served with the characteristic avuncular generosity of the vice-chancellor. Loud Wagnerian music dismissed us from the vice-chancellor's lodge to our meal, and here the company was regaled with a critical appraisal, not only of the specialist teaching hospitals, and of the National Hospital, Queen Square in particular, but yet again of the lack of contribution made to the clinical specialty by the EEG and the related electrophysiology of the peripheral nerve.

I was fortunate enough, after qualification and what would now be described as preregistration house jobs, to postpone two years of National Service (later serving in the RNVR) in order to act as senior house officer to Dr Alan Ogilvie and his assistant physician, Henry Miller. During that year, as chief and junior, we became firm friends and I believe it was then that those of us working for him were taught some of the secrets of hedonism and the gusto of life. It was apparent that success demanded intense application from time to time. Through his generosity I was able to meet several of medicine's senior and most revered practitioners, and was introduced to a wide circle of Henry's friends both in and outside medicine. There was an opportunity to drive one of the first Ford Zephyrs to be fitted with the Raymond Mays's conversion, an exciting experience; I remember vividly the day that I was directed to the private obstetric nursing home in Newcastle in order to take some blood for one of Henry's private patients, and was dismissed in the Zephyr with a brief warning regarding its performance. The machine was quite terrifying and it was not until later that I learnt that Henry had put paving stones in the boot in order to keep the back wheels on the ground as he accelerated away (as was his wont) showering the bystanders with pebbles and loose debris from the driveway.

He regarded the Membership as something to be acquired quickly and my own personal satisfaction in obtaining the diploma was enriched by his obvious delight that one of his "boys" had succeeded under his tutelage. He took a great interest in National Service experiences, and would match RNVR tales with even more hilarious anecdotes from his time in the RAF. I lost direct touch on returning to Newcastle, to the then professorial department of medicine, and only after a rather disillusioned year sought his advice about a career in neurology, realising that not only the subject of one's chosen specialty, but also the senior colleagues in the specialty, were factors profoundly influencing one's own intentions. A thoroughly irreverent letter from Henry to Michael Kremer, Dean of the Institute of Neurology, allowed easy access to Queen Square and it was during this period of training that our friendship grew closer, for Henry was always interested to know what was happening at the specialist hospital and I enjoyed many lunches with him, and, after joining "the house," would often attend the Royal Society of Medicine, where he was a frequent speaker and member of council. My wife and I spent evenings in the flat with Henry and the late Hugh Garland before they went their separate ways by sleeper from King's Cross to the North. These evenings, although somewhat clouded by ethanol, are particularly remembered, for through the obfuscated atmosphere poured an unceasing monologue of amusing anecdotes interrupted only by the occasional intervention of Morpheus.

By this time, Henry had entered the second phase of his career. He had eschewed the financial rewards of successful private practice and turned his attention to building up the department of neurology in Newcastle upon Tyne. He attracted John Walton, now Dean of the Faculty, as his first first assistant, somehow managed to extract a ward in the teaching hospital from an avaricious academic department of surgery, and founded the famous (at least in Newcastle) Ward 6. John Hankinson came from Queen Square to join the neurosurgical team of Rowbotham, Lassman, and McIver, and Gordon Gryspeerdt was attracted from St Thomas's Hospital to found what has become a very busy and expanding department of neuroradiology. With this clinical band, Henry set about attracting research workers to his department. His magnificent personality enabled him to woo local philanthropists to such good effect that the Demyelinating Research Unit was founded, to which E J Field came as first director before being appointed to a chair in the university.

The flow of clinical papers did not ease but now more acceptable papers on scientific research were presented to the establishment. The local students' "rag" contributed to the founding of a research fund in multiple sclerosis, and from this the first major survey of the condition in this country was undertaken. A series of controlled trials in the management of multiple sclerosis followed, and there was no shortage of younger colleagues and junior devotees. Later, he was appointed to a personal chair in neurology and, after the death of Andrew Lowdon (then Dean of the Faculty), Henry, having worked as clinical sub-dean in his spare time, became Dean of the Medical School and subsequently Vice-Chancellor of the University, the last of the three phases in his life about which others will be writing in extenso.

It was traditional to serve on the house at Queen Square for at least two and a half years, during the latter part of which one was designated resident medical officer. Henry, however, considered that 18 months was quite long enough, and I was persuaded to return to Newcastle before I had completed my attachment to the National. In the meantime, the ebullient David Poskanzer (now of Harvard and the Massachussets General Hospital) had gone up to Newcastle from the Square, and when I returned to Newcastle in the October of 1960 it was to enjoy perhaps the three best years of my own clinical life. For here we had a rapidly expanding, active department, enjoying a high standard of clinical neurology, always goaded, abused, and inspired by Henry's attention. He allowed his first assistant a free range of clinical responsibility, and for this I shall always be grateful. When errors were committed, the perpetrator was left in no doubt that he had been indiscreet, but when a modicum of success was enjoyed, then equally there was generous recognition.

By this time the Regional Neurological Centre had opened in Newcastle, and neurology and neurosurgery had combined in the one building on the old General Hospital site. Henry, however, preferred to stay at the RVI and John Walton developed his own separate interests at Newcastle General—in particular, research into muscular dystrophy and other neuromuscular diseases. The popularity of the department was apparent in the teaching hospital group and became known because of the personality of its head, and also because of the publications which began to flow from the research workers and clinicians whom Henry had attracted. Especially enjoyable in these years were the entertainments provided by Henry and his visitors from all over the world around the dinner table. The Friday night dinner parties following the research meeting with the flags on the table honouring the nationality of the visitor, and with fare which demanded of him a very high gastronomic capacity, will always be remembered; in later years, when the university developed its own catering establishment, many of us in neurology will remember evenings in the "Alnwick Room" with Henry at the head of the table entertaining his department and its famous guests.

After his accession to the deanship and later to the vice-chancellorship, we did not have much contact at the clinical level but would always look forward to enjoying his company at local meetings, conferences, and especially the international conferences. Perhaps the most enjoyable of these was the International Congress in Rome, which others will undoubtedly describe. My first Congress with Henry was in Barcelona and I recall with great pleasure one hilarious day when, after emptying the bedroom fridge of its contents (a very mixed selection), Eileen, Henry, and I spent an afternoon and early evening at the bullfight, surprisingly his first ever. He was by this time not in the best of health and I remember our concern at being unable to obtain transport back to the cocktail party of the conference. On the last evening of that conference, with typical generosity, he organised a birthday party for his original first assistant; we all suffered during the journey home the following day, and how we suffered.

Many have regarded Henry during the last few years as something of a maverick, not to be taken too seriously, but when he wished to be serious he could be very serious and his latter writings in *Encounter* on "Medicine and Society" and his articles in the *Listener* give evidence of this facet of his personality.

For Henry, life (and medicine in particular) was fun. He loved the clinical and research razzamatazz. His clinical teaching was anecdotal, his examination of the patient perfunctory at best, but with his very quick mind he very rarely missed anything remediable. He despised ill health, not only in himself, but in juniors and colleagues. He cynically regarded holidays as a waste of time. A Geordie at heart, he loved North-Eastern society and the Newcastle Medical School, and often declared that he would always work in Newcastle out of preference, but there were only three other places in the world he would be prepared to settle—Oxford, Hong Kong, and, rather strangely, Canberra in Australia, but no doubt others will talk of his Australian trips. He had great delight in small events, the tailormade silk pyjamas, a gift from a one-time patient and later close friend, his election to the Athenaeum, his enthusiasm for Rose Hill in West Cumberland, his Marks and Spencer ties, and Savile Row suits.

Often declared by his peers to be ambitious for national recognition, his fame was international, totally without pretension. I feel that the honours that appeared to elude him were to him of little consequence, and it would have been no surprise, had he been offered some honour, to hear him decline it in his best Churchillian prose. Clumsy with the practical matters of medicine, and never a laboratory benchworker, he had immense admiration for surgical expertise despite his public condemnation of the surgeon and his perfunctory dismissal of their intellectual standing in medicine.

In his final few months, he realised only too clearly that his congestive heart failure would ultimately overcome him but, for those of us with such affection for this personality, the anguish was quickly dispelled by Henry himself, either with a shared bottle of champagne or a few gins; those of us who survive him in Newcastle hope only to continue the high standards he set himself and others, and maintain an active, busy and attractive department, which in itself would be his best and most desired memorial.

J B Foster is a consultant neurologist at the Newcastle General Hospital.

John Gilroy

I enjoyed dining and lunching with Henry at the Garrick Club, as he was always such an interesting, serious, and witty conversationalist. I always wanted to paint his portrait but could never determine a positive expression which conveyed his character. Eventually I persuaded him to sit for me, as I wished to present the painting to the university. He remarked at the time in good Geordie dialect, "Why waste time on my mug—but at least you'll enjoy painting the bonny robes and frills." He was a very enthusiastic sitter, but hopeless at keeping a definite expression and remaining still.

His conversation was vital to me. He had an interest in everything I asked, but I found it difficult to get him to remain static. I painted several expressions, but only after the third sitting did I realise the true characteristics which are in the final portrait now hanging in the university. He was so anxious to co-operate that he travelled from Newcastle upon Tyne specially for an afternoon sitting, and returned the following morning. At this particular session I was very concerned about him as he looked so ill and seemed a different person altogether from that of the earlier sittings.

One evening at the Garrick Club will remain memorable. We dined together and then proceeded to the outer lounge and joined Lord Cohen, Sir Melford Stevenson, Richard Crossman MP, Lord Justice Charles Russell, and Dr John Tilley (all of whom were members). The atmosphere was electrified by a continuous flow of club port. Sir Melford and Richard Crossman were the star entertainers and what was said at the time is now sacred to those who were present.

Henry fanatically admired Sir Thomas Beecham, and he implored me to part with the studies I had made of Sir Thomas many years ago. I was delighted for him to possess them. I loved to exchange Geordie repartee with Henry but, alas, I was always second rate.

My last evening with him was at the unveiling of his portrait. It was sad in one way: he was ill, and about to fly to America for a special conference. My fears were unfortunately verified as this journey speeded his death. He was a wonderful friend and I am honoured to have recorded him for posterity.

John Gilroy's portrait of Henry Miller now hangs in King's Hall, University of Newcastle upon Tyne, and is shown on the front cover of this book.

George Godber

John Walton in his obituary referred to him as "the one and only Henry Miller," and apologised for describing him as an unforgettable character. Those comments came at the end of an eulogy that was not fulsome and was wholly justified. Henry was not a cultivator of bureaucrats but he was such a friend as would discount one's bureaucracy. In nearly 30 years of growing friendship my admiration only mounted; even when he was wrong it was in some splendid way—and he would admit it on exposure to the evidence. Most of us do not do that; it takes real stature to accept and act upon correction. Admittedly, Henry was the producer of the correction more often than the recipient.

Contributors

Henry had to fight for the creation of his department, even for his first recognition as a neurologist rather than a physician with an interest in neurology. Thirty years ago Newcastle, like a lot of other centres, recognised few of the medical specialties outside general medicine. William Hume had established cardiology firmly enough for those who were to follow, but George Rowbotham's development of a fine neurosurgical service almost obstructed the evolution of medical neurology. It was Henry's range and skill which established it. In later years I had the good fortune to meet at intervals an informal group of registrars, who used to come to sit round in my room and tell me how wrong I was. Once we were discussing the pecking order among teaching centres, which advisory appointments committees seemed to have engraved on their minds. Queen Square was an experience, they said, which every aspirant in neurology must be able to claim. But, they also said, if you want to know modern neurology you must go to Henry Miller. That was the statement of a young London graduate, not of some visitor from the north. How seldom does one meet the teacher who really does excite the taught and leave them in that state of idolatry which John Walton described.

I really got to know and appreciate Henry while we were trying to find a way round the rules to use NHS funds to support an academic unit. He wasn't habitually a patient man, but he didn't approach the problem like a surgeon, knife in hand, so we found a way through, and NHS money went to a development of clinical service which freed enough to help the university do its part. He knew when not to explode or back away. After that we used to meet at short intervals and always there was some new step Henry wanted to take, and surely soon did. Many people have a single limited objective which they gain and on which they rest out a clinical career. With Henry the exciting thing was to watch the way a gain was only the justification for reaching out for something now visualised even farther on. It was difficult to be sure how much had been foreseen earlier but undisclosed, and how much was new and fresh inspiration. The longer one knew Henry the more certain one became of his length of view.

Among British centres Newcastle stands out, over the years, for the close links of the medical school with the major municipal hospitals. John Charles and his chairman Walter Thompson, later to be respectively CMO and first Chairman of a Regional Hospital Board, helped, through their remarkable development of the City Hospital to establish a home for James Spence as the first professor of child health in Britain, and later for the regional neurosurgical service, the department of cardiology, the department of radiotherapy (with the first of the new linear accelerators), and the professorial unit of psychiatry. Here was a unique partnership of the designated teaching hospital, under its board of governors, and a major regional hospital housing most of the regional specialist centres. It was Henry who saw the commonsense solution of a single management committee under the regional board managing two main university hospitals. While too many other self-styled centres of excellence were organising campaigns—predestined to failure—against the simple sense of unified management within a regional plan, Newcastle, under Henry's guidance, was anticipating one of the good points of the 1974 reorganisation. They were making the allegedly unacceptable work to advantage.

The framework of the NHS is rigid, and that can be both a support against attack and an obstacle to progress. It takes tolerance and insight to find ways round the obstacle without losing the support. In retrospect one can only regret that Henry's health kept him from more active intervention in some of the events which 1974 and 1975 were to bring.

Henry fell foul of central policy over one aspect of NHS development which brought him sharply into friendly conflict with Dick Crossman. Both were able debaters and both could be abrasive, but this was not the problem. Ministers—Nye Bevan and Dick among them—usually react against too large institutions. They see the potential oppressiveness of size in a caring establishment, where the medical scientist is apt to see first the benefits of bringing the different aspects of science together. Both are right, so the solution has to be a compromise. Henry, like the Bonham Carter Committee, wanted to go too far one way. Later, David Owen wanted to go too far the other way. The confrontation in Newcastle was to come over the arguments about the size of a rebuilt RVI and the need for a Walker Gate hospital. This was one of the few occasions when Henry's rationalism brought him down too strongly on the university side. The dialectics that ensued were remarkable, and they were not yet subject to the constraints that a falling capital budget were to impose. This is an argument that had to take place and one from which we are now emerging with a reasonable compromise. In the end, the arguments for a reasonably human scale have to prevail, but they must not be allowed to destroy the minimum medical scientific base for specialised medicine. The claims of what the Americans call high-technology medicine are apt to end in stressing the science more than the benefits it confers. There is a revulsion against medical science among some people; Ivan Illich does not lack supporters nor, wholly, reason. I think we will miss Henry's contribution more than most to the compromise that must result.

The other side of this picture is provided by Henry's contribution to the BMA's Board of Science, of which he was the first chairman. That was an event that occasioned surprise and expectation duly fulfilled. Intensive care was one of the earlier subjects studied, but so were aids to the handicapped and the primary care team. There was and is every reason to be critical of the unorganised state of provision of aids—from powered prostheses to commodes or wheelchairs. It is not simply that effort is not made, but rather that generalisation of best current practice is not achieved. Too often development is duplicated with minor variations that are expensive and not readily introduced in a marketable form. High technology medicine may lead to advances that can be generalised at lower cost, but more often inflates cost for marginal benefits for the few who have access to it. The Board of Science under Henry's influence was not used to promote modern medical techniques so much as to encourage the generalisation of best current practice. That could be a valuable lesson from the truly modern medical scientist.

Henry had his conflicts with the psychiatrists, but Newcastle during his deanship and vice-chancellorship gave Martin Roth the facility to build up a university department of the highest quality. Moreover, Henry was one of the few academics prepared to entertain the possibility of a chair mainly concerned with mental handicap, its causes, and prevention. It did not emerge—not from lack of will, but of the man for the job.

The Newcastle school has always been distinguished by its broadly human approach to medicine. Perhaps James Spence was the best known protagonist of that, but the influence spread far beyond child health. The school benefits from its links with regional hospitals and with general practice to an extent which only Southampton yet parallels. Henry was critical of that endless academic game of musical chairs known as reviewing the curriculum. But, none the less, the work of those like George Smart and Andrew Lowdon was continued by Henry himself as dean and, supported by him as vice-chancellor.

Looking back at communication over more than 25 years, my recollection is one of excitement and stimulation to fresh thoughts, of robust but friendly exchanges; of an uninhibited contribution to public debate on health, without destructive intent on an increasingly beleaguered NHS. With it all there was friendship above the conflict, which is the best memory of all.

Sir George Godber was Chief Medical Officer at the Department of Health and Social Security until 1973.

John Hankinson

It is just 20 years since I joined Freddie Rowbotham in Newcastle, and first met Henry Miller. Henry gave me a very warm welcome and smoothed my path in every way. He proved an ideal medical colleague

Contributors

for a neurosurgeon, and my early years in Newcastle were very happy ones, largely owing to the pleasure and stimulation of working with Henry Miller and the very full social life which we enjoyed. His pragmatic approach to neurological problems was admirably suited to those aspects of neurology which ultimately are of interest to the neurosurgeon, and we established and maintained a most satisfactory professional relationship with almost none of the friction which sometimes occurs.

I will refrain from anecdotes as most of the events and people who would figure in them render them unsuitable for publication. He was always amusing and original; I was sorry that, in the latter years of his career, he inevitably spent less and less time in clinical medicine and I was deprived of a great deal of entertainment as well as his robust commonsense and experience. In the words of the song he has indeed "gone, like our youth, too soon."

John Hankinson is Professor of Neurosurgery at the University of Newcastle upon Tyne.

Gordon Macpherson

"Many thanks for your kind note. I have recovered from the disease and am now busy recovering from the treatment! Unfortunately I am stricken by mental torpor and cannot yet summon the energy even to write a book review. However, I think this is passing. Take grandfather's advice and relax."

That letter encapsulated Henry for me. It was his response to a commiseratory note I had dispatched when he fell ill in 1972. By chance this reply surfaced in my desk, along with what, sadly, turned out to be his last letter to me (of which more later), shortly after the invitation to "remember" Henry had arrived. So it seemed a providential text for doing just that.

The letter demonstrates his aptitude for constructing brief, clear, and attractive prose. Perhaps constructing is an ill-chosen adjective, with its implications of carefully planned, polished phrases. Polished yes, but I recall arriving early for one of my first meetings with Professor Miller, as he then was, and waiting in his room while he dictated some letters to his secretary. The sentences of perfect English flowed out with no pauses for construction or reflection. Even a Welshman would have applauded, and I wondered with some alarm whether I would ever do anything but flounder miles astern in the wake of this remarkable man.

35

Contributors

Our paths had crossed in 1967, when he had accepted an invitation to direct the BMA's brave new Planning Unit, which I had been detailed to service as secretary. At the time I knew of Henry Miller but had not met him. Later, I often pondered why he—a seemingly archetypal BMA non-member—had accepted the post. It struck me as a curious amalgam: the bustling, acutely intellectual, international physician of socialist convictions and the BMA, an organisation generally renowed for its spirit of compromise and conservatism. Yet Henry relished a challenge —in his letter one can almost sense his challenging his illness—and he was perceptive enough to foresee that harnessing a collection of bright, forward-looking doctors and lay experts to the BMA's servicing and public relations capabilities would ensure a stimulating performance. In short, he thought it could help medicine. Though obviously biased, I think he was proved right and his astute political sense led him to insist in advance of accepting the directorship on freedom to publish the unit's reports uncensored by the BMA's hierarchy of committees. Yet when it came to presenting his unit's reports to the Council of the Association, and later to the press, he handled the occasions with a deftness, humour, and, in an odd way, humility that disarmed critics, even some of those most determined in advance to be difficult.

Certainly, it was his sharp sense of sceptical humour—well displayed in the latter—that helped him to persuade the most unlikely people to join him in the novel enterprise of planning with the BMA. To my knowledge, none regretted succumbing to his pressure and very few resisted. His selection of chairmen for the working panels was masterly and having demanded his freedom of the BMA he, in turn, gave the chairmen and their colleagues their heads as to how they prepared the reports. Not unnaturally he had clear ideas of his own—for example, he resisted any suggestions of a grandiose replanning of the NHS or its financing—but was willing to listen to contrary opinions, relishing the ebb and flow of argument. And he had a healthy realism about the limitations of medicine—that too is clear from his letter—which kept even the most idealistic members firmly on the ground.

I know that the report on primary care, the most ambitious of the unit's studies, did not convert him from his futuristic view of large hospitals as the focus of medical care. But he listened with respect to the panel's arguments and as an ex-GP I like to think that these modified his reservations about the future of general practice. That report, more so even than the others—on intensive care, computers, and aids for the disabled—influenced developments in medicine and all of them became established references. There was, however, one disappointment. A study of priorities in medicine was a project he had dearly wanted to launch via the Planning Unit. But a series of practical problems and his own impending retirement from the unit resulted in a rushed and, hence, inadequately researched commentary—it barely justified the title of report—which cast a shadow over what turned out to be the final days of the unit. Even so, the publicity accorded to the concept of medical priorities, which Henry had rightly forecast as a looming challenge for doctors and society, helped to launch a public debate that still bubbles furiously. So, even this "failure" planted the seeds of success.

To an extent my recollections of Henry Miller are not so much a film, more a series of snapshots: greetings or farewells as he descended or ascended the Newcastle night sleeper (which at times seemed the axis of his life); entertaining dinners at the Garrick (opening with that characteristic habit of tucking the four corners of his napkin flag-like across his waistcoat); "working" breakfasts at the Athenaeum ("only meal they serve worth having, my boy"); brisk Planning Unit meetings from 4.30 to 6.00 ("serve the gin at 4.30—it'll oil the meeting and give the BMA establishment something to talk about"); and occasional enjoyable trips to his home territory of Newcastle (I dare to count myself a converted Novacastrian).

Mention of that night sleeper reminds me of a casual aside one day after a typically Henry yawn: "I only managed one book review on the train last night." For him to admit, as he did in his letter, an inability "even to write a book review" showed how low his illness had felled him, somewhat belying the letter's otherwise optimistic tone.

His success owed much, not only to persistent optimism but also to his natural facility for "getting on" with people. I cannot imagine anyone he met or any venture in which he took part being unaffected by his verve and irreverence for "status." "Grandfather's advice" in his letter was a personal touch that I chuckled over if only because I knew that he would be the last to heed it.

Henry Miller belonged to that fascinating genre, the eighteenth century polymath. That age of inquiry and conversation, of large personalities and large appetites, of artistic enjoyment and political controversy, would have suited his literary and scientific talents admirably. It was our good fortune to have him in twentieth century medicine, where, as well as his skills in art and science, he mastered that other technique so essential to modern academic success: administration. With Henry in the room, even that tedious chore the committee became bearable and even entertaining. With him in the chair, a meeting could acquire that other uncommon characteristic: brevity.

Why do I remember Henry? Well, it was his unusual blend of intellectual acuity, humour, and humility that really captured my admiration. The last was not, perhaps, an obvious quality, for it often hid behind that trenchant wit. May I persuade any doubters to my view by concluding with a paragraph from his last letter to me written only three months before he died: "I am very bored with being a vice-chancellor but am obviously too old for any genuine form of gainful employment, so will probably see my time out—if spared—which will probably be about three years. Perhaps I could then come and be your office boy?" I like to think he really meant it: what fun it would have been for the *BMJ*.

Gordon Macpherson is now Deputy Editor of the *BMJ*.

Denis Matthews

I am certainly not qualified to discuss Henry's prowess and renown in medical circles. But he had a well-known personal passion for music. It was over the question of music that I first met him in May 1970 at the Garrick Club, one of his regular London haunts. As Vice-Chancellor of Newcastle University he had invited me for an informal chat about the future of its department of music. It was proposed to establish a chair on the retirement of the existing head, Dr Chalmers Burns. Dr Burns, it must be added, had built up quite a thriving department from the days when King's College, Newcastle, had been officially a "division" of Durham. Meanwhile, independence had arrived, and Henry was keen to bridge the gap between academic and public music by having a practising performer in charge. "Not that I have the slightest influence over selection committees," he said, "but I think you would suit the job and the job would suit you." More of that anon. It was clear to me at once that Henry was a popular character at the Garrick, though I was unprepared for an outspokenness that I soon came to expect and enjoy. Needless to say, he was a generous host. "The pursuit of happiness," he later said to me, "is a waste of time—but I do think a chap is entitled to enjoy his misery with a large gin in his hand."

On the subject of musical education it was clear that Henry had little use for non-performing "ologists," as he called them. It was equally obvious that his musical tastes differed considerably from mine. The once-accepted "three Bs"—Bach, Beethoven, and Brahms—were certainly not his. One of *his* musical Bs, though hardly a composer, was undoubtedly Sir Thomas Beecham. That having been registered it was far easier not take take Henry's remarks at face value, though—as with Beecham—there was often a grain of truth in his most outrageous opinions. After a while, however, I did begin to wonder whether his debunking of Beethoven was intended to put me *off* Newcastle as a possibility. The next March he wrote suggesting that I should visit the

38

university "to have a look round and meet some of the folk." Having been met at the station by him, and royally lunched, I found myself ushered into a well-peopled committee room. There was a long and friendly session, after which Henry congratulated me on "having interviewed the committee very well." Back at the Vice-Chancellor's Lodge, the subject of opera having cropped up, I was challenged to conjure up the Prelude to Act 3 of *Lohengrin* on his ornate Steinway. In view of Henry's general antipathy to the "great" German masters his enthusiasm for Wagner surprised me. Beecham, however, had also been quite a Wagnerite in his own way.

To cut the story short of my eventual appointment at Newcastle I must record Henry's words of welcome at an official Senate dinner to "our first professor of music—whom we appointed in the teeth of fierce academic opposition." This went down splendidly with laughter and applause, enhanced by his parallel with the dismay that might greet a surgeon "who had actually performed an operation." Our next important meeting was the occasion of my inaugural lecture, over which Henry presided. He seemed alarmed that I had chosen Brahms as my topic. "Keep it to 50 minutes," he said, though, knowing that he had no means of escape, I talked and played for 95 minutes. "I keep hearing nauseating praise," he added next day, "and to make matters worse I've had to go and buy a record of some of those confounded intermezzi you played." I felt delighted to have made a semi-convert.

During subsequent years I saw much less of Henry than I would have liked. Apart from his duties as the V-C and travels to conferences and so forth he was taken seriously ill in 1972. He was, of course, reluctant to "slow down." We had many plans for public concerts in the university, which did mean occasional meetings and frequent phone calls. He still attended recitals and concerts, especially when they included request items of his own. "Music is largely a nineteenth-century affair," he would say. He enjoyed piano virtuosity and was happy when John Ogdon came up to play a whole string of paraphrases by Liszt, Busoni, and Godowsky. John also included a sonata by Hummel, one of Beethoven's much lesser contemporaries and therefore "preferable" to Henry. This was in the University Theatre, Henry's favoured venue. It had comfortable seats and a licensed bar, a prerequisite for a successful concert. Knowing of Henry's passion for the Russian nationalists I included Mussorgsky's *Pictures at an Exhibition* in one of my own recitals. He then persuaded my wife, Brenda McDermott, to learn Balakirev's *Islamey* for him, a feat duly relished by him. *She* had the misfortune to precede it with Schubert's impressive but austere *A minor Sonata*, D784. I sat near enough to Henry in the audience to hear him mutter "like Beethoven at his worst." The César Franck *Violin and Piano Sonata*, on the other hand, was one of his favourites. Ralph

Contributors

Holmes and I worked at this specially for him in a programme with *Prokofiev No. 1* as the centrepiece. The Russian magic failed to work here: "a very strange sandwich with a large chunk of bread in the middle."

Henry's enjoyment of barbs and banter did not allow his own likes and dislikes to influence his support for music in general. I had to visit him, cap in hand, when a series of twentieth-century concerts ran into financial trouble. He helped to bale us out, but commented that the university could not continue to underwrite programmes of non-music for audiences that did not want to listen to them. A few months after our own arrival in Newcastle we found a large house suited to our musical needs but almost within earshot of the V-C's lodge. "Obviously *we* shall have to move," he said, though in fact it meant that we met rather more often for neighbourly drinks and discussions on Sunday mornings. He was full of musical reminiscences and would reinforce them by dipping into his large collection of records, usually played at full blast. Then, to one's surprise, he would sit down at the piano himself to illustrate a point—perhaps the charm of that neglected eighteenth-century Tynesider, Charles Avison. Or it might have been Godard or Arriaga.

Of conductors he had much to say. Even established names were liable to be written off as "ineffectual" or "non-starters." Though loyal to Beecham, Henry did concede that Toscanini's performance of Elgar's *Enigma* was surprisingly good "for a Wog." Yet Beecham's love of Mozart seemed to leave him, at this stage, rather cold. The *Jupiter Symphony*, one of Beecham's favourites, irked him. "Thank heavens medical science didn't save Mozart—otherwise he would have started writing symphonies like Beethoven." Poor Beethoven, poor Mozart. Henry loved an argument. One could always tease him for preferring Bizet's early but slight *Symphony in C* or a handful of charmingly trivial Beecham "lollipops." One could learn to remain undisturbed by his dismissal of *Fidelio* as "fiddle-ee-oh." "I know you don't take to these serious heavy-handed German types," I told him. "That's why you get on so well with Wagner." Yes, Henry was always a tonic. Two other remarks of his would have given Beecham pleasure. After all, it was Sir Thomas, was it not, who described the harpsichord as "playing on a bird-cage with a toasting fork?" Henry seemed similarly allergic to the organ: "I prefer to listen to music through my ears and not my buttocks." When I expressed disappointment that he had not been able to attend my début as a choral conductor with the Newcastle Bach Choir, he said he would have found it an unthinkable ordeal to "sit through long stretches of unaccompanied choral music of a religious nature."

All the same, I am delighted that the department of music has acquired Henry's Steinway. It will be a constant reminder of his stimulating and often salutary personality. I regret that we never succeeded in pinning him down to give a lecture to our students about his musical tastes. He would have been splendid on Russian opera or on Beecham, but even a randon collection of his Desert Island Discs would have been healthily provoking. I doubt whether he would have included any of the late Beethoven quartets. Yet we had many serious discussions about the possibility of having a resident quartet in the university, frustrated by lack of funds. Admittedly he would be apt to change direction and ask me about the feasibility of getting Arturo Benedetto Michelangeli to give a piano recital in the University Theatre. That certainly would have broken the bank, even with a full house. So let Henry have the last word: "I used to think surgeons were the most mercenary people I knew, but I have come to the conclusion that musicians and architects have them beaten to a frazzle."

Denis Matthews is Professor of Music at the University of Newcastle upon Tyne.

W B Matthews

In the immediate post-war years, when the lower rungs of the neurological ladder were crowded with ambitious aspirants, the Olympian heights were first occupied by a band of immortals. While, no doubt, essentially benevolent, from the nether regions they could present a somewhat forbidding aspect: "safe and proud above the hot struggles of the poor." Poised, for even in those days one could scarcely say floating, at an intermediate level, was the formidable, fearless, but entirely approachable figure of Henry Miller. This was an exciting time in medicine in Britain. Large numbers of comparatively mature doctors were leaving the armed Forces, in great need of training and of opportunities to put this training to use. The NHS was imminent and many well-entrenched and long-established traditions were under attack. Although, of course, already qualified to form part of the establishment himself, Henry was also in a position, which he used effectively, to voice the discontent of the rising generation who would staff the NHS. All his life he remained in many ways an anti-establishment figure.

I believe that the first time we spoke was after I had, with trepidation as an invited speaker, undergone the considerable ordeal of presenting a paper to the Association of British Neurologists. He suggested that my paper would make an admirable contribution to the *Journal of Negative Investigation,* but, characteristically, took in good part my more carefully

Contributors

phrased hint that his own communication would make headlines in the *Journal of Ineffective Therapy*. In 1960 I was privileged to be a member of a group of six British neurologists, organised under some obscure banner by Hugh Garland, to visit Rumania. Henry was of the party and, while our hosts had unmistakably been hoping for a solid phalanx of prewar classics, Henry and Hugh, at least, compensated for any disappointments they may have experienced. They could scarcely be expected to enjoy to the full the scintillating interplay of repartee between these two masters of the art, but there was a more serious side to this foray to terra incognita. Henry's paper on the increased incidence of multiple sclerosis in social classes I and II was possibly not entirely appropriate in a country where both the disease and the social classes referred to were at that time rare, but no less so than Roger Gilliatt's paper on the neurophysiological diagnosis of the carpal tunnel syndrome —a condition that had not yet made its appearance in Rumania at all. It was, however, in that most exacting phase of any visit to a foreign centre, that of the conducted tour of the laboratories, that Henry showed to enormous advantage. Such tours resemble an attempt to see the whole of the Prado at a single visit. With the best of intentions interest begins to flag as fatigue increases. With practice it is possible to maintain the aching facial muscles in an appropriate smile of international amity when presented with fleeting glimpses of other people's research. Henry's approach was different. Without, I am sure, a shadow of pretence, he was interested and informed, intelligent, and interrogatory on an astounding variety of scientific inquiry. His apparently inexhaustible energy, genuinely directed to the increase of knowledge, put his younger colleagues to shame and must greatly have enhanced the pleasure of our hosts. Unfortunately Henry's many commitments enforced his leaving the expedition early and we were denied the spectacle of his accompanying Hugh Garland, dressed up to the nines as usual, shooting duck from an insecure punt at dusk on the Danube delta on the Russian border.

I never had the opportunity to see Henry at work as a clinical neurologist, but his impact on the subject was evident to all. He was insistent on the introduction of scientific method to clinical neurology, in particular the techniques of epidemiology and of the properly conducted therapeutic trial, and in many of his most important papers he collaborated with others on these topics. He did not acquire personal expertise in any investigative method but had no difficulty in detecting the inflated claims made for some techniques. He was, perhaps, a little inclined to prejudice and I remember that his faith in peripheral clinical neurophysiology never recovered from being told that motor nerve conduction velocity was entirely normal in a girl virtually paralysed by porphyric neuropathy. My personal contacts, and therefore my memories, were mainly on the subject of medical writing. It is not easy here to display sufficiently becoming modesty, no doubt because I still feel a pleasing glow of satisfaction that Henry approved of my prose and wanted to collaborate with me. Others in this volume will no doubt be recalling his written and spoken wit. The two modes of expression were indeed more than usually closely linked and Henry wrote as for the spoken word. To read one of his papers, particularly those not too elaborately prepared, is to hear again the pointedly, artistically articulated cadence of his speech, in intimate discussion or in impromptu or deliberate oratory. Henry was a professional writer, a great advantage in a collaborator. With him there was no question of broken deadlines, inaccurate references, or texts of immoderate length. Co-authorship was not, however, entirely without hazard, as Henry's insistence that trigeminal neuralgia should be included with epilepsy as a paroxysmal disorder clashed with my own view that it belonged with the section on the cranial nerves. This led to our text-book reaching page proofs without the condition being mentioned at all. Despite his professionalism Henry was, in my view, a little lax about indexing. He thought it perfectly in order that the well-known sensation sometimes experienced by those with loss of posterior column sensation should be indexed as: "String, tied round toe, sensation of." Perhaps, after all, he was pulling my leg.

I never heard Henry expound any general principle of teaching, but he clearly relied on the not altogether inappropriate belief that what is not remembered cannot be said to have been taught at all. He did not go as far as the bold statement that: "History is not what happened but what you remember," but he certainly had much sympathy with this view. The memorable, indeed unforgettable, aphorism, forms either a solid basis of knowledge or, if subsequently modified or even contradicted by experience, is a stimulus for discussion or controversy. Although, like the rest of us, Henry liked to be right, I am sure that he felt at least as much achievement if he aroused scientific, that is to say knowledgeable, antagonism. In his writings he was severe on anything that he regarded as pretentious or unsound. Like Samuel Johnson, Henry taught and wrote to win. Similarly he hated cant and was not always too delicate in the expression of this aversion.

Henry was less happy in the constraints of the systematic description of disease. His knowledge of the clinical aspects of multiple sclerosis for instance must have been almost unrivalled but a mere catalogue of symptoms and signs did not inspire him to the best writing of which he was capable. He was more in his element when, for example, he was dilating on his deliberately provoking views on psychiatry.

Of all Henry's writings, that which had the most influence on myself was a paper on "Neurology in the General Hospital" (*BMJ*, 1958, 1,

477), written before he had achieved worldwide fame and before he was overburdened with administration and the imperious demands made on the successful author and orator; written from the experience of a skilled intuitive neurologist, intellectually and emotionally concerned in the fascination of the infinite variety of neurological practice. To my mind, this was the basis of Henry's later more glittering achievements.

W B Matthews is Professor of Clinical Neurology in the University of Oxford.

J H D Millar

I met Henry on many occasions since the war and always enjoyed his stimulating and amusing company; and I look back with pleasure to many cheerful occasions. The first time I saw him was at the Association of Physicians Meeting in Belfast in 1949. He read the last paper of the meeting on "polymorphic collagen-vascular disease." I can't remember what he said, but I do remember his witty and racy style. At that time it was customary to hold clinical demonstrations of interesting cases and, as neurological registrar to Sydney Allison, I was responsible for a few patients. Henry with, I think, Raymond Daley had a slight confrontation with me over a case which I now see in the programme labelled as "congential diffuse haemangiomatsis." He later visited Belfast on several occasions and in 1966 read a paper to the BMA on "post-traumatic syndrome," one of his favourite and more controversial topics. He was an active member of the Association of British Neurologists and attended most meetings of the Association of Physicians, being president in 1974. I always regret not being able to attend on his presidential year. Many members will remember the entertaining paper he gave on musicogenic epilepsy at the Bristol meeting of the Association of Physicians in 1961.

Over the years we met at various meetings on research into multiple sclerosis, at first in London on a small committee set up by Professor Payling Wright and Douglas McAlpine; Sydney Allison, David Kendall, and others would attend about once a year to discuss research. Later, we both served on the Medical Advisory Panel of the Multiple Sclerosis Society, of which he was chairman from 1963 to 1967. Multiple sclerosis was probably the disease which interested him most and he was considered an international figure, chairing discussions at meetings at home and abroad; he was Florence Tong lecturer in 1963. With his colleagues at Newcastle he published many important contributions on multiple sclerosis and related subjects, with Stanton and Gibbon on parain-

fectious encephalomyelitis, with Poskanzer and Schapira on epidemiological studies in Northumberland and Durham and conjugal multiple
sclerosis. With the latter he published in 1963 an important paper in the
Lancet comparing the epidemiology of poliomyelitis and multiple
sclerosis, suggesting that multiple sclerosis like paralytic poliomyelitis
was due to a lack of protection from antibody acquired early in life.
There were also papers on the effect of trauma, inoculations, and vaccination and not least therapeutic trials with Ridley and Newell using ACTH
and prednisone and, with Millac, cyclophosphamide. There were also
several joint papers with Professor Field from the MRC demyelination
research unit at Newcastle.

He made much of the idea that he was a "central" rather a "peripheral"
nervous disease man and pretended that he wasn't interested in medical
electricity. At first he was slightly suspicious of me because he thought
I was too much concerned with EEG work.

Like others, I was concerned about his health: he was very overweight
and a coronary seemed inevitable. After his first attack he made efforts
to reduce but a "slim life" never became him. I last saw him at the
International Neurological Conference in Barcelona in September 1973.
He was in splendid spirits and except for being a little out of breath
appeared in good health. Eileen and he were as usual generous hosts and
he enjoyed all the social occasions. He read a comprehensive and
masterly review on neurological disorders associated with disease of the
gastrointestinal tract and was co-chairman with Huston Merritt at the
meeting of the International Federation of Multiple Sclerosis Societies.

When he became Vice-Chancellor of the University of Newcastle
upon Tyne he continued to be actively interested in neurology. I am
sure he will always be remembered as a clinical neurologist, deeply
concerned about the welfare of his patients. He used his considerable
talents to further the interests of his specialty and to stimulate and inspire other neurologists to carry our research. Above all he remained a
warm friend and a compassionate doctor.

J H D Millar is a consultant neurologist at the Royal Victoria and Claremont
Street Hospitals, Belfast.

Michael O'Donnell

One of my personal treasures is a crumpled notebook (W H Smith
$5\frac{1}{4}$ x $3\frac{1}{8}$ narrow feint) filled with near illegible phrases. I scribbled them
one night in December 1975 after I had dined with Henry at his
favourite London hotel, the Howard, and the reason that my scrawl,

normally difficult to decipher, verged on the impenetrable was that the evening included a challenge from my host that the pair of us drink our way through one shelfload of the "minibar" in his room. My handwriting suggests we succeeded.

It was an evening I shall not forget. Henry was in his most expansive, ebullient form, eager for company, eager to talk. And he said so many things I wanted to remember that when I eventually made it back to my own room I reached for my Biro and my Smith's narrow feint. I have my notes in front of me now and, though I recall—and can see—that we spent a lot of time in deliciously scurrilous gossip, one or two items are fit (just) to be preserved in print.

Henry, for instance, had no doubts about his greatest achievement as vice-chancellor; the Denis Matthews appointment as professor of music. Nor did he have any regrets about what more sedate members of our profession called his outrageous behaviour. He enjoyed his reputation for unconventionality, though he was a mite dismayed that some colleagues accused him of being insensitive, of too often saying the right thing at the wrong time or before the wrong audience. Most of his lapses into "bad taste" he claimed were deliberate. I noted one of his remarks: "Some occasions demand that the 'wrong thing' be said because they are themselves 'wrong' occasions that offend reason and breed complacency."

Outraging people, he claimed, was a good way of compelling them to think, to re-examine the received truths that lay dormant in their minds. He loved to challenge people to argue—for he always sought argument rather than agreement—but admitted he was sad that the sharp edge to his remarks, even when he delivered them with a smile, had made him enemies. When I suggested that people who reckoned it an insult to be challenged to cerebrate were safer to have as enemies than as friends, he said: "If anyone asks you to write my obituary, please include that." I did.

He had derived great pleasure from his jousts with the psychiatrists "Many of my best friends are psychiatrists," he told the World Psychiatric Association in 1969. "They are the sort of psychiatrists who send the patient back to me with the polite suggestion that I have another look for the cerebral tumour—and they have an infuriating habit of being right."

He gave me the notes from which he made that speech and I've just re-read the paragraphs in which he challenged psychiatry's extraterritorial demands.

"There are many quite well educated people who believe psychiatrists have special and mysterious methods of finding out what is going on in patients' minds, that are denied to the rest of us and indeed to the rest of humanity. Does the psychiatrist know more about the roots of normal

human behaviour than anyone else? When he moves outside a professional relationship it seems doubtful whether his views are more
interesting or his conclusions any more reliable than those of the rest of
us. They are certainly less illuminaing than those of the poet, dramatist,
or novelist.

"One curious phenomenon concerns insight. My careful personal
observations confirm that the practice of psychiatry in any of its forms
does not necessarily confer any insight whatever. Whether mechanist
or psychoanalyst, there are many psychiatrists who manifest that insightless insensitivity to audience reaction that is the hallmark of the bore."

Reading the last sentence I can see him delivering it with the question-
ing smile that challenged anyone present to get up and try to give him
back as good as he had given.

Over dinner we talked a lot about music—"Radio 3 is what distinguishes Britain from the less civilised world"—and at one moment,
when he was deep into a Rabelaisian tale, he suddenly raised his hand
and said: "Sh. We must listen to this." The pianist in the Howard's
dining room had just embarked on the opening Allegro from the
Schubert Sonata in A major. Six minutes later, when the last note had
been played, Henry resumed his story at the exact phrase he had
interrupted.

We also talked a lot about the abstract area of diagnosis and discovered
with glee we had both been friends of the late Evan Jones, the quirkily
eccentric St Thomas's physician who seemed to bring supernatural
percipience to the diagnosis game. Henry eulogised the wizardry of
Evan in phrases that later proved beyond recall for this ataxic Boswell
but admitted he agreed with Robert Platt that clinical decision was a
more useful gift than diagnosis. He described with relish how one
neurologist he knew (expletive and name deleted) would write long
long letters to GPs describing every lesion from which their patients
might be suffering and arguing at length the pros and cons for each.
"Every argument is sound," said Henry, if my notes are accurate.
"Every letter is long. Indecision is so well camouflaged with erudition
that the poor GP is quite impressed until the patient asks him what he
should do."

He contrasted those letters with others written by a friend and
colleague in Newcastle. "Maybe only four lines. He has gone through
the same thought processes as X but has forced himself to stick out his
neck and pick a winner. Sometimes he's wrong but at least he's trying
to do what a consultant's there to do."

The evening ended with us resolving for the umpteenth time to
publish a joint paper on the "Lump Scale"—an idea born after another
dinner years before. The scale would be used to measure the effective-
ness of medical reassurance. At one end is a tiny lump so small that

47

any competent Dr Finlay can reassure its possessor that it is harmless; at the other end the lump has become a large, fluctuant, pulsating mass which even the most avuncular Dr Cameron could not dissuade the patient from taking to a surgeon and demanding high technology medicine. Between the two we felt lay territory worth exploring.

That territory will now remain untrampled, but I remember my night and early morning at the Howard with enormous pleasure because it encompassed everything I like to remember about Henry: the excitement he created around him, his impish observation, his delight in extravagant behaviour, and the vigorous challenge of his conversation. His death deprived us of qualities already in short supply in medicine: his irreverence in the face of hollow pomp, his detestation of ill-founded tradition (coupled with a respect for traditions that had proved themselves socially or professionally useful), above all his dedicated and often courageous assaults on complacency.

History has already proved him wrong in some of the causes he argued most passionately. But even when he was wrong he ensured that those who were more nearly right had constantly to re-examine their defences. Few dogs slept in his presence.

Last month I dined again at the Howard. It seemed a greyer, chillier place than I remembered.

Michael O'Donnell is Editor of *World Medicine*.

A G Ogilvie

I hope that it will not be considered to be out of order if I start my contribution to *Remembering Henry* by remembering Eileen. When in 1940 I was President of the Durham University Medical Society, the Secretary of the Society was a Miss Eileen Baird, who made the society run so smoothly that there was really nothing for anyone else to do. At a later date Dr Eileen Baird became my house physician, and made things in the wards run just as smoothly. On one occasion during her period of duty in this post she asked quite casually for a weekend off, from which she returned as Mrs Henry Miller. I am glad to be able to report that her work in the clinic did not deteriorate in any way following this change in her condition.

It was later on that I first became aware of Henry's love of music. I learnt then of the method by which Henry and Eileen, and the baby, enjoyed concerts. During the first half Eileen took charge, either in the foyer or walking about outside, while Henry occupied the seat. During the second half a "cox and box" arrangement came into force and Henry took over, while Eileen took the seat.

After the war (in 1946) two new assistant physicians were appointed by the Royal Victoria Infirmary, Newcastle upon Tyne, and Henry was appointed as one of these. He was attached to my clinic, or rather became part of it, and remained with me until he rose to higher things, and created a department of neurology. I did not know him at all well at that time and simply wondered how things would turn out. All I knew was that he had impressed his chiefs in the Royal Air Force, and that he was a fine judge of a wife.

Over the succeeding years, on which I look back with pleasure and affection, I got to know much more. I came to appreciate his true generosity and his kindliness, sometimes overlaid by his (at times) apparent intolerance. This, as I came to understand, was due to his contempt for what he called "mealy-mouthed sentimentality," of which he was determined not to be guilty. Essentially and outspokenly honest in speech and action, he disliked the lack of it in others—and no doubt this also accounted for his "intolerance". His opinions were expressed without reserve, and even occasionally with some exaggeration.

As time went on, I observed that men joining the clinic (whether in the capacity of registrars or house physicians) as normal human beings, would leave, when the time came, as neurologists. He was a great encourager of the young, and always appreciated straightforward effort: though it has to be admitted that he was irritated by stupidity of the denser sort, and frankly disliked humbugs of whatever sort.

He had an uncanny facility for gathering around him eager students and junior officers who were anxious to work with him and for him. He seemed to exert an effortless attraction, due in part, one feels, to his interest in their ideas and his wish to further them as he could: and he had a remarkable ability to find jobs, or at any rate openings, for men wishing to work, which not only suited them at the time, but as they were going to be. And all this was done easily and naturally without any fuss or strain.

As can be expected from what I have already said, he had always a great and genuine interest in students, and this no doubt contributed to his success as clinical teacher, dean of medicine, and later as vice-chancellor. To them he was always "Henry." When medicine lectures became voluntary, the attendance fell off dramatically, and this affected all lecturers, both "goodies" and "baddies." On one occasion (reported to me, as, of course, I was not present) only six students turned up. Henry looked round and then said, "Is there a pack of cards among us?"

His brain worked with amazing speed, much faster than he walked, and he walked fast. It did in fact work rather too fast on occasion, leading to a comment or retort which on reflection might, perhaps, with advantage have been withheld, as it might well have been in the case of a slower thinker. Occasionally, a brilliant remark may have been released because the temptation was too great. The late George Bernard Shaw, whose love of music was well known, once said that music was the brandy of the damned. This was not a considered opinion, but something he felt was too good to waste.

Henry was a fine clinician, and took much more trouble over a case than often appeared. But he had a special interest in research. Here he had not only natural ability, but also immense energy, which was not obvious except in the result. Genius, of course, makes laborious and difficult things appear easy and simple, but also tends to disguise the real effort which has gone into the work. But others can speak on this aspect with greater authority.

Occasionally he would make some quite outrageous remark, with the simple curiosity to see the effect. When, for example, in a committee on staffing, he said, "There are too many surgeons anyway, let us shoot a few," there was nothing personal in it. In fact, none of his remarks, whether "off the cuff" or not, were really made with any intent to wound or embarrass: there was nothing he enjoyed more than a similar retort, provided of course that it was intelligent and preferably amusing.

Henry was a good driver, but one had a strange desire to hang on to the seat or anything else that was handy while he himself was calmly oblivious of this. I myself always enjoy a holiday, but his attitude to holidays was one of humorous detachment. "It's such hard work enjoying yourself," he would say, though he enjoyed music, literature, and above all medicine, and new ideas.

Whatever view we take of Henry Miller, we must recognise him as being a large man with a large personality and a large intellect, who occupied a large sphere of activity, and who must leave a large space behind him which will be difficult to fill. To me latterly he was one of those whom, though seldom seen, one was glad to think of as still in the same world, which is all the poorer for his loss.

A G Ogilvie is honorary consulting physician at the Royal Victoria Infirmary Newcastle upon Tyne.

Robert Orton

In 1948 I was appointed lecturer in the department of psychological medicine at the Royal Victoria Infirmary. On the same day, and in the same waiting room, was a tall handsome man, who turned out to be

Henry. He was appointed lecturer in neurology to the same department (he was already a consultant physician on the staff of the infirmary). So began 28 years of professional and personal friendship.

At that time the late Alexander Kennedy was professor of psychological medicine. He insisted on the title "department of psychological medicine," as opposed to "department of psychiatry." He was firmly of the opinion that psychiatry was a branch of medicine so that, strictly speaking, our titles were consultant physicians in psychological medicine. Henry agreed with this concept. He had already done a considerable amount of psychiatry and had, of course, been a neuropsychiatrist in the RAF during the war. In the RAF, he had come under the influence of C P Symonds, who was a firm believer in the title neuropsychiatry, holding that psychiatry was really a part of neurology. Henry subscribed to this view and, to a large degree, so did Alec Kennedy and myself. In those early days Alec Kennedy was largely concerned with developing the department and I was left to get on with the job of doing the clinical work. In this way I came to know Henry very well indeed: I was really his psychiatric consultant. To start with, Henry used to work in the department of psychological medicine half a day a week and we used to joke over tea and say that most of the cases he saw were psychiatric and most of the ones I saw were neurological. So began a professional relationship, in which we boxed and coxed over the years.

It goes without saying that those who knew him well soon realised that he was a brilliant neurologist: his diagnostic ability and astuteness were very much part of the man. In addition, he was wise about deciding what to do with people, something which was not always recognisable from reading his articles. On one occasion I questioned what we should do about an old lady who, between us, we had discovered had a cerebral tumour. His comment was easy: "What good are we going to do her? If they operate on her she might die immediately; on the other hand she might die a cripple; at the moment she is tolerably well physically, but she is depressed—you treat her depression, Bobby. That, at least, will make her end reasonably happy." He loved to have his eye wiped, and nothing amused him more than my turning up and saying, "This patient is not a hysteric, but has in fact got such and such a disease . . ." Equally, he was pretty quick to tell you that the "hysteric" you saw yesterday had in fact got a cerebral tumour. All this was done in an extremely friendly bantering way, which led one only to feel an increasing respect both for his ability and for him as a man.

Henry had an encouraging quality too, for those who worked with and for him; undoubtedly many people owe him a great debt of gratitude because of the encouragement that he gave them. He did not become a great man by overriding other people in a ruthless way to gain his own ends—quite the opposite. He encouraged those whom he could see were good at their jobs and progressing well. He was never mean with his compliments, and his generosity knew no bounds. I, for one, will remain ever grateful for the encouragement that he gave me. On occasions the patients that he sent me were incredibly difficult to treat, but a successful outcome was praised by Henry in a quiet, sincere way. Praise coming from Henry really did mean a great deal.

His banter about psychiatry always drew laughter in the coffee room; if I arrived when he and his team were having coffee, it wasn't long before he was teasing me. He had firm ideas about psychiatry and respected it greatly, but thought that some bits of it were absolute nonsense. He was at some pains in numerous writings to point out some of the pieces of psychiatry which he thought would not stand up to critical examination. He felt that it wasn't Freud (who was, of course, originally a neurologist) who wrote most of the nonsense, but his disciples. He was very pleased when I used a reference from Freud in which Freud had pointed out that psychoanalysis was but a superstructure which would one day have to be laid upon its organic foundation. He was sure that Freud would have been one of the first to accept that things such as ECT and tricyclic antidepressants were significant advances in psychiatry.

In these views, he was largely supported by Alexander Kennedy and myself. His views on neurosis were very much sounder than most people appreciated. His work on compensation neurosis is quite a classic, and he was aware that the dividing line between hysteria and malingering was very thin. One famous anecdote is about a compensation case of his, when a man he believed to be malingering both muteness and deafness was pursued by a registrar of Henry's on to the train from Newcastle to Darlington. When the registrar returned he told how he had sat in the same compartment where the man and his compensation secretary chatted away quite happily all the way to Darlington. On the other hand, he realised that the psychoses—the serious illnesses of psychiatry—did show unequivocal response to the skilful use of appropriate pharmacological agents, or even ECT, and it was because of this that he took the firm view when lecturing that these were greater advances than the mumbo-jumbo of psychoanalysis and such things.

In an article in *World Medicine* Henry once mentioned that he was one of the two founder members of the Society for the Abolition of Psychiatrists. This all arose in rather an amusing way: he gave a lecture to the medical students called "Do it yourself psychiatry," in which he made a plea that there was too much psychiatry to be done by the psychiatrists, and that a lot of it would have to be done in future by general practitioners. He was, further, very complimentary about certain psychiatrists when he said, "Watch them. I have never met a good psychiatrist yet who was not also a good physician and they'll wipe your eye for you." After the lecture, Henry, his wife and I were chatting as we walked along the corridor and I expressed the view that it might be a good thing if psychiatry in general hospitals developed in the same way as other subspecialties in medicine; that people should be trained as physicians and then do cardiology, neurology, gastro-enterology, or psychiatry, and so on as their special subjects. I said that I thought all physicians should really know more psychiatry than they did, and equally, of course, that perhaps all psychiatrists should know more medicine. Henry fell in with this view and said, "Let's form a society for the abolition of psychiatrists—you and I will be the founder members." Next morning, when he was having coffee with his registrars, one of them remarked "Fancy Orton having the nerve to walk up the corridor with you after that lecture," and Henry replied: "You should have heard what he said. Between us we have formed a society for the abolition of psychiatrists."

His views on psychiatry were not really as outrageous as all that: he felt that psychiatry had frequently given itself a bad image. If psychiatry confined itself to the small amount of knowledge that it had got; if it used the weapons that had already been developed by the pharma-cologists; and if it kept its feet firmly on the ground, it would indeed be thought a very important branch of medicine. He did once express the view to me that all trainee neurologists should do at least six months' psychiatry. He believed that neurologists by gaining some first-hand experience of psychiatry would, in fact, become better diagnosticians and more able neurologists. There is no doubt, as he realised, that it is often considered respectable to send a psychiatric patient to a neurolo-gist, but not respectable to send a psychiatric patient to the psychiatrist. Because of this, he felt it was essential that neurologists should have a reasonably good grasp of psychiatry—they should then be able to deal with minor psychiatric cases quite well but, on the other hand, be able to recognise those that did in fact require the expertise of a consultant psychiatrist. He himself, of course, had this ability to a considerable degree.

As a man, Henry was great value. In a social setting one was never dull in his company. I will always remember the parties at his house— he was always very hospitable. He chose his guests with care, and his parties were extremely jolly. He sometimes gave two parties on succes-sive evenings, so that those who did not get on with one another could at least go to separate parties. His jesting then knew no end; although I think sometimes some people were slightly hurt by it, most people took it in the way it was meant—namely, as friendly banter. Later in life, he used to tease me about my size and I, of course, him about his. He was about a foot taller than I and over twice my weight. We must

Contributors

indeed have looked a very comic pair. When I went on his ward to see a patient for him, I feel sure that sometimes, behind the scenes, his registrar found the sight of us highly amusing.

During all this, however, one must never forget his charming active wife who, though she must at times have had a difficult life with the great Henry, was always a great moral support to him, and when he became sick her responsibility towards him must have increased a great deal—throughout all this, she was clearly extremely steadfast. He bantered, of course, about his illness. After I had had a coronary thrombosis, he said to me at a party, "Ah, at last you've joined the club, Bobby, how are you?" When I said I wasn't to bad, he said, "Ah, but you're not fibrillating yet."

One looks back on all this with a feeling of sadness: the world has undoubtedly lost a great man. He is a great loss to medicine, and a great loss to the University of Newcastle. Clearly, only a great man could have inspired the putting together of a book of this kind, with his many friends and colleagues being asked to contribute to it. It's not often that editors put pen to paper after someone's death, and to see articles about Henry—not even Henry Miller, just Henry, because everybody knows who is meant—makes me proud to have been a friend of his. I for one, owe him a great debt of gratitude. He is indeed a great loss.

Robert Orton was a consultant physician in psychological medicine at the Royal Victoria Infirmary and Newcastle General Hospital. His comments were made in a tape recording.

Harry Platt

Although my encounters with Henry Miller were comparatively few, and usually all too brief, when in his company I always felt I knew him well. On such occasions the gap between our ages—almost a complete generation—seemed to be non-existent, for he saw that I was one of those elders unshaken by his impish banter. I have no doubt that in the beginning it was his concept of the unity of neuropsychiatry that attracted him to me. For me, once house surgeon to a great pioneer neurosurgeon, William Thorburn, a teacher of anatomy under Grafton Elliott Smith, an intimate friendship with Geoffrey Jefferson—a life, so to say, in the corridors of neurology—it was the admiration of the amateur for the supremely gifted professional.

If I did not see Henry, the man, very often, I could in the last few years enjoy his mind in his brilliant writings in the *Listener* and in

54

Encounter. In some of these major critiques his Swiftian shafts of wit were a joy to read. As I remember him, there was no one quite like him, and for British medicine to lose a man outstanding in science and in letters, still in his intellectual prime, is indeed a tragic happening. He had looked forward to an early retirement from his vice-chancellorship, and if he had been spared to us, what a second career it could have been.

Sir Harry Platt, Bart is Emeritus Professor of Orthopaedic Surgery at the University of Manchester.

Lord Platt

If these tributes to Henry were all to paint a picture of a beatified being with no human failings, Henry would be the first to dismiss them as a mere addition to the already overflowing archives of *de mortuis nil nisi bunkum*, and if he is now looking down upon us from some celestial plane he would not take us too seriously. Incidentally, if he *is* occupying some celestial plane, all I can say is that it will never be quite the same plane again. Look at him as you may, Henry was a disturbing character in any society: he made you ponder, even think; and that is disturbing to most of us.

He would have little respect for a volume which made no reference to the numerous people who disagreed with him from time to time. Was it not one of his chief functions to stir up controversy? Many other contributors will, I hope, praise him, for he deserves praise, for the good things which he did, for his wit—sometimes scalding—and his humour—never lacking—and his brilliance, and his neurological skill.

What I have to describe must have started in 1957, I suppose, when I was the newly elected President of the Royal College of Physicians. E D Acheson, who has since proved his worth as the very successful Dean of the new Medical School of Southampton, wrote a scathing letter to the *British Medical Journal*, denigrating the college for its examinations, its conservative and anachronistic outlook—in fact, for most of its work. This may have been justified criticism, but I thought it very cruel, considering that I, as a very unconventional President, and a whole-time professor of a provincial university had, by consent of the electorate of fellows, been given a mandate to reform the college. Had it been a letter of welcome spurring the new President on to the road of reform I could not have complained. Henry followed this up with a scurrilous letter to the *BMJ* (which in those days was the enemy of the college), supporting Acheson's condemnation, and this, I felt, was most unfair, although in retrospect I can see that even destructive criticism can be a spur to achievement.

It so happened that Henry and I met (I think after a comitia meeting) in the cloakroom of the old college in Trafalgar Square very soon after these letters had appeared, and I remember saying "and as for you Henry . . ." but I forget the words which followed; and only remember that I threw my hat at him which was a somewhat unpresidential thing to do. (Presidents wore hats in those days—soft ones, however.)

After that we met occasionally, of course, at meetings of the college or the Association of Physicians, and I think we rather avoided each other until some years later we found ourselves face to face and Henry said, "I think we should carry on the feud a little longer, don't you?" and I said to him, "Of course, Henry, one must always have a good feud in progress." You can't really go on disliking a chap who says that kind of thing. In the years that followed, we met many times, always on the best of terms, but always making a point of continuing what had become in capital letters THE FEUD. I remember introducing him to my wife and referring to the fact that he and I were in a perpetual state of feud.

Yes, he was a controversial character, was Henry, and I sometimes wondered how well his unusual qualities and his various idiosyncrasies entirely suited him to being Dean of Medicine, and later, Vice-Chancellor of Newcastle University. Those who elected him to those posts were taking a risk, as I am sure they knew, and I hope that they feel that the gamble came off.

A very human chap, Henry, and on that note I end a memoir, a reminiscence, which has, willy-nilly become almost a eulogy.

Lord Platt was Professor of Medicine at the University of Manchester and President of the Royal College of Physicians.

David C Poskanzer

I have never met a man with the intelligence and quickness of mind of Henry Miller, quite apart from his humour and energy and the sheer joy of living that characterised each day of working with him. It was my privilege to be his first assistant in neurology at Newcastle upon Tyne in 1959 and 1960, and thereafter a collaborator in research concerning multiple sclerosis.

On my arrival in Newcastle in 1959, Henry picked me up at my hotel in his car and said, "Come along, we are off to see a patient across the river and on the way we will look around for a place for you and your wife to live." He drove down through the centre of industrial Newcastle and out along the Scotswood Road. Those were the years before urban renewal, and we passed row after row of dingy little houses, the legacy of the Industrial Revolution for which Newcastle was notorious throughout Britain. My heart sank as we travelled further through slum areas. With a gloomy expression, relieved only by the twinkle in his eye which I had not yet learned to recognise, Henry turned from his driving and said, "I'm sure we can find a place for you to live around here." It took several days for me to recover. Now I know that he must have been chuckling inwardly at my discomfiture.

Once I settled in Newcastle, Henry's morning rounds became the highlight of my day. When I first took over the direction of ward 6 I arrived with typical American dogged devotion to work for its own sake at 7.00 am, only to be rejected by Sister with the comment, "Young man, come back at a respectable hour." It took a day or two to learn to make rounds at 9.00 am, and prepare for what we came to refer to as "the second coming." At 10.00 am it was almost as if an alarm had sounded. All of us—housemen, senior house officers, and registrars deep in examination and conversation with the patients—would hear some silent signal. Eyes would brighten and faces would smile, and, with shoulders straightened, off we would march to Henry's consulting room at the end of ward 6, to meet him as he charged down the hall with the propulsion of a locomotive.

He would fall into a large chair behind his desk, put himself into an erect position, straighten his tie, and tap the bottom of it into place with a characteristic gesture then turn with the cool grey eyes that missed nothing and a single word, "Well?" At first I presented a systematic rendition of each patient's condition, the status of bowels and the soundness of his sleep, and was met with a quick wave of the arm and the question, "Is there anything important?" It became apparent immediately that the delegation of authority was one of his major attributes. I finally learned to greet him only with some off hand statement such as, "Well, there is a lady in room 12 who may have multiple sclerosis, or amyotrophic lateral sclerosis, or a stroke, or a brain tumour, or depression: I think perhaps you ought to have a look at her." Leaving his desk, entering room 12, and posing two or three critical questions, the testing of the two or three neurological signs, and the return to the desk might encompass an elapsed time of five minutes. He would then turn to me and say, "Multiple sclerosis and depression; don't they teach you anything at Harvard?" The smirks on the faces of the housemen who were struggling to control their laughter were relieved when he broke into his usual laugh, shared by everyone as morning patient rounds concluded.

The next hour was devoted to brilliant conversation that ranged from research projects under way to those projected, from incisive observations on presidential politics in the United States to a dozen other subjects, and then, perhaps, comments about the loss of ten million neurons a day due to senescence in the British Cabinet or the sad state of psychiatry in the United States. The rapid-fire monologue continued as we followed him to his car, terminating in mid-sentence as the door closed, the motor roared, and he was off to some university meeting.

We spoke among ourselves about "the third eye," an imaginary faculty situated in mid-forehead in Henry Miller so that not a gesture or a word escaped him no matter how tired he was, no matter how deep in conversation with another person, no matter how quickly he passed. He was a master at sizing up people and, I suppose, at reading what we refer to now as "body language." He seemed to know exactly how far he could tease, joke, quip, and say outrageous things without destroying the egos of his associates. But he enjoyed nothing so much as intellectual argument and dialogue.

In working with him on research projects only a few sentences were required before quite complicated concepts were within his grasp. His comment was often, "Yes, yes, just give me what you have written and I will turn it into English." On trips to Carlisle along the military road his joy of living was often expressed in driving more than 70 miles an hour while carrying out a conversation at more than 100 miles an hour. We were planning an extensive research project in Carlisle in association with Charles Rolland. How well I remember Henry turning to me and saying, "This is the fun of medicine, this is the intellectual stimulation. You just can't go on seeing patients all day; somehow we have to put these things together."

Of an afternoon he might be faced by an hour or two of clinical teaching, the room often packed to the doors by medical students who knew a superb teacher when they heard one. They braved fixation by those steady eyes, and his crucial questions that often nailed a medical students to his seat. Henry might say, "What would you do if this patient were unconscious—rush off and call a doctor?" But his affection for the medical students and his juniors was overwhelming. The class of 1961 at the University of Newcastle Medical School will not forget the aftermath of their final ball, when it was decided that a trip to the coast was indicated. Picture, if you would, Tynemouth at 4 o'clock in the morning as the first rays of the sun came over the horizon and Professor Henry Miller, his first assistant, and perhaps 50 medical students, all in dinner jackets and long ball gowns; joyously immersed in the freezing waters of the North Sea. It started off as a harmless sentimental look at the dawn, followed by timorous wading on the part of a few, progressing, owing to the enthusiasm of the senior member present, to total immersion and the return to Newcastle of a bedraggled, sopping, and happy group of people.

He could be just as perceptively gentle and kind. Just as we were finishing our research and I was preparing to bring the final manuscripts to him and Dr Kurt Schapira, my car was stolen from the Peter Bent Brigham Hospital in Boston, the only drafts of the six manuscripts in the boot. I phoned the police and, because it was an off day for news, my home was so deluged with reporters that I hid out elsewhere. Sixteen hours later my car was found far from where it had been stolen and to my amazement the manuscripts in the boot were intact. I was leaving for London that morning and was so upset about the theft that I had not yet bothered to inform Henry or Kurt. Unfortunately, a stringer for *The Times* picked up the bit of news and, without my being aware of it, my collaborators in Newcastle read about the theft in their morning paper. I had decided not even to mention the matter. When I arrived at Newcastle station, however, instead of being met as I usually was by Henry and Kurt there was no reception committee. I phoned Henry. He said, "I'll be right down," and said not another word. He arrived at the station with a big smile and said, "How nice to see you, how are you," and a dozen other British courtesies which he unfailingly observed. As we moved off toward his car he turned to me casually and said, "Did you lose anything?"

Memories of Henry stretch over the years. I recall one evening phoning him from Boston and starting the conversation by saying, "I hope I haven't disturbed you." He replied, "No. no, I was watching a Greek drama on television." "Which one?" I asked. "ΙΡΟΝΣΙΔΕΖ." It took three days before I realised which "Greek drama" he had been so deeply interested in.

His visit to Boston was again a great pleasure for us. We arranged a programme which we thought he might enjoy, and that meant he wanted to see everything despite the fact that he was already not well. We travelled to Concord to see the bridge at which the American War of Independence began. (Henry always referred to this engagement as "the war in which a group of British colonials defeated a large number of German mercenaries.") He wasn't up to a long walk across the bridge and into the woods, but on our return from that walk we found him quietly reclining, eyes closed, hands clasped on his chest on top of a stone which carries the words of a lesser American poet—"They came 3000 miles and died/to keep the past upon its throne/unheard behind the ocean tide/their English mother made her moan," and the date 19 April 1775. Whether Henry rested from fatigue or from the sheer banality of the commentary, I am not sure, but the tableau of the Vice-Chancellor of the University of Newcastle benignly reclining at full length on the monument was a startling one.

Contributors

Treating him as the visiting dignitary he was, and as an intimate friend of many years, we sent a flying squad to Cape Cod to bring back live lobsters, dug out the finest champagne in the cellar of Boston's best wine merchant, and prepared a feast for Henry and Eileen, knowing that few people in the world would appreciate it so well. The rich conversation, his happiness in conversation despite his illness, still echo in warm memories.

Was it the Inca emperors who had snow brought from the mountains hundreds of miles away be relays of runners to cool their drinks? No Inca emperor deserved more than this mighty man who brought so much natural talent, energy, enthusiasm, and love of life to so many around him. On occasion when he was irritated he would refer to me fondly as the "American gorilla." I never took offence then, and since he left us I have never bothered to ascertain through the mistiness whether gorillas really cry.

David Poskanzer is Associate Professor of Neurology at Harvard Medical School, Boston.

Stuart Prebble

In common with a number of my fellow students I first met Dr Miller at a party. It was one of his annual get-togethers for up and coming student officers. And it was among my first impressions of the man that he obviously knew how to throw a party. By the end of the evening he and his wife were playing the piano and singing; and I recollect being inspired to awe by this huge fellow dressed in a massive dark suit, with his head and neck bulging red from his too-tight collar, singing his heart out.

Not the kind of vice-chancellor I'd expected to meet at all. Far from the polite and sophisticated university official, Dr Miller loved to surprise you, or more particularly to shock you. At our first meeting he surprised me by knowing my name—then shocked me with his witty irreverence to conventionally respected institutions. Not least in his attitude to the then Secretary of State for Education to whom he constantly referred as "that bloody woman Thatcher."

Meeting with Dr Miller in the more traditional relationship across the desk was an ambiguously entertaining and yet challenging business. In those days he was a big man in every sense, and his bulk obliged him to sit way back from his desk so his body slanted in a shallow gradient from his mouth to the edge of the tabletop. And he had a disconcerting habit of throwing his head back with such gusto while searching for the right epithet that he seemed in constant danger of toppling backwards. A danger only outweighed in gravity by the potential problem of getting him up again.

On formal, and informal, occasions Dr Miller used to like having the registrar, Mr Ernest Bettenson in—with, I suspect, a threefold purpose. The first was as an entirely reliable witness to the conversation (he is said to record minutes of his dreams); the second, more called upon, as a walking manual of facts, statistics, and histories of the university, and third, most called upon of all, was as a straight man for Dr Miller's constant witticisms and jibes. Mr Bettenson winced and giggled in response—then almost invariably added "I think what the V-C is trying to say is. . . ."

While constantly monitoring the smallest shift and detail in the political mood of the students, Dr Miller rejoiced in giving the impression of total indifference. If you went to him with the threat of several thousand students withholding their rent and occupying the administration building, he'd reply, "I'll leave the confidential files open if you buggers promise to leave my cocktail cabinet alone." But, equally, if you went with a story of an individual student's hardship, the chances were in favour of his already knowing the details and having already dipped into his personal fund to help.

When Dr Miller became seriously ill a cloud of gloom descended over students as well as staff. Though some of our more radical groups disliked his views, Dr Miller was unanimously respected. And, in a way, Dr Miller personified part of the character of Newcastle University— big and busy, diverse and constant. He was a Geordie, forthright and deep, down to earth but with vision. His death has been a huge loss to his family, his colleagues and the University, the city, and those who miss this big man.

Stuart Prebble was President, Newcastle University Students' Union, 1971–2, and now works for BBC TV in Newcastle.

David Pyke

I remember Henry at the meeting of the Association of Physicians in Newcastle in April 1974, when he was the president. It was, as always, an enjoyable meeting and easily the best part of it was his chairmanship. Perhaps it was a little hard for those he dropped on, but it was great fun for the rest of us. By the end of the session people were only half listening to the papers: they were waiting for Henry's comments afterwards—and they were not disappointed.

Contributors

He was unfair, of course. He could be very cutting, but without meaning to hurt. Sometimes his incisiveness was justified. There was, I recall, one paper presented by the junior of the two authors. The senior author was a well-established physician but the junior, the man who was actually giving the paper, was a young man from the Far East whose command of English and of his subject were both imperfect. After the first critical question, to which the young man had replied that it should be directed to the senior author, Henry said in his commanding voice, "Where is the senior author?" and, when he identified himself, Henry said to him," Do you believe this stuff?" It was, of course, the right question and reflected the feelings of many of the people in the audience, but none of them I think would have expressed themselves quite so directly, nor would they have had the effect of getting to the heart of the matter so swiftly.

He didn't always carry the audience with him. There was one paper on anorexia nervosa in which the author developed the not very original theme that the condition might have something to do with psychiatric causes. Psychiatry was a red flag to Henry, and it was not surprising to anybody else, nor, I expect to the presenter, when he got a rough ride afterwards. It was obvious that Henry thought the condition was purely endocrine. But when he demanded contemptuously of the audience at large, "Has anyone ever seen a case of anorexia nervosa in a male?" and a dozen hands shot up, he said "Next paper."

It was rather fun at the meeting of the committee which met to select papers for the next year's programme. We had offered a paper this time and were rather pleased with it. When we came to our paper's turn for selection or rejection I said, braggingly, "I think this is a pretty good paper—in fact we weren't sure whether to offer it to the association or to the Royal Society, but we finally decided on the association." Henry looked at the paper, looked up and said simply, "I think you were wise."

One more thing about him—his diction. You could hear every syllable he uttered, in those descending tones which kept you alert until the very end—just as well, because that was where the sting came.

A last story. I forget where the meeting was, I think it was the RSM. It was a discussion of medical ethics—whether people should be kept alive when their condition seemed hopeless, or whether euthanasia was justifiable. "I hope there won't be any discrimination on grounds of religion in all this," said Henry. "I am an atheist and the world has a long history of persecution of members of my religion."

David Pyke, a former Secretary of the Association of Physicians, is a consultant physician at King's College Hospital, London.

Clifford Richardson

I met Henry Miller in London and Edinburgh about 25 years ago, but came only to know him better after about 1970. I joined his spellbound audiences on several occasions, hearing him speak to the American Neurological Association in Los Angeles, and as a frequent guest speaker in Toronto. He was the McLaughlin lecturer and made a trip across Canada under the auspices of the Royal College of Physicians of Canada in, I believe, 1972. He was a visiting professor at our Toronto University hospitals. In his hospital rounds he showed sound instructive clinical opinions, embellished by his many witty observations and reminiscences. He was also a leading speaker at a meeting of the Multiple Sclerosis Society and was well known for his special studies and knowledge in that subject. His address on accident neurosis to the Medico-Legal Society of Toronto was based on earlier papers published in the *BMJ*. It was a huge audience with attention firmly held by his brilliant rhetoric. As might be expected, his opinions were highly regarded by defence lawyers, and less appealing to the plaintiff advocates.

Vivid in my memory are the more personal and special meetings between my wife, Freda Richardson, and Henry and Eileen. There was immediate rapport and persisting friendship. In 1972 we had a rather hilarious trip to Niagara Falls, which is famous and popular here with visitors from afar and with newlyweds. There, when we were dressing in sou'westers for a trip through the caves under the falls, Henry kept us amused with a running jocular commentary. On seeing a young couple with four children, for example, he said: "Honeymooners, I presume."

Our happiest sojourn with Henry and Eileen was a few days spent with them at our island and cottage at Lake Temagami some three hundred miles north of Toronto. At first we thought Henry was being rather arrogant in not helping us haul food and luggage in and out of the boat. Eileen then confided that he had developed auricular fibrillation some months before—the beginning of the end for him.

J Clifford Richardson is a consultant neurologist in Toronto.

George Richardson

Henry's father had died at a very early age and he entered medical school on a scholarship, although later (while still an undergraduate) his income was moderately enhanced by an inheritance of shares in an iron and steel foundry. So that shortly after I met him (1934), at the beginning of our clinical studentship, he became the proud owner of a second-hand Austin 7, which he drove with characteristic élan and disregard of such refinements as double declutching. This acquisition enlarged his already wide horizons and increased his considerable social attractions. At that time he was a slim fair-haired youth, voluble, aggressive, and displaying a considerable knowledge of English literature as well as an apparent academic interest in socialism, enriched by the friendship of the Trevelyan family, while already enjoying, through inheritance, some of the fruits of capitalism.

Henry never gave, or sought to give, the impression of being a dedicated medical student, but he did make the fullest use of the facilities open to students in the university and in the city's cultural activities. With little apparent effort he was always well to the front in all competitive examinations. His secret, as I learnt later when we shared rooms, was the complete use of his time and his astonishing ability to concentrate on the task in hand in spite of surrounding distractions. As an undergraduate he gave the superficial appearance of being a somewhat dilettante student. He had usually left the wards by 11 am at the latest, and could then be found enjoying the greater attractions of the Union. He took a full part in student organisations and was active in union affairs. Certainly, his rather brief attendances in the wards did not escape the eye of the clinical sub-dean, who was quick to notice a student's inactivity. Henry characterised the less attractive teaching rounds as examples of shifting dullness. He became highly selective in distributing his patronage to consultants' teaching rounds. Surgically, he preferred F C Pybus and enjoyed Norman Hodgson's organised outpatient sessions, which were immensely popular because of their clarity and relevance to examinations, at the same time enabling extroverts like Henry to display their rhetorical skills and recently acquired knowledge. Medically he patronised J C Spence, who was undoubtedly a stimulating teacher and ready to display his knowledge of current writing in a manner to excite a student's interest.

Spence was certainly impressed by Henry's intellectual ability and general knowledge far beyond that of the average student. He became a regular visitor to Spence's house, discussing medicine, social affairs, politics, and listening to classical music. He also stayed at Spence's cottage in the Lake District and was then a participant in Spence's enthusiasm for fell walking and rock climbing. Henry never had an abiding interest in outdoor activities or athletics of any kind, and rock climbing was a short-lived episode. He explained to me once that in associating with consultants it was especially important to gain the support not of the present most senior individuals, but rather of their juniors, who, by natural selection would have the power and influence when he himself would be a candidate for a staff appointment.

Henry was equally selective over attendance at lectures, which were often of poor quality and relayed information which was easily and more comfortably obtained from a textbook. Afternoon lectures were often avoided in favour of the cinema. The medical school was conveniently placed for at least three large cinemas, at the nearest of which a seat in the stalls in the afternoon cost only sixpence (2.5 new pence). In one particularly dull week of lectures we saw the Marx brothers in *A Day at the Races* three times. He was also an enthusiastic supporter of the People's Theatre, an amateur organisation using a converted chapel in a sleazy area of the city and giving many outstanding performances of both classical and modern plays. Music was his great addiction, and he rarely missed an opportunity to attend concerts, ballet, or opera in Newcastle. For a student he spent a lot on classical records and was the proud possessor of an EMG gramophone, enjoying the ritual sharpening of the fibre needles. When Henry found that I planned to take "conjoint," which entailed visits to London, he decided to do likewise. In my own case this was an insurance against possible failure in the Cambridge MB. For Henry the possibility of failure in an examination never entered his mind, but a visit to London meant the opportunity to go to the opera and ballet. Our first visit was for pathology and he was determined to use his time in London to the full. This left only minimal time for the examination and he did not envisage the three-hour paper requiring longer than an hour, though it was obligatory to remain in the room for half an hour. After precisely half an hour Henry rose and, to the accompaniment of loud stamping, handed in his completed paper. Of course, he passed. He never completed "conjoint," having duly passed the MB at the age of 21, preceded by a prize (the Goyder) for the best student in a competitive clinical examination in medicine and surgery.

Henry had his future career carefully planned and in this he had the active and increasingly powerful support of Spence. While we were residents together Henry told me that after that year he proposed to do a six months' HP post at Great Ormond Street and a year in pathology at Johns Hopkins under Arnold Rich. The fact that Ormond Street HPs usually had the MRCP did not deter him. Indeed, he had already decided on completion of the first part of his programme to apply for— and get—a post as medical registrar in the RVI, during which time he would get the MRCP. The possibility of failure did not enter his calculations. All went according to plan, including the MRCP at the first attempt without a final viva. He received a characteristic note from Spence on a postcard "Congratulations on the M. Now for the F." I only know of one academic failure. During his year in the USA he decided he would have sufficient opportunity to collect the material for an MD thesis. This he did with the considerable facilities that Hopkins provided for examining previous necropsy material. He prepared a paper on cirrhosis of the liver which was elegantly printed, lavishly illustrated, and attractively presented. It was rejected, probably because the adjudicator could not accept the idea that a medical graduate of $2\frac{1}{2}$ years, including only one year in a department of pathology, could possibly have sufficient direct personal experience to justify an acceptable thesis on a pathological subject. Rather than continue the topic and resubmit an extended thesis he rapidly obtained the MD by examination. Although a graduate of Durham University, he was quick to establish a claim to be the first holder of the MD Newcastle since, while Dean of Medicine in the first year of the formation of that university, he so described himself in the *BMJ*.

Immediately after graduation Henry and I, with Linton Snaith, went for a motoring holiday in the south-west ending in rooms in Cornwall. There he seemed to enjoy all the usual activities of bathing, scrambling on rocks, sunbathing, and drinking in the local pub. Subsequently, he avoided formal holidays as unrewarding, unnecessary, and largely a waste of time. He himself travelled in university vacations, but almost invariably with definite academic objectives. In later life, when increasing weight and deteriorating health were of more concern to his family and friends than to himself, I mentioned that by dieting he would live longer. "Yes," he replied, "and it will seem longer." One of his last visits was a long and exhausting lecture tour through Australia, when his health was obviously declining. Henry commented that if he were to die a great deal of trouble and expense could be saved by offering his body to the sharks of Sidney harbour.

During the early months of the war we were together again in Newcastle and occupied the same digs, where we shared a sitting room. The room was filled with books so that they overflowed about six deep on to the large table in the middle of the room. There was just space also for his gramophone and collection of records. Among the books English literature rather than medical texts were prominent, and there was a substantial number of political books, including those from a left-wing book club. Medical texts were mainly confined to pocket editions, since Henry did most of his medical reading in the ten minutes in the bus to and from hospital, and reading current literature in the library. The table top was covered, save for two alcoves side by side for our meals to be served. And splendid meals they were: a large breakfast and three-course evening meal five days a week with full board at the weekend. For this we each paid 35/- a week but received a rebate of 5/- if away for the weekend. Not only did we have a splendid landlady, but the bus into town stopped on the corner and opposite was a cinema and a pub. Henry had been a sprightly, slim young man weighing about 10 stone, but later with the combination of professional and economic success, and his love of good food and drink, he expanded physically.

I left our commune when I married in 1940 and Henry was my best man. During that year a vendetta developed between the junior doctors and the pathology department. The registrars, ably led by Henry, organised a boycott of the department of morbid anatomy, which was under the autocratic dominion of Professor Bernard Shaw. Two weeks passed without a single necropsy being done and the professor was becoming concerned—the more so since a survey of the mortuary showed no fall in the hospital death rate. At that stage the consultants, realising the cause, ordered that necropsies should be requested on all deaths and normal service was resumed, but with a rather more co-operative department.

I was called up into the RAF medical branch in 1941 and a year later Henry followed. After the birth of my son I received a characteristically phrased note from Henry "You are a ballsaching bastard not to tell me you had given birth. Hearty congratulations. What do you call it? I have a bit of news I am proceeding on attachment to Halton for assessment as a clinical pathologist. I can get back to bomber command but refused a permanent station job in favour of neuropsychiatry. PS. Oh—also, I am getting married in Cambridge on Friday (by licence) to Eileen. I knew there was something else to tell you."

When Henry became Vice-Chancellor of Newcastle University we lived within a hundred yards of one another in the parish of St George's. Parish surveys were done annually and it fell to my lot to visit the V-C's lodge with the forlorn aim of interesting him in the affairs of the church. In addition, a small form had to be left for the occupant to complete giving some family details. The form was left one evening and returned to me by his chauffeur the following morning:

Others in family . . . Four souls and one cat.
Would you like to be involved with the church . . . Certainly not.
Is there any way we may be able to help you? . . . Lend me money.

"I think this sort of inquiry is an atrocious impertinence.
By all means call back, but for a drink."

Unfortunately, he was declining rapidly and I was not able to enjoy our farewell drink.

George Richardson is senior physician at the Newcastle General Hospital.

Kurt Schapira

Shakespeare may have been correct in his belief that the good done by men lived after them, yet there can be little doubt that their wit, humour, and warmth endure longer in the hearts and minds of their friends.

It is not difficult to remember Henry, since he was my teacher and one of the most memorable men it has been my good fortune to have known—a privilege I shared with many others. He was larger than life, with a zest for living, intimately linked with a remarkable talent as a teacher. First and foremost about Henry's teaching was that he obviously thoroughly enjoyed it. He had a deep fondness and a healthy respect for students who, in their turn, instinctively recognised a brilliant yet kindly master, whose witty tongue would at times lash out merely to show that he could still hold his own. He taught principles and not minutiae; the latter he felt could be better learned from textbooks, perhaps refreshed from time to time by a little alcohol, and in the quiet of one's own room. He was a brilliant and popular teacher whose lectures and clinical demonstrations were superlative performances. Clearly he was fond of us poor ignorant students, though, as he often said, we were not as "couth" as he was. When we failed to come up to scratch, a witty and scathing comment would spur us on. Sometimes, however, it failed to succeed, as with the student who could not recall the name given to a fixed and irregular pupil. The atmosphere was transformed into that of a Roman arena. The victim in the ring was totally unresponsive to the helpful whispers of his friends in the amphitheatre. After what seemed an eternity, Henry leaned forward, smiled sweetly, and suggested: "Armstrong Siddeley?" The class exploded into laughter, and the crisis passed.

In his undergraduate teaching he followed very much the style and methods of his own teacher and friend, James Spence, believing that only essentials should be taught to undergraduates in the most simple and direct way. He felt that specialists were far too active in undergraduate teaching and that elaborate biochemical investigations such as the estimation of the "serum rhubarb," one of Henry's favourite investigations, were more pertinent to postgraduate studies. Unlike some of our teachers at that time he did not believe that his specialty was all-important in the medical curriculum. Indeed, he often said that neurology was an easy and relatively unimportant subject; easy because, after all, the big toe could only go either up or down. He himself, as I learnt over the years, could do much more with a Babinski response—albeit, he maintained, only when using his Bentley car key.

He enjoyed the cut and thrust of witty conversation, even or perhaps especially, when he was at the receiving end of a barb. I recall the occasion on a ward round when a brilliant registrar seconded from Nigeria made a number of suggestions about the diagnosis of some of the patients, suggestions which were not altogether to Henry's liking. The young man had just passed the Membership examination at the first attempt and was not unnaturally in a somewhat euphoric state. After some time, Henry turned on the poor fellow and said to him in the most acid tone of voice that he could muster: "Why don't you go home and become a witch doctor?" "I would really like to," came the reply, "but unfortunately I am not quite good enough." His initiation ceremony into the firm had taken place; they became lifelong friends and admirers.

Others, no doubt, will write of his contribution to research, of his brilliance and energy which transformed Newcastle into an international centre of neurological research within the space of a few years. It was in 1956 that I was appointed his first research fellow (*sic*), a title he himself bestowed upon me in an attempt to anglicise me once and for all, and to legitimise my receiving what he called a music-hall salary. The next three years were among the happiest of my life, notwithstanding the occasional dire threat of being relegated from coauthorship to a footnote if the data required for the next paper were not on his desk within 48 hours. Although I translated many a German neurological paper in connection with our research projects, Henry never really believed that I knew a word of the language, no doubt because the teutonic circumlocution could not easily be turned into the crisp phrase he would have used. His conversion took place in a Viennese wine cellar, when my expertise as interpreter facilitated an evening of gastronomic delights. Subsequently, I was allowed to teach him the only German word he ever used: "Zusammenfassung." I was delighted to hear him use it many years later, as always to great effect, when chairing a university committee appointing the Professor of German.

So far I have written little about Henry as a friend; this aspect of our relationship is more difficult to write about. I enjoyed his friendship for some 20 years—"man and boy," as he often used to say. He was kind and generous both with his time and ideas, although it was clearly understood that his generosity was never to be mentioned or even alluded to, since any reference to it embarrassed him and was likely to produce some fond and abusive remark. Generous gifts were always made under some pretext or guise, such as that he already had 14 copies of the book, or that he didn't particularly like this gramophone record because it reminded him of a certain maiden aunt. To play the game was to accept the gift without too many thanks; the understanding was clear, and nothing more needed saying.

One of the most remarkable things about him was that he never

Contributors

changed. Our friendship began when he was an assistant physician, and continued without change throughout the years, during the last of which he was the vice-chancellor of the university of which I was a lecturer. Inevitably, his heavy commitments reduced the number of meetings we had, but on each occasion when we did meet the old warmth and sense of fun were there.

By any standards, Henry Miller was an unusual man. He enriched not only the profession to which he was happy to belong but also the lives of his many friends, colleagues, and students. Of the many things he taught me, perhaps the most significant was that a career in medicine was above all a privilege, and that it could at the same time be a most enjoyable profession. It was the human aspect of medicine, which saw patients as people, which gave him the most intense satisfaction, enjoyment, and often amusement. He practised "whole man medicine" long before the term was invented. Soon after joining his firm, I remember accompanying him one warm summer's evening to a peripheral hospital to see a patient who presented a most difficult diagnostic problem—not an unusual event in the practice of neurology. The clinical picture was that of a peripheral neuropathy, of the kind that Professor Garcin, another of Henry's friends and admirers, used to classify under the heading of GOK (God Only Knows). It was almost midnight when we returned to Newcastle and I shall never forget his parting words, "Medicine is such fun and the extraordinary thing about it is that they even pay you for doing it." A silent click of the car door and the Bentley glided away into the night.

I have said nothing of the evenings of music, stories, and of the discussions into the early hours about all manner of things, nor of the panache, coupled with some inaccuracy, with which he played the piano, nor of his conducting Verdi choruses played so loud that the walls would vibrate and no champagne glass was safe. Such happy memories are some consolation in our loss. For him, nothing has changed—he was a legend in his lifetime, he remains a legend still.

Kurt Schapira is a consultant psychiatrist at the Royal Victoria Infirmary, Newcastle upon Tyne.

D A Shaw

"Better by far you should forget and smile
Than that you should remember and be sad."

Rossetti

For someone living in his city, working in the university over which he presided, and practising neurology in the department that he

70

created, memories of Henry Miller are not occasional reconstructions of the past. They are everyday experiences, informed, sharpened, enriched, and invariably illuminated by memories of Henry so vivid that they are part of the experiencing moment. The two volumes of Kinnier Wilson in the bookcase have his pencilled underlinings and annotations on nearly every page; other, less worthy, texts on the reference shelves carry a variety of irreverent marginal comments. In the clinics there are patients whose early case sheets are headed— Dr H G Miller. The initial outpatient histories and follow-up notes are often recorded in his familiar black ink handwriting, and in an abbreviated but characteristically lucid style. One such patient, a woman with multiple sclerosis and rather a favourite of Henry's, is in the ward at the time of writing. Another patient currently attending is a man who in the late 1950s was liable to psychomotor seizures whenever he heard the chimes of Big Ben on his wireless. Henry was intrigued by this history, and would describe how attacks could be aborted if he switched off in time, but how circumstances sometimes prevented his rapid access to the wireless set, in which case he would hope to drown the sound by pulling the lavatory chain. His family doctor recently referred him back to the clinic on the day in May that the BBC re-instated the Westminster chimes before the news bulletins. He had not had a fit: he had bilateral carpal tunnel syndrome.

There is a room on Ward 6 that we refer to as Henry's room. On one wall is the Bjerrum screen, and beside it is the desk where he would sit and sign his letters, watched over by members of his staff. Among them in the mid-1960s was a young Nigerian, now a neurologist of great distinction, whom he particularly liked, and whom he particularly tried to provoke into verbal exchanges from which he did not always emerge unscathed. On one occasion, this young man made the mistake of addressing a singularly penetrating question to the seated figure while he himself stood with his back to the large black screen. Henry's "Why, B . . . , I thought you'd gone," successfully diverted attention from the original question.

Across the corridor is the room where most of the talking and coffee-drinking is done. On the walls are photographs, each inscribed to Henry, and bearing the signatures of Charles Symonds, Houston Merritt, Henry Cohen, Russell Brain, Raymond Garcin, Francis Walshe, Ludo van Bogaert, and Arnold Rich. In this room Henry talked for many hours and first had pain one Saturday morning after coming in to see a boy with SSPE. Generations of SHOs, registrars, and first assistants have homed in on this room, or in earlier days on sister's room, on getting the word that "Henry's in," to enjoy the brilliance and the fun of his conversation and his story-telling.

His style was unique. It embraced all the arts and devices of which sophisticated humour is compounded. He had an eye for incongruity, perhaps one of the main ingredients of humour. Thus, he would recall the first occasion on which, as a student, he was invited by a senior surgeon to look through a cystoscope. The patient had had a suprapubic cystostomy and the examination was being conducted in a room on the periphery of the hospital, and in an age when the surroundings of the Royal Victoria Infirmary were rather more rural than they are today. Henry, who made no claims for his delicacy in the handling of instruments, on being pressed somewhat impatiently for a description of his findings, reported that what he saw was a cow upside down in a field. Apart from its element of incongruity, this tale of his reminds me of his great delight in defusing an overcharged atmosphere or deflating a pompous one.

Although it had so many different aspects, Henry's humour was essentially verbal. He did not depend much on vulgarity, but he could use profanity with great effect. He loved words. He liked the sound of them in the same way that he liked music, and in his story-telling and his writing he was a master of poetic association as well as of luxuriant phraseology. He also delighted in playing with words and his manipulations and transpositions, particularly of the names of his colleagues, were often extremely funny. This fascination with words never led him quite into the realms of fantasy of an Ionesco, with word associations depending solely on sound. Nevertheless, he could not resist some flights of surrealism in his verbal antics—though, mostly, he remained loosely anchored in reality.

My memories of Henry are not of events, performances, or particular achievements. All of them are inspired by some aspect of his remarkable personality and they are etched on the mind of his own artistry. Without that artistry, I cannot reproduce and share them as I should like to. They are abundant, and they are precious. Perhaps Henry's greatest legacy is that we can remember him and smile.

D A Shaw is Professor of Neurology at the University of Newcastle upon Tyne.

Norman Shott

One of the most rewarding features of a career in university administration is the experience of association with highly intelligent people with distinctive and mostly stimulating personalities. Just occasionally one finds oneself working with someone with such personal qualities that, because of the pleasure derived from the association, the experience seems, and too often is, too good to last.

Contributors

Thus it was for me when Henry Miller was appointed Dean of Medicine in 1966 after the untimely death of Andrew Lowdon and after completion of the somewhat mystic procedures adopted at that time for the appointment of a new dean. These might have been said to resemble the former procedure for the appointment of a leader of the Conservative Party, combined with the procedure for the appointment of a new Pope —a particularly inappropriate mixture, it might be thought, in the case of the appointment of Henry.

The next $2\frac{1}{2}$ years during which Henry was Dean were, without doubt the most enjoyable ones of my career as faculty executive officer (a post designated by Henry as managing director, manager, or station master according to the function of the moment) I think perhaps the reason for this was partly the daily consultation of faculty affairs, which almost invariably brightened my day despite the sometimes dull nature of the business, and partly because of the way in which Henry delegated responsibility to me for running the faculty on a day-to-day basis, wishing to be concerned himself only in matters of considerable importance requiring policy decisions at top level. This willingness to delegate responsibility to his subordinates, and his very generous recognition of their work, imparted immense job motivation and satisfaction.

Henry Miller's impact as Dean of the Faculty of Medicine was to some extent less than might have been expected, having regard to the highly controversial views he held on so many matters which concerned the faculty. This was partly because he was in office for a comparatively short period, but mainly because at the time he became Dean the medical school was in a period of consolidation rather than active change. An integrated undergraduate curriculum needing radical reorganisation had been introduced in 1962, and had to be given a chance to settle down.

Nevertheless, Henry clearly had a pronounced influence on the faculty. His controversial views, and unconventional ways of expressing them, were not always easy for some of his senior academic colleagues to accept, especially those on the receiving end, and at times when he pressed home his attacks the flak was thick and accurate. There is, however, little doubt that he stimulated argument and appraisal of traditional attitudes to an extent perhaps not previously experienced in the faculty.

There are many things for which I shall remember Henry Miller; for his lively encouragement to younger members of staff, particularly those who had already shown special ability and needed opportunities of extending themselves; for his popularity with students, which was akin to worship; for his ever-open door and friendly welcome to all who wished to see him; and for so many other personal qualities about which so much has already been written. I shall, I think, especially remember

Contributors

him for the way in which he so often livened up rather dull discussions, and his ability to relieve so wittily any undue tension which may have crept into the proceedings and restore good humour to all.

I shall remember him for a typical contribution he made in May 1966, when he was clinical sub-dean, towards the end of a fairly long and rather dreary discussion on the curriculum. Professor Hale Ham, who at that time was Dean of Western Reserve Medical School (where the integrated curriculum had been introduced some 13 years earlier), was visiting the medical school as Jacobson lecturer to take part in discussions with the faculty, so as to compare the curriculum at Western Reserve with the undergraduate curriculum which Newcastle introduced in 1962. Professor Ham gave two public lectures on the Western Reserve pattern of teaching and these were succeeded later in the visit by a round table discussion with heads of our main teaching departments. In view of the rather special occasion, I had decided to record the whole discussion. This consisted of a monologue by Professor Ham followed by comments and questions by each head of department. This exchange of views of the two curricula was no doubt of great value and interest to all present, but it created an atmosphere of mutual self-satisfaction and congratulation, and, by any stretch of the imagination, the proceedings could not be regarded as lively. Henry was then invited to speak and I give below a verbatim account of his contribution which was received with much laughter and enjoyment by everyone present. To what extent he had his tongue in his cheek at the time is, of course, a matter for conjecture, but the answer may lie in the fact that when seven or eight months later he became dean it was clear that he was wholly in agreement with the principles of the Newcastle curriculum and became its staunch supporter.

"I think it would be a pity if no jarring note was struck at this meeting, although I do not actually intend to strike it. I think the great virtue of these things is the enormous ability of man to resist education and we are certainly putting this to a very thorough test in this enormous orgy of factual indoctrination which goes on four afternoons a week. It is very interesting, but if you take a group of doctors in their 30s they will have had very widely different training, and if they are working in the same field there is very often very little to choose. Admittedly, the American doctor starts his training at 22 and qualifies at 26 and by that time the English doctor who qualifies at 22 has had four years of postgraduate work but less pregraduate education but in fact by the time they are both 32, if they are good, they would both be very much the same and would have very much the same approach and attitude.

"In other words, I think that people resist education and I myself very much doubt whether this sort of exercise with the enormous amount of time which is spent on rearranging the presentation of the facts—which is what this is really all about—is a fruitful expenditure of time. We have not been at it very long and I do not suppose we would have discovered a cure for cancer if the time had been used more fruitfully, but if Western Reserve has been doing it for 13 years I am sure that enormous advances in medicine might have been made if all these chaps had devoted themselves to pursuing their arts instead of discussing what in any case is a very dubious theory, since there is really no scientific method of measuring results of education. This is quite obvious from the questions round the table. How are these things measured and what do we do to make changes for better or for worse?

"Curriculum changing is well known to be an occupational disease of deans, which is recurrent and remittent with occasional periods of freedom. I unfortunately missed Dr Ham's lecture last night, but on Wednesday Dr Ham wrote down in three columns on the blackboard the factual teaching that was carried out at Western Reserve. This rather lacked some of the softer sciences which we have dragged by the scruff of the neck into stage I here, but otherwise it contained the kind of facts that we all learnt at medical school, arranged in different columns. The same facts and, regrettably here, the same teachers. Is it really going to make all that much difference and if it is how on earth will you know? So, despite the aura and ambience of self-congratulation and premature publicity which surround the whole exercise described in words like courageous, outstanding, original, fresh, dynamic, all this really amounts to is presenting the same facts with the same teachers in a different order and I do not honestly see why it should take three chaps to teach about the corpus striatum any better than one chap who ought to know enough about anatomy and physiology for a medical student.

"I think that these chaps are drowned in an absolute miasma of facts, although from what I gather Western Reserve students are a little more receptive because they are a little older, but our wretches sit there with glassy eyes while someone from the physiology department goes into the chemistry of the products of pituitary degradation. So I regard the whole thing as not so much a curriculum—more a waste of time."

I think that very few deans of medicine prepared for their appointment with pronouncements like this, which partly explains why I shall always remember Henry Miller.

Norman Shott is Deputy Registrar at the University of Newcastle upon Tyne.

Contributors
Sam Shuster

Henry was a convention breaker and would have been pleased to see me follow where he led. So, instead of the conventional obituarial blanket of praise decked with a few surface decorations in tasteful colour, I propose to put the old rug up to the light. When I first showed my cartoon "Henry IX" locally it almost passed off without a nod. I put this down to the well-known soporific effect of my lectures, or perhaps my audience mistook it for the original Holbein, but it was simply they knew it wor our Henry and that it was apt beyond comment. He was our monarch beyond doubt. Henry wasn't at the lecture, and I sent him a print: news came back that "we are not amused." Now this is the vital clue to Henry's character: humour was a central part of the man and he loved jokes—but he preferred to make them himself. It was not that he didn't like to be upstaged; the ambivalence was the essence of his big, contradictory self. He despised convention yet lived by it; he attacked office but attained it; he hated formality but couldn't renounce it; he spoke well but debated poorly; he loved people but hated persons; he was not sympathetic to the academic idea yet he worked for an academy. Like so many outstanding people he was massive in his contradictions—which is why there are two big opposing Henry factions and no neutrals.

So what was Henry's contribution? To me it was his determination to puncture pomposity and to put the good earth back under authority's feet, and this I think helped to create a new attitude to medicine. He made the starched collars (which he could also wear) flap in the breezes of life. In this respect the force and humour of his utterances—and that force did much for the self-esteem of Newcastle medics, as well as for the popularity of its school—was far more important than the content which was often banal. Indeed, I often felt that his enormous humour contributed to this very failure of content: the humour became primary and too often he seemed to take a line because it was the more amusing and startling, only to founder in the impossible defence of the consequences. He was a stimulator and not an innovator, and he stimulated by his abrasive ego-puncturing wit. Henry's approach was just right for medicine as it used to be when he was at his deflationary prime. But what was so good for medicine was bound to fail in the less rigid and more sophisticated university community. Henry became an amateur of the academic—oh, how I wish he'd stayed as the Master of Medicine.

Sam Shuster is Professor of Dermatology at the University of Newcastle upon Tyne.

George Smart

I knew Henry for the whole of my professional life, and for all but a few years we worked together as colleagues. We were students, housemen, and medical registrars together; we were both in the RAF during the war, and for part of the time we were both stationed at Halton; from 1951 until about six years ago we were colleagues in the teaching hospital and medical school at Newcastle. Life with Henry around was at once a serious business and a hoot.

Henry was so amusing and provocative that one must guard against giving a string of highly amusing anecdotes—but any account of him would be incomplete without some. Characteristic is the story he told of the time when he was driving his car far above the speed limit to visit a patient and suddenly realised he was passing a police car. With characteristic presence of mind he seized his stethoscope and dangled it out of the window. On returning from seeing the patient, the same police car was still parked at the side of the road. As Henry passed, the officer dangled out of *his* window a pair of handcuffs.

While this jocular side of Henry's character was undoubtedly very prominent, it should not be allowed to overshadow the very real contributions he made to our profession and to the University of Newcastle.

Even in our student days Henry clearly stood out because of his intelligence and quick and amusing wit, and because he was clearly a man who was determined to stamp his mark on affairs. I am reminded of an occasion when we both served on the Students' Representative Council. The election for the Council's president was in the offing and a prominent member of the Rugby XV talked as if it were a foregone conclusion that he would be elected president. This did not suit Henry at all, for he had his own ideas about the best man for president. Accordingly, not only were the rugger braggart and Henry's choice nominated as candidates, but also another and popular member of the rugby team. This effectively split the rugby vote and Henry's man sailed home.

His capacity for rapid thought, and the pithy fluency with which he could express himself, both in speech and in writing, were certainly among his more memorable characteristics. He tended to see things as black or white and the pungency of his remarks could be very funny to those not on the receiving end. The fact that they also tended to be down-to-earth, no-nonsense observations, with a good dollop of underlying truth, didn't make them any softer. I remember, for example, one occasion when, as vice-chancellor, he was taking the chair at a meeting of senate during a debate on filling a chair of English literature. When someone suggested the name of a very widely read author, another senator remarked in a disparaging tone that it wouldn't do to have a man like that. Henry at once observed that apparently the one disqualification for an appointment to a chair of English literature was to have written anything which somebody had actually read.

I suppose it was in the RAF that Henry became interested in neurology—certainly he was very much influenced by Sir Charles Symonds and became one of Symonds's band of neuropsychiatrists. Perhaps this was the experience which ultimately inspired his lecture called "Do-it-yourself Psychiatry," in which he had everyone in his (standing-room only) audience rocking with laughter—except the psychiatrists, who became progressively more furious.

Although during student days Henry's love of music was quite apparent, it was during our time at Halton that this was such a joy to everyone, for he had a marvellous collection of records (78s, of course) which groups of us spent many evenings listening to. One or two of us had made an amplifier from old radar equipment which was an early version of hi-fi. Many a time we attended the Sunday concerts given by Thomas Beecham in the Stoll theatre.

Henry was not by any means a medical scientist, but he had a great deal of flair and intuition and these, coupled with his intelligence and drive, enabled him to follow so effectively in the footsteps of Nattrass in contributing to the establishment of a first-class neurological centre at Newcastle. He started his consultant work, however, as a general physician, only later moving wholly to neurology. He then initiated the epidemiological study of multiple sclerosis in the north—particularly around Carlisle—which led to the suggestion that the disease might result from an infection with a very prolonged incubation period.

When he was awarded his personal chair he could quite easily have hived off neurology as a separate department from that of medicine, but he did not. On the contrary, he firmly held that neurology was a part of internal medicine and that it should be so in an administrative sense too. He may, perhaps, have carried this idea too far, since medicine was beginning that rapid advance which made specialisation inevitable, but, as Professor of Medicine, I had every reason to be grateful to him, for the amount of money we could apportion as a subdepartmental grant was ludicrously small; he never once complained, but set about obtaining badly needed finance from outside sources.

To develop a combined neurological and neurosurgical clinic, a ward of the Florence Nightingale type was turned fully into separate cubicles and Henry's consulting-room was at the end; it had a washbasin near the window. It was alleged by Henry that a note arrived from the sister of a ward overlooking his asking him if he would kindly remember in future to draw the curtains before he washed his hands.

Henry became Dean of Medicine at a very critical period in the medical school at Newcastle. The new curriculum had been introduced (one was never too sure that Henry regarded it, before be became Dean, as a change for the better, but, as ever, he learnt quickly—vide his article *Fifty years after Flexner*), but there were many problems—mostly connected with the entrenched positions adopted by the heads of two or three key departments. Henry took a very firm line and I well remember a meeting, chaired by him with a great deal of glee, which included non-professional members of the departments concerned as well as the professors. Skilfully stoked by Henry, the whole thing developed into a massive interdepartmental slanging match and it was from that date that the despotism of departments in determining what should be taught to undergraduates began to crumble. Soon, for example, the subject working parties, which determined how their particular subject should be presented (so that all disciplines took part in an integrated and logical sequence) were empowered to ask whoever they felt was *best* to take part in the teaching, informing the head of the man's department; previously they had had to ask the head of the department to nominate someone—and often got unsuitable people. There is little doubt in my mind that Henry consolidated the changes that had been made and successfully resisted the inevitable counter-attack from those who did not see eye-to-eye with the exchanges—in doing so he did not always endear himself to those concerned.

But he made up for it in many ways, just one example being a dinner party he gave to heads of departments just at the time that the breath-alyser test was being introduced. Neatly and correctly placed among the cutlery, each guest had a breathalyser tube and it was shattering to see how many turned green at the end of the dinner—tubes, I mean.

When Henry became Vice-Chancellor he did so with pleasurable anticipation, but I often suspected that he never really enjoyed the job as much as he had enjoyed being dean, or as much as being a consultant. The trappings of the job, the restrictions it imposed, and the ritual, must have been irksome to someone with such a sense of irreverence. We had, of course, involved the students in the medical school very closely with the curriculum and with affairs in general and, although Newcastle had never had any student trouble, Henry felt that there should be student representation on the senate. It was quite a struggle to achieve this, but Henry won the day. At a meeting of senate shortly after they had become members, which happened to be at Easter, the students showed their appreciation by presenting Henry with a crumpled paper bag in which there were two smallish Easter eggs. Henry was delighted.

With his wit, his literary leanings, his down-to-earth common-sense, his proclivity for debunking, his zest for life, and, latterly, his regrettable tendency to overeat and put on weight, Henry seemed in some respects to resemble Samuel Johnson. Unfortunately I am no James Boswell, but I have tried my best to sketch out something of a friend who certainly added much enjoyment to my own life and to whom I owe a great deal.

George Smart was formerly Professor of Medicine at Newcastle University and is now Director of the British Postgraduate Medical Federation, University of London.

Andrew Smith

I never worked with Henry, but from our students days was fascinated by his style. Most clinical teaching then was on the classical model—routine questions and routine examination leading inexorably to diagnosis by exclusion. Not Henry. He listened to the patient, interjected pertinent questions, did a quick selective examination, and diagnosed by informed guesswork. It is, after all, how most doctors work (but few teach), and it is the exciting side of clinical medicine.

He was an outstanding lecturer and debater, but an even better after-dinner speaker. He spoke quickly but distinctly, carrying one along by the sheer pace with which he developed his theme. His fluency, wit, and verbal extravagance left one informed, astonished, and roaring with laughter by turn. All delivered at tremendous speed and apparently off the cuff. Rolling in the aisles is a fair description of the reaction of his audiences. I remember a bankers' dinner in Newcastle, a vast formal affair with hundreds of guests and a top table of local notables. Henry and a judge, who had a reputation for such occasions, were the principal guests and the connoisseurs were evenly divided about who would make the better speech. I thought Henry did, but the ribaldry of some of his sallies was too much for bankers. "Not what one expects from a vice-chancellor," said a stuffed shirt near me. But exactly what one would expect from Henry. The sight of so many serious dinner-jacketed dignitaries was bound to provoke his iconoclasm. He had to shock them.

As a writer he was as good, but with quite a different style. The verbal pyrotechnics were replaced by lucid sentences in beautiful English; the outrageous remarks by balanced judgments—as if he realised the exaggerations of some of the things he said and on reflection moderated them. There are few extreme views in *Medicine and Society*, though some of his phrases are devastatingly pointed. "Except for a handful of outstanding individuals in each generation, medical officers of health have always tended to be both a depressed and a rather depressing section of the profession," is an example.

There were other contradictions in his character. As a proclaimed life-long socialist he was radical in many of his attitudes, but he was a traditionalist in others. He was in favour of liberal abortion laws long before most of his colleagues had got beyond Victorian restrictiveness (he was the first prominent doctor to use realistic "abortion on request" instead of emotive "on demand"). He was against parsimony in prescribing analgesic drugs, castigating those doctors who prescribed too little to relieve pain, as being neurotically afraid of addiction. He was for the legalisation of cannabis, a subject most doctors still do not even think about.

His conservative side showed itself in his professional life. He chose neurology, the traditional specialty of the clever but conventional young doctor rather than (as they were regarded at that time) upstart paediatrics, or not scientifically respectable psychiatry. He had the DPM and, despite his assertion that psychotherapy did nobody any good but the therapist, a therapeutic personality. In his early days as a private consultant he was my first choice as a second opinion for depressed patients. One of them, who also had early Parkinsonism, told him she couldn't see why I had sent her to him, because she knew he could do no more for her than I could. He agreed, listened to her, made her laugh (which I had failed to do), and prescribed a phenobarbitone hyoscine mixture. Years later, when more effective drugs for Parkinsonism were invented, I sent her to another consultant who recommended one of them. She said it didn't do her any good and went back to Henry's bottle. She didn't trust professors, she said, and, when I told her Henry was now a professor, she said firmly in a tone which brooked no contradiction, "Oh, but he was a good doctor." Now in her 80s, she still sends for repeat prescriptions of Dr Miller's mixture.

Henry's attitude in 1962 to the new curriculum at Newcastle was not progressive. "Curriculum review," he said, "simply results in the same subjects being taught in a different order." Though there is an element of truth in this, it was not so in this case because there was a proposal to introduce something quite new—general practice under the title of family and community medicine. It had been a popular voluntary option for some students for over a decade, but not an official part of the curriculum. The Northern Faculty of the Royal College of General Practitioners was pressing hard for its inclusion, strongly supported by Professor Donald Court, who converted other influencial academics. But not Henry. Discussions were still going on after the new curriculum had started, and I was one of five general practitioners invited, together with the professors of medicine, paediatrics, obstetrics and gynaecology, and industrial health—and Henry—to decide the issue. The Dean,

Contributors

Andrew Lowdon, the surgeon, dined and wined us well, reminded us that we were there to talk about the possible introduction of general practice into the curriculum and invited Henry to open the discussion. He did this in his most brilliant debating style.

What a barrister he would have made. He was witty, generous in his praise of the best GPs but made it clear he thought there weren't many of them (only about a score measured up to the exacting specification of personal physician of first instance, he was to write later in *Medicine and Society*). He painted a hilarious picture of medical students doing country rounds with bumbling old GPs, if not in horse and buggies at any rate in ancient bull-nosed Morrises. Great fun for them to see how the other half lived, but surely nobody could believe that they would learn anything that couldn't be taught better by specialists in hospital? Much of what he said was true and common ground between us—but we thought things could be improved by better medical education. So brilliant was his delivery and so convincing his argument that I despaired of refuting even what seemed false. We did our halting best, though none of us could match Henry's debating skill, and the vote was nine to one in favour of a course in family and community medicine in the next academic year. Only for four weeks and, on Henry's insistence, only as an experiment. It was characteristic of him that 18 months later, when the students' representatives asked for a longer course, he said to one of the GP tutors, "I see you have pulled the wool over their eyes." When he became Dean a year or two later he did nothing to curtail the expanding activities of the general practice teaching group, and, later still, as Director of the BMA Planning Unit, he wrote in his preface to the report of the Working Party on Primary Medical Care (an able group of advocates of general practice selected by him) that the proposals for restricting general practice outlined in it should be put to the test.

An extraordinary man, Henry. Medicine is not the same without his shafts of pomp-shattering perceptiveness or, after advising physicians to steer clear of euthanasia, such sentences as, "It might be more appropriate for an enthusiastic prelate to conduct the patient to the Elysian fields."

Andrew Smith, a family doctor, is a lecturer in family medicine at the University of Newcastle upon Tyne.

David Stafford-Clark

I shall never forget Henry. He was one of my greatest friends—but of a very special kind, somebody whose personality seemed somehow to complement and supplement my own. Our first meeting occurred when he was a medical specialist on the staff of the RAF hospital at Halton. I had just been posted to Halton after $4\frac{1}{2}$ years in Bomber Command, and, before that, 18 months with other combat units, so I came as an experienced RAF medical officer in contact with an experienced physician who wore an RAF uniform but otherwise had not greatly had to change the pattern of his life to comply with the needs of the service. I think that Henry respected the work that I had done in Bomber Command, and the fabric of understanding that I had built up about the realities of combat flying.

I think also he felt that during the war I had inevitably been side-tracked into a very special branch of what could be my future profession, and that some cold water needed pouring on my aspirations to become a pioneer in aviation psychiatry since, as he trenchantly pointed out, I had no qualifications in psychiatry and none in aviation medicine. We became friends really because we never had to pull our punches.

There must have been other people with whom Henry enjoyed this relationship but there was nobody else in my life whom I could admire with such an uninhibited, affectionate, cheerful, outrageous exchange of badinage in speech and writing; in fact, Henry and I were perfect foils each for the other.

From the outset Henry felt that if I wanted to become a doctor of any importance I had to get higher degrees. The sine qua non was the Membership, which, of course, he had and I hadn't.

Naturally Henry plied this advantage mercilessly; in the course urging me to make up my mind about my future he suggested a number of careers which I could easily follow when the war ended. For example, I could stay in the Service (I should amass braid and ribbons, but I should never become the kind of teacher, or pioneer, or researcher that he thought I wanted to be)—a service career would, Henry assured me, as the years went by, find me no longer flying, no longer outstanding even in aviation medicine, creeping up and down the steps of various London teaching hospitals (whose staff I might otherwise have adorned), bearing a briefcase, and uncertain of my role. I have the greatest respect for the Royal Air Force, but eventually I decided, after careful thought and some further advice from Henry, to decline with real thanks their offer of a permanent commission. Henry had other goals for me, which I knew he expected me to explore, reject, and come back to him for clinching advice.

Contributors

So, when I left the Air Force, I became a houseman; took the Membership, which I was fortunate to pass in six months; and acquired the MD in general medicine at the University of London. I had wanted to take my MD by thesis and submitted one called "Morale and flying experience—a study of operational air crews in Bomber Command."

Whoever was given my thesis for a preliminary assessment, with that unfailing bureaucratic bias which so many university administrators and examiners display, reported that this was clearly an attempt by a serving medical officer to write a psychiatric dissertation and, although it was interesting, it did not display much evidence of specialised psychiatric knowledge. This was not surprising because, of course, I didn't have any. The examiners, however, were quite adamant that if I wanted to submit this as a thesis for an MD I must be prepared to take the written and oral parts of the academically rigorous MD examination in neurology and psychiatry as a special subject. I had no hope whatsoever at that time of passing that exam and, after I got the Membership, I decided that those conditions were essentially unfair since this was the work of a general medical officer in the Air Force, not a specialist, and if they would only accept it as a specialist psychiatric thesis, then I would take the MD by examination in general medicine and write the unseen essay as an alternative—which is what I did. Henry's comment on this was: "Once you become a university administrator, you become a bureaucrat; which sooner or later involves your making ponderously wrong decisions; and the awful thing is, David, that I see the whole of that future stretching in front of me if I succeed."

In retrospect, remembering Henry, that future, but without those limitations, did extend before him. But I think it's true to say that I never doubted that Henry's loyalty to the university in accepting the Vice-Chancellorship (a very great honour) was not unmixed with regret that it took him so far both from clinical medicine and the time to travel, to meet old friends, to renew transatlantic acquaintances; to be, in fact, Henry at his most fully extended. I am quite sure that he gave the university not only of his best, but of that superb best which perhaps few but he could have given, but I regard his Vice-Chancellorship almost as a martyrdom for the university to which his loyalty was unwavering.

Henry and I continued to correspond and to meet after the war, and, as I gradually surmounted the various hurdles and became a consultant at Guy's and the Institite of Psychiatry, we became in effect professionally on an equal footing. But Henry always treated me as his special pupil in one respect, and as his special and treasured antagonist in another. As a psychiatrist who had learned neurology he respected me. As a psychiatrist who had not abandoned psychiatry for neurology he felt somewhat ambivalent about my fulfilment of his intentions for me,

84

and as a neurologist he never fully understood the unconscious element in psychiatry. Had we not been so fond of each other we couldn't have communicated personally as we did. Anybody else reading our correspondence would have thought that we were carrying irony and outrage to a point where friendship might be threatened, but of course that wasn't so. Henry wasn't like that and nor, I like to think, am I.

Perhaps two excerpts from that correspondence right at the beginning and almost at the end will exemplify what I mean. The first excerpt is fairly soon after we gained what I might call academic and professional equality. I had published what was to prove a remarkably successful book, *Psychiatry Today*. Henry was very enthusiastic about this book—he recommended it to all his friends, all his pupils, and all the consultant psychiatrists of his acquaintance. It contained in one chapter a quotation from Trudeau and one of my readers raised a difficulty with me which I was bound to refer back to Henry.

May 22 1952. "My dear Henry, A little while ago your astonishing erudition landed me in a slight difficulty. . . . I had lifted a quotation from Trudeau . . . in the book that you and Raymond Daley have edited and I inserted it in my own book *Psychiatry Today*. You understand that it was Trudeau that I was quoting, rather than yourself, not that I do not regard most of your literary work as eminently quotable, even perhaps classical, but simply that Trudeau could fulfil my purpose at the time. The quotation . . . was: 'To cure sometimes, to relieve often, to comfort always.' I thought this a most apt and well-chosen quotation and was grateful to you for having discovered it for me. But a little while after the book had been published . . . I received a letter from a genial old scholar in the Isle of Man who apparently knew my mother well when she was a girl, had read the article, and written to me both to remind me of this connection with my family and to inquire specifically from what part of Trudeau's writings I had succeeded in finding so penetrating an observation, and particularly what verbs Trudeau had actually used in French. This has floored me completely. I have not been able to find any original of Trudeau's works in the library here and so I am turning to you to know whether you can supply me with the information to send on. I should perhaps tell you that I confessed all to the genial scholar . . . but I did promise to try and trace the quotation for him, if necessary seeking your help."

Henry's reply dated 27 May: "Dear David, I have taken Counsel's opinion as to the propriety of having your name and address on the outside of your envelope. He says it amounts to a medical advertisement but I am glad to tell you that, although he thinks this is sailing pretty close to the wind, he does not feel that we should take action at this time, but merely keep you under observation.

"I'm sorry I cannot help you. I cannot give you the original French

85

because I found the quotation in Arabic in a Persian medical journal and translated it myself. In actual fact, I can't quite remember, but I probably invented the whole thing. I've seen it elsewhere since, but they probably copied it from my book. In any case, you should not encourage your mother's old boyfriends, nor would I advise you to mix with scholars, in which case your hollow pretensions may be publicly exposed.

"I think that I have almost the success that I deserve, but, of course, not quite. Do come and see me if you're ever called up here to correct one of my diagnoses."

28 May 1952: "Dear Henry, Thank you for your characteristically outrageous reply to my letter. Knave that you are, I should have known that you would treat me thus. I now find myself in the unenviable position of the snake in the grass treacherously stabbed by a broken reed, and I shall write to the scholar renouncing all pretensions to literary research. . . ."

That correspondence and our meetings went on in this way from 1952 to the time of Henry's death. The last excerpt from correspondence before I retired was late in 1970 when I had been asked by a publisher if I would collaborate with Henry in a book to be called *Medical Ethics: their psychology and practice*. I gathered I was to provide the psychology and he the practice. I wrote to him asking what he thought about it. Referring to the publisher, I said "He is undoubtedly an afficionado of yours, and gave me a reprint of something you had written for *Encounter* or some other . . . propaganda sheet, called "New Doctors' Dilemmas." It was, of course, brilliant, polemic, pungent, and penetratingly thoughtful underneath the gloss. . . . The idea of our collaborating on a book is a pleasant one and I would certainly be willing to consider it if you can spare the time yourself. Indeed, as the rhinoceros said to the game warden 'I'm game if you are.' If this suggestion reads like a Mills bomb to you, throw it back before it explodes." And the reply: "Dear David, Alas, I would simply love to bask in your reflected glory and would greatly enjoy collaborating with you, but my job has become as time-swallowing as it is (and all too often) boring: so I just couldn't fit it in. It is all I can do now [he had recently been promoted to vice-chancellor] to knock off the odd (very odd) lecture, to say nothing of a book. The fact that I don't know what an ethic is, is neither here nor there. Love, Henry."

And that is how I remember Henry. That last remark, putting me in my place in one sense, and in another reminding me of the pretentiousness of words like medical ethics, is quintessential Henry Miller. I have never known another man quite like him. His love of music, his pilgrimages to concerts, not only all over England but, when he got the chance, all over the world; his sensitivity; his remarkable kindness; the inspiration he was to my youth; and our companionship throughout our maturity, I shall never forget. Even now, as I complete this contribution, I shall always be glad that I have had the opportunity of knowing and remembering Henry.

David Stafford-Clark was Chairman of the Division of Psychiatry (now consultant emeritus), Guys Group of Hospitals and now lives in Kantara, in North Cyprus. His comments were made in a tape recording.

John M Sutherland

I suppose that if I had not come to Brisbane in 1956 I might not have become a friend of Henry Miller. At any rate, in 1961 my wife and I, accompanied by our two children, decided to spend a few months in Britain and, while my wife and family made post haste for Scotland, I arranged to visit a number of neurological centres. At this time my neurological colleague and friend, the late Kenneth Jamieson, and I were in the process of creating a department of neurology and neurosurgery in Brisbane, and I felt that I would benefit from the experiences of other established and highly regarded units.

Thus it was that after a hegira to Queen Square, London, and a visit to my old friend and mentor, Douglas McAlpine of the Middlesex and Maida Vale Hospitals, I visited Ritchie Russell and Charles Whitty at Oxford, Sydney Allison and Harold Millar of Belfast, and J D Spillane of Cardiff. The last stop on my itinerary was Newcastle upon Tyne, where I had arranged to spend some days with Henry Miller—John Walton was unfortunately overseas at that time. I, of course, knew of Henry Miller, who had already become something of a legend in neurological circles; I had read his papers; and I had been made fully aware of his dynamic personality by William Gooddy in London, and by others encountered on my travels. Nevertheless, my first meeting with Henry Miller was at the Royal Victoria Infirmary in late June 1961.

An attractive lady doctor met me. "Good afternoon," she murmured. "Please come through. Dr Miller is expecting you." I was ushered into an office and had my first view of Henry.

"John Sutherland" he intoned, as if pronouncing a benediction and making me feel that I was being mistaken for someone of importance. He held out his hand. "Welcome to Newcastle." "Thank you very much, Dr Miller." "Henry, Henry, please. Now, let me show you around. We have Spillane coming to examine DPM candidates with me in a few days' time. He's a first-class clinician and we mustn't let him put anything over us."

Contributors

Henry was a large man. Not flabby, but big physically, and big in presence. With his ready grasp of things, his eloquence, wide knowledge, and clinical sense, ward visits with Henry proved an unforgettable experience. The ward visit over, and tea taken, I was returned to my hotel. "I'll pick you up about 6.30, take you home to meet Eileen, and have a drink. Then we will have dinner somewhere." And with that he breezed off to a meeting.

At Henry's home that evening, Professor Martin Roth came in and was introduced, "Meet Martin Roth. He is an unfrocked neurologist." This in reference to Sir Martin's eminence as neurologist before he devoted his interests to psychiatric medicine. "Dinner somewhere" proved to be a lavish meal at a club. The food was excellent, the wine superb, and, a characteristic Miller touch, the centre of the table was decorated with British and Australian flags. On leaving the club we made our way to where the Bentley was parked. Henry patted the gleaming bonnet affectionately. "Home, girl," he said.

Memorable days, accompanying Henry at work and at play, followed. I felt that emulation was impossible. There could be only one Henry Miller. The entire unit emanated a fascinating combination of clinical expertise, acumen, foresight, business ability, driving ambition, and efficiency. When I complimented him on what had been achieved, Henry commented, "You have to keep moving with chaps like John Walton breathing down your neck."

As my day of departure became imminent, Henry said, "You will have to stay another day. I would like you to meet a chap who is coming over from America. He has a peculiar name. I think he is an Eskimo." I did as I was bid. The "Eskimo" turned out to be David Poskanzer of the Massachusetts General Hospital, a long-time friend and colleague of Henry, and whose friendship I now value highly.

In 1963 Henry Miller accepted an invitation to be the Sir Edwin Tooth Visiting Professor in Brisbane. His visit was a signal success. Henry was no cold, sterile academician. He imparted knowledge and wisdom with consummate oratory, both at teaching rounds and at formal lectures. During one teaching round we were discussing the nature of a sixth cranial nerve palsy, which had afflicted a middle-aged lady from North Queensland. The cause of the palsy remained uncertain, despite angiography and other investigations. "You know, John, you *do* over-investigate your patients," Henry commented. I swallowed. "Is that so? You must remember it is over 700 miles by air from Townsville, where this lady lives, to Brisbane—rather more than between Carlisle and Newcastle," I replied somewhat smugly. "No excuse. The aetiology of idiopathic sixth nerve palsy is equally idiopathic in Townsville as it is in Carlisle."

His lectures on "accident neurosis" attracted huge audiences and the views he expressed were, by design, provocative. Indeed, the correspondence which subsequently flourished in the columns of the *Medical Journal of Australia* did not cease until terminated by the editor in June 1964. Sometimes trenchant, but always good humoured in his replies to critics, Henry scored heavily with strokes such as " It is still difficult to regard psychiatry as in any sense a science," or "The psychiatrist's subjective interpretations of the patient's subjective experiences, thought and motivations is often intriguing," and "Psychodynamic reasons can certainly be unearthed, adduced, imagined— or fabricated. . . ."

Socially, Henry Miller was a tremendous companion. His ability as a a raconteur, his skill in friendly debate, his tolerance and good humour made him the best of companions. While in Brisbane in 1963, we arranged for Henry to spend a weekend cruising in Moreton Bay on a cabin-cruiser jointly owned by Dr David Henderson, a senior physician in Brisbane, and his brother, a well-known Queensland stockbroker. In addition to the Hendersons, Henry and myself, the "crew" also included an eminent QC and a senior orthopaedic surgeon. After dropping anchor on the Friday evening the ship's company dined, wined and talked well into Saturday morning.

It was on the Saturday that Henry made a diagnostic blunder—in my experience the only one he committed. I awoke from sleep in the grip of a migraine attack. Hearing moans of agony emanating from my bunk, Henry glared balefully at me. "Sutherland, you have got a hangover." And then, in an airy aside to the others, "Lets have a nice dry Riesling with our scrambled eggs."

I had, however, some measure of revenge. On the next day, while our companions were preparing lunch—and prelunch cocktails—in a rather desultory manner, Henry and I elected to enjoy a swim off the boat. While so disporting ourselves Henry remarked, "I have just seen a huge fish." Now, in Moreton Bay all "huge fish" are sharks in my book until proved otherwise. Therefore, with a degree of speed unusual in a middle-aged neurologist, I returned to the safety of the boat. From this advantageous position I informed Henry conversationally of my views on the probable species of the large fish he had seen. The speed with which Henry George Miller covered the few yards to the boat, the agility with which he flung himself on board, and the wealth of abuse to which I was thereafter subjected live with me to this day.

As Professor Eric Saint, a lifelong friend of Henry's, has written, "He lived his life from beginning to end with an infectious gusto. Miller was to remind us that medicine can be great fun and that to do our work well, to be creative, we don't have to be conventional, stiff, or pompous; there is room in our life for panache and gaiety." Those of us in Australia who have known Henry Miller, or who have received training in his unit at Newcastle upon Tyne, remember him in this way and pay tribute to a great man.

John M Sutherland is an honorary consultant neurologist at the Royal Brisbane Hospital, and honorary Reader in Neurology at the University of Queensland.

W H Trethowan

Henry Miller's views on psychiatry are best summed up in his own words: "neurology without physical signs." In this he adhered to the traditional pattern of British neurology, which, until relatively recently, seems to have regarded the neurosis as its prerogative and not a matter for psychiatric intervention.

But Henry differed from most of his fellow neurologists in that he had acquired a Diploma of Psychological Medicine. This, he clearly believed, entitled him to pronounce widely upon psychiatry and psychiatrists, which, whenever a suitable opportunity presented itself, he never hesitated to do. But, despite his DPM, there is no record of his ever having spent any part of his career in a purely psychiatric setting. It appears that he obtained such training in psychiatry as was necessary to allow him to sit the examination during the war, while serving in the Royal Air Force Neuropsychiatric Unit. Despite an interest in psychiatry engendered presumably during this stage of his career, Henry remained a neurologist through and through. As a result of this, his various pronouncements on psychiatric topics characteristically reveal the neurologist's matter-of-fact approach. Thus he strongly eschewed woolly theorising, particularly by those who were psychodynamically inclined. Indeed, it could be said that the Freudian concept of the "unconscious" was almost his favourite anathema. This comes out clearly in his Milroy Lectures, for which he chose the subject of accident neurosis. In these he compared the different attitudes of neurologists and psychiatrists to the problem, stating that the former approached the subject pragmatically, laying considerable emphasis on the hope of financial gain as motivation for the syndrome, while most psychiatrists tended to consider such an interpretation as unsubtle, their own views leaning much more heavily on the distinction between conscious and unconscious motivation.

I think there are many today, perhaps even some neurologists, who might feel that Henry's views on accident neurosis were somewhat extreme. Although he recognised that head injury could sometimes precipitate an attack of endogenous depression, he may not have taken sufficient cognisance of the other kinds of depressive symptoms which

Contributors

may come after industrial accidents, where the injured man may entertain considerable fears about himself, his future, and that of his family—
fears often enhanced by the long-drawn out tedium of the legal process
with its many and repeated medical examinations by a variety of
specialists, none of whom reveal their findings to the sufferer, or offer
him much in the way of cheer. All in all, it was clear that Henry
regarded accident neurosis as less of a psychiatric condition than a
social disorder, referring to it as "an unfortunate accidental byproduct
of well-intentioned and essential legislation to compensate the injured
person."

Despite his apparently irresistible tendency to tease psychiatrists,
including me, as if to see what stuff they were really made of, such
teasing never gave real offence for, even when his comments bordered
on the outrageous, they were always offered both with good-humoured
exuberance and entirely without malice. He regarded me, he said, as
"one of those sensible psychiatrists," a statement which, if you think
about it closely, could be considered as a somewhat backhanded
compliment in that it constituted an invitation to agree with him or
run the risk of his disfavour. Good-humoured banter was, however,
the order of the day and his pursuit of this was skilful enough to be
hard to outwit.

Nevertheless, I did succeed in doing so once. This was at a meeting
of the 1942 Club, soon after it had become known that he was to be
appointed Vice-Chancellor of the University of Newcastle. One of
Henry's customary digs at psychiatrists provoked me to offer him a
dose of his own medicine, and comment on the current state of neurology.
What I said, in effect, was that, as neurosurgeons were now dealing with
the operable cases, and psychiatrists with the functional ailments,
neurologists were being ever more left to cope with the hard core of
degenerative disorders for which they could do little or nothing. "And
why had Henry Miller decided to desert the sinking ship?" This
silenced him, which was no easy matter.

But it was psychoanalysis especially which excited him to ridicule.
The time when he most clearly revealed this was on the occasion of a
radio broadcast in 1968, later published in the *Listener*. This, for me
at least, turned out to be a memorable occasion, one that I shall
certainly never forget. Apart from Henry and I, the other contestant was
Dr Tom Main, then Director of the Cassel Hospital. The intention was
that Tom Main should make the case for psychoanalysis while I should
present an opposing view, claiming the need for an eclectic approach
and the virtues of other forms of psychiatric treatment. Henry was to
be chairman, but this as will be seen, was not how it turned out.

On the appointed day we repaired to Broadcasting House, where our
lady producer had laid on an excellent cold collation, together with an

ample amount of various alcoholic beverages apparently with the purpose—which certainly turned out to be successful—of loosening our tongues. All three of us enjoyed good appetites, although Tom Main and I were not quite in the same class as Henry. Lunch having been finally disposed of, we retired to the studio where we sat close together around a small circular table with a microphone hanging down between our three faces. The proposition was that we should talk for as long as we felt able, after which our producer, who was to record the proceedings, would edit the tape and reduce it to a suitable length.

Now, while I would not regard myself as exactly lacking in verbal fluency, it became obvious from the start that I was no match for the other two. As soon as the red light came on Henry leapt to the attack. Then, when he at last ran out of steam, Tom Main immediately took over. This to-ing and fro-ing continued for what seemed to me almost an eternity, during which I tried several times to get a word or two in edgeways, while finding myself somewhat in the position of a referee trying to avoid actually getting bowled over by two giants in an all-in wrestling contest. Indeed, it at once became apparent that the role of chairman, having been abandoned by Henry, had been tacitly assigned to me, although as time went on the other two, wearying a little perhaps, appeared to concede that I might be allowed to express an occasional opinion. It must have been at least an hour and a half later when we finally ground to a halt, upon which in came our lady producer, white-faced, haggard, and obviously aged by a number of years. If I remember rightly what she said was: "Goodness knows what I am going to do with this lot"—her task being to reduce the whole thing to a reasonably comprehensible 20 minutes or so.

The broadcast contained many notable "Millerisms." Thus (in reply to Tom Main): "My own terrifying nightmares may be due to some ugly goings-on in my unconscious but if I find that these goings-on remain unconscious so long as I don't combine hot lobster and cheese soufflé for supper, I think it would be a more logical preventive medicine to avoid the lobster than come to your consulting room four times a week for four years to have my personality remodelled."

Later, when the discussion ranged over the possible psychosomatic factors underlying duodenal ulcer, Henry deftly disposed of this by diverting the subject to that of inguinal hernia. When Tom Main suggested that hernia could be the outcome of man's moods being expressed by posture and muscles Henry expostulated: "The result of this may or may not be inguinal hernia. This is the fallacy of an all-embracing theory. Psychoanalysis can not only account for homosexuality, bad dreams, but for inguinal hernia."

The suggestion that the findings of psychoanalysis were ignored by all the leading professions was, for him, an opportunity too good to miss:

"Of course they're ignored and ignored for a very good reason, and that is that it's an entirely subjective mythological interpretation based on no controlled observations. If I peddled a form of treatment that was as lacking in any controlled evaluation as psychoanalysis, I'd be laughed out of court."

Here, too, is Henry's view of the influence of early childhood experiences as a later cause of neurosis: "It may be . . . that you can readjust the adult patient by bringing to light a lot of things that did happen in the cradle. But if you can deal with the biochemical end result which causes the symptom by using an appropriate drug, then it seems to me commonsense. I would in no way support either of you that it's a terrible disaster that we don't have a psychoanalyst at every street corner."

While this was not what either of us had actually said, Henry was a good enough debater to know the value of putting words into the mouths of his opponents. All in all, and in the frame of reference of this particular context, I think it must be conceded that it was Henry's day. He may not have won on a knock-out, but he certainly scored a victory on points.

W B Trethowan is Professor of Psychiatry at the University of Birmingham.

George Waller

For a period of 12 or so years from 1952 to 1964 my acquaintance with Henry was as a medical expert in personal injury cases on the North Eastern Circuit. Sometimes it was a paper acquaintance, and I would be advising on the basis of a written report which he had made; sometimes I would be calling him as my witness; sometimes I would be cross-examining him as the witness for the other side.

He was a very useful man to have on your side. Not because he was a good expert witness, though he was—the term "good expert witness" sometimes carries overtones which would not apply to Henry—but because he gave an opinion which appeared to be completely uninfluenced by other than medical considerations.

An expert medical witness, particularly in a neurological-psychiatric case, is almost always influenced by those who put the case to him. Those representing the injured workman stress the pessimistic side of the case, and those representing the insurance company stress the optimistic side or perhaps say the whole thing is imaginary. The witness would barely be human if he did not reflect the instructions to some extent. Of course, some witnesses reflect more than others.

Contributors

Henry Miller was, in my experience, quite outstanding. Of course, this was partly because giving evidence or writing medicolegal reports formed a comparatively small part of his professional life. With a small exception, which I shall mention in a moment, Henry appeared to be uninfluenced by the side he was on. When you had a report from Henry Miller you knew it represented his opinion and unless the other side were able to introduce a fact which was new to him, it was an opinion which would remain unshaken under cross-examination. Furthermore, if you were appearing for a badly damaged man Henry had a way—unequalled in my experience at the Bar—of explaining the full effect of the plaintiff's disabilities in a way which brought home to the judge trying the case the disastrous effect of the plaintiff's injuries. But, equally, if he did not regard the injuries as serious he would say so.

If he was giving evidence for the plaintiff, and I was cross-examining him, there would be a frank discussion which would usually end in Henry's opinion looking stronger than ever. But if something were put to him that made him doubt his original opinion he would at once say so.

His Milroy lectures on accident neurosis in 1961 were of great interest, not only to the medical profession but to lawyers, insurance companies, trade union officials, and others interested in personal injury litigation. Their publication did appear to offer support to defendants' insurers whenever they received a claim with psychological effects of which they were sceptical. Frequently when the insurance companies had such a case they would send the man to Henry. On the basis of the history produced, and of his consultation and examination, there was a period of a year or so during which I got the impression that he rather readily formed an opinion that here was another case to illustrate his thesis of accident neurosis. But in court, and this is my abiding impression of this great man, there was never any question of defending his opinion at all costs. Every question in cross-examination was answered frankly and independently.

A typical occasion arose from the following facts. The 50-year-old foreman in a Tyneside shipyard was walking across the shop floor when a bolt fell on his head. It was not very heavy and did not cause a fracture, but the foreman was stunned for a short while. He was off work for a few days, then returned to work. Within a few weeks, however, he found, or said he found, that he no longer had a head for heights. Walking along beams 30 feet above the ground was a frequent and essential part of his job, so he could no longer do his work as foreman and took work at a much lower wage which did not mean leaving the ground. The insurers did not believe this was genuine; they sent him to Henry, who could find nothing wrong and expressed the opinion that it was accident neurosis, that it was not the result of the accident but motivated, perhaps subconsciously, by the prospect of damages. The

94

foreman was my client and I had to cross-examine Henry (whose opinion was likely to carry more weight than that of my consultant). I used the Royal Air Force wartime metaphor of operational tiredness and suggested to Henry that the foreman's nerve after years of walking at heights was perhaps near breaking point and that, in these circumstances, this comparatively trivial injury might well genuinely be the last straw. Henry thought for a moment and then said, "Yes, I think that could very well be the case."

I have always treasured this memory of Henry. There was no trick, no pressure in the question. It would have been as easy for him to have said, "It's just possible, but in my opinion it was not such a case" because, up to that moment, that was his opinion. It was an aspect which had not previously occurred to him. Nobody in the world could have criticised him for adhering to an opinion which he had honestly formed. Why should he change it? But not Henry. His hesitation before answering indicated to me that he was saying to himself: "Have I been unfair? Perhaps I have," and then gave the answer which I have mentioned. The answer made a difference of many hundreds of pounds in the award to the plaintiff.

As a medical expert witness in court Henry Miller was in the highest class. He was not one of those whose natural sympathies resulted in his becoming either a plaintiff's witness or a defendant's witness. He was called by both sides. His manner of giving evidence, not overconfident, conversational—almost as if he were discussing the case with a colleague —gave to his evidence a quality of reliability, and this was enhanced by his readiness to make the kind of concession I have mentioned above.

Finally, I remember his personality. A big man with a lively intelligent face and a matter-of-fact manner. You had the feeling in court that here was the master talking. This was not showmanship, although to a casual observer it might have appeared so. He gave the impression that he knew as much as there was to be known about the subject, because he did know. And if it was something unusual or outside his specialty he was ready to give an opinion making clear the limitation in its authority. The interesting thing was that, with all its limitations, this was often a very valuable addition to the problem.

He was a powerful ally if he was on your side, he was a powerful opponent if he was giving evidence for the other side. But whichever it was, a day in court was the better if Henry had been a part of it.

Sir George Waller is a Lord Justice of Appeal.

Marjorie White

My first remembrance of Henry was as a student nurse, just about 1947, when he first came back from the Air Force—I think he was then the senior registrar. He came to give us drug and dietetic lectures, which are rather boring subjects but anything but boring the way he did it. And I always remember, and I used to bring this up on many occasions, that he used to stand there—he was very personable in those days—and say that the only cause of obesity was overeating, and our rather fat tutor came to the first lecture and didn't appear any more.

I next came in contact with him when I'd been a sister for about a year. I went to the private ward as sister-in-charge, and he was then an assistant physician, but had quite a private practice, and I've known him ever since. He was a very hard worker, and a marvellous person to work with from the nurse's point of view. He looked after his patients so well. He came in every day; if he had a patient he was at all concerned about he'd be in twice a day. Also, we would be told that if we were at all anxious, or if anything happened, would we ring him at home, and the night staff were told this too, so you never had any worry about his patients; you knew that you always had someone that you could call on. On several occasions I came on duty at 8 o'clock and he'd been there, because he'd been called in. He also used to do all his own procedures, though as the years went by and he got busier he had to delegate to others, but whenever he could he did the personal thing himself and looked after his patients very well.

Also, he had such a clear mind that when he rang up to book a patient in for investigations he always had a long list of what investigations he wanted; he'd give me the whole list and I'd book all the things in the right order and his patients could get more done in three days than most got done in three weeks—it was people's money that was concerned, too. This was in about 1951. He was marvellous to deal with and also very approachable; if you had any worries or problems you could ring him up and he wouldn't mind. The thing was that he also loved his work—I remember some years ago that he told me that it was extraordinary that he should get paid for doing something that he enjoyed so much. He felt that it was such a privilege that you almost should be paying to do it.

Eventually when he got his own department, which was ward 6 (the neurological ward), he had a very small medical team—a first assistant, senior house officer, and a houseman—and I always remember that one first assistant hadn't been here all that long when a job came up elsewhere, a very suitable job for him, and Professor Miller, as he was then, said that he ought to apply and pushed him for this job, but knowing very well that he would have no one to replace him; for six months he was on call for 24 hours a day seven days a week. He did all the ward rounds, all the clinics, everything, and he was on call, with his private practice as well, and wrote numerous articles—I just don't know how he did it and yet, if you met him, he gave you the impression that he had time to talk. With some doctors you feel they're almost counting the minutes, but he was never like that and he had a great sense of humour, of course. He never changed from the time he was an assistant physician until he became dean.

He had a big private practice, which he had to run down gradually when he became Dean. He was always as approachable and easy to get on with, and considerate to work for, and he was always extremely kind to me. Underneath his outward blaséness (as it was in many ways) he was terribly soft hearted and kind to the patients and very concerned for them. He always got on very well with the students, as he was very tolerant and very good with them. He never had any problems with students up here when other universities were having them, because he understood their point of view.

As Dean, he did a full ward round every Saturday morning—apart from being very interesting, these were entertaining. He was very sad at having to give up medicine when he became Vice-Chancellor and liked to keep up with what was going on. Christmas was never the same without him and he practically always came in, all of his family with him—and I've seen the children grow from babies.

He always got rather interesting and amusing patients—I often used to think that the consultant got the type of patient that seemed to go with his personality. One afternoon he rang me up to ask if I had a bed, which I had, and he said he'd tell me about the patient when he got there. This was very unusual but anyway he rushed over with this woman, an American, and we pushed her in a room and then he whisked me up the corridor and whispered, "Her husband's going to murder her, he doesn't know she's here, and he mustn't find out." I had visions of an irate husband with a hatchet. This woman had married in her 40s; her husband had died, by which time she was about 62, so she decided to come and visit her husband's brother in the North-East, and came over from America. He was about 72 and after three weeks they got married. It obviously wasn't working out. She'd gone to visit some other relations nearby, left her luggage at the station, and nipped up here. Henry said she wasn't very well, anyway, and needed a few tests doing. I didn't care for her much, we chatted a bit, and, as she came from America she was used to central heating, fridges, freezers, electric blankets, and everything (this was 15 years or so ago and these things were not so general here). She found life rather uncomfortable, but her husband had managed all his life without these luxuries, so he

Contributors

wasn't going to spend any money on them. Anyway, he eventually found her and came—a little meek and mild man, but, as Henry said, Crippen was meek and mild. Anyway, we had a hilarious week making arrangements to get her back to America.

I was rather uneasy about the legal side. One evening I was going to see a friend, a solicitor, and also a friend of Henry's, so we decided to ask him about it. He said, "Tell Henry to be careful," so I told him. Next, this woman told Henry she wanted to change her will, so we called this fellow in. He was another character with a great command of the English language and together they were tremendous. He said he had a friend, a travel agent, so he rang him, and fixed up for her to go back to America, but by then she hadn't finished all her tests. These three kept meeting on the ward and having a great time. I was suspicious because one day I discovered that she had a friend in America whose wife had died since she had left America, and I think she was rather upset because I'm sure she had her eye on him. Anyway, we dispatched her off to America and none of these three charged her a penny; they were thoroughly enjoying themselves and said it was worth it for the fun. She never even had the decency to write and thank them, and we never heard another thing.

Kurt Schapira was another great friend and every time the three of them—Henry, Kurt, or Leslie—met they would sing the duet from *Don Giovanni* "La ci darem la Mano"—it was hilarious, like a signature tune, and if I heard it I knew they were there. Kurt has a marvellous sense of humour and he and Henry got on so well.

To show how considerate he was about patients: he always asked anybody's opinion—he would ask my opinion, his houseman's opinion. He might not agree with you, but he was always willing to listen to someone else's point of view. He didn't think he always knew better than anybody else. He had a lot of psychiatric cases because he had a Diploma in Psychological Medicine, and, of course, a lot of people who can afford to pay would rather say they were going to a neurologist (it was more respectable in those days) than to a psychiatrist. He was qualified to practise both, anyway. He had a lady from a nearby town, who, in spite of everything, went from bad to worse until she couldn't walk. He asked a psychiatrist colleague to come and see her. Part of the hospital called Claremont House in the hospital grounds is where psychiatric patients are treated on a weekly basis, and very often they will treat hospital patients on a day basis—returning them to the ward in the evening. This fellow said he wanted her transferred to Claremont House. We weren't too happy about this as she'd be going from the private ward, where you have a single room, to sharing a four or five-bedded room with some very odd people, helping with chores, and making her own bed. Henry didn't feel that, having asked someone else to see her, he

98

could interfere. I rang them up and asked for an ambulance to take her over, but they wouldn't hear of an ambulance, though I told them she couldn't walk.

I spoke to Henry, who said he'd take her over, so we took her and left her, though I wasn't happy about it. Then her mother and an aunt came to visit her, and two or three hours later the sister rang to say she'd taken her own discharge. I was furious: if she had rung when she was going, I'd have rung Henry, who'd have rescued her. Henry was furious too—she hadn't even seen a doctor, and it looked as if he'd just handed her over and hadn't cared what happened to her. That weekend Henry went down to her home to see and apologise. I don't know anyone else who would have done that.

Every Christmas Henry used to give a party at home, usually on 13 December, which was his birthday, so it doubled up very nicely with a birthday-cum-Christmas party. It was always a very popular party—I don't think anybody ever refused. There were always hordes of people there, and usually a hard core would be left behind, so that his poor wife used to be landed with having to produce some food. They had a job to get rid of the hard core. Henry used to play the piano, it was great fun, and you had great difficulty getting out of there on two legs, sometimes at two or three in the morning.

One of the most striking things about him was his ability to say the rudest and the most offensive things to people without giving offence. From anybody else you'd have been mortally offended, but from him you took it in the way it was meant. He used to introduce me to patients either as Poppy or the manageress, which very often blackened my character before we started. Another very amusing thing he used to do sometimes: if you were doing something on the ward, he'd rattle in his pocket, bring out a penny, and put it in your hand—"Thank you, that's very good," he'd say. However, one day he slipped up and it was half-a-crown, so he stopped doing that.

He also used to treat a number of alcoholics, whom he gave Antabuse to before breakfast. We'd put them on Antabuse for a few days, then Henry would come trundling in with a bottle of their favourite tipple, pour out a good generous drink, and the medical staff would retire and knock back the rest. The patients used to be very ill. At this time we had a patient who didn't really want to stop drinking, but his wife asked if she could dissolve the tablets in his drink. You couldn't do this of course, as they made the patient too ill, but we had a discussion about whether they would dissolve. One of Henry's fallacies about losing weight was that he wouldn't have coffee mid-morning, he'd have Bovril. We were having coffee one day—the other sister on Pavilion 3 with me at the time, and me—and Henry was having his Bovril. He was telling us he was going out for drinks and lunch. My colleague suddenly

Contributors

got up and peered into Henry's cup and said, "They do dissolve," and I said, "By jove, they do; there isn't a trace of it." His face was a picture—the thought of having to be on tomato juice all over lunch. He looked as much as to say, "They wouldn't dare . . . but would they?"

Henry very much enjoyed music. I'm very fond of opera and it was Henry's favourite and I learnt a lot about music and opera from him. He introduced me to Mahler, and to Carl Orff. One of the GPs, I think, had given him the records of *Carmina Burana*, which he had never heard before and he lent them to me. He would go to the ends of the earth for opera. He and his wife would leave at 5 o'clock at night and go to Leeds for an opera; often they did the same to Edinburgh, and they used to go backwards and forwards to the Festival; they would sometimes leave here at five and go over to Rose Hill, the little theatre in Cumberland, where I went once when he and Eileen took me one Sunday as my Christmas present.

I clearly remember the last time I saw Henry was about April 1976, when I was invited to the Schapiras for a meal. We knew then that he hadn't been well for some time and Kurt didn't think he'd stay very late. But he was in cracking form. He told us he'd been talking to some colleague from the South and they had been discussing neurological bladders, and this chap had been telling him about a new electrical device. These neurological bladders don't work, so you can fix them with these small transmitters, and then every so often they go to the loo and press a little button that triggers off the nerve. This man lived in a coastal town and apparently the coastguards were getting an awful lot of false alarms and it was some time before it dawned on them that this chap's electrical device was on the same wavelength as the coastguard's—so that every time he went to empty his bladder the coastguards got called out.

Henry didn't go till midnight or later. He played hard all his life. If anyone ever enjoyed life Henry did, but he would have hated to be an invalid. If ever he was ill, he just disregarded it. He would ring you up at work and say "I'm in bed," but it didn't keep him quiet; he'd be ringing up about this and that. He hurt his ankle and couldn't walk once, but he had himself wheeled in. He wouldn't give in. He is a great miss and no one will ever take his place.

Marjorie White is a nursing officer at the Royal Victoria Infirmary, Newcastle upon Tyne. Her comments were made in a tape recording.

Henry Miller at different ages (photographs kindly lent by Mrs Eileen Miller)

Henry in the RAF (photograph kindly lent by Professor George Smart)

Top: Henry with King Olav of Norway   Bottom left: Henry with Eileen.
Bottom right: Henry as Public Orator (photographs kindly lent by Mrs Eileen Miller)

Henry IX

(photograph kindly lent by Professor Sam Shuster

Accident neurosis *

HENRY MILLER, MD, FRCP, DPM

Physician in Neurology, the Royal Victoria Infirmary, Newcastle upon Tyne.

Lecture I

At a time when fever hospitals are being closed and accident hospitals planned or reopened, the fact that several recent lectures in this series have been devoted to various aspects of accidental trauma would not have disconcerted Dr Gavin Milroy. His "suggestions" to lecturers of 80 years ago reveal an urgent preoccupation with what was topical in State medicine, and he could not be impressed today that two short decades have witnessed the virtual displacement of the contagious fevers by trauma as a major epidemic scourge of our civilisation. Each year more than a million people in Great Britain are injured at work or on the roads. Figures of such magnitude pose major problems of organisation to the Health Service, but the functional nervous disorders which sometimes follow accidents have an additional importance to State medicine, since it has been widely argued that their very occurrence is in some way related to the machinery that society has evolved to deal with them.

The literature of accident neurosis is scanty, and it has received little attention from formal psychiatrists. Most papers on the subject are in the nature of occasional contributions, often more conspicuous as expressions of opinion than for their factual content. Indeed, the subject is so fraught with prejudice that it demands a conscious effort to maintain a clear distinction between fact and interpretation. This I will endeavour to do, and my material will fall into two parts—first, the presentation of clinical data derived from personal experience, and, secondly, a discussion of its possible medical and social significance.

The question of terminology is a vexed one, and the inelegant prefix of the title has been adopted reluctantly but advisedly. The term "traumatic neurosis" was coined by Oppenheim (1889), who attributed the condition to neuronal damage of a molecular nature. Whatever validity such a concept may have to the problem of cerebral concussion, it is clearly irrelevant in the present context: accident neurosis may arise quite independently of physical injury of any kind. Furthermore,

*From the Milroy Lectures for 1961, delivered before the Royal College of Physicians of London on February 7 and 9.

Accident neurosis

the subsequent extension of Oppenheim's term to cover the results of so-called "psychic trauma" as well as physical injury has so far deprived it of any clear meaning that it is best discarded. The terms "compensation neurosis" or "litigation neurosis" have the virtue that litigation is a more constant feature of these cases than physical injury, but they prejudge the issue of aetiology.

The evidence presented here is based on personal experience of about 4000 patients examined for medico-legal assessment after accidents during a dozen years of consultant practice. It includes an analysis of 200 cases of head injury recently examined for this purpose, and a follow-up study of 50 patients in whom gross neurotic symptoms after an accident had been found on examination more than three years previously.

NEUROSIS AND HEAD INJURY

The material under review in this connexion comprises 200 consecutive cases (152 male and 48 female) of head injury first referred for medico-legal examination between 1955 and 1957. The ages of these patients ranged from 2 to 84 years: 90%, however, were between 20 and 60, the average age being 42. All social strata were represented, from unskilled labourers to the peerage. The average interval between injury and first examination was 14 months. Ninety-four injuries were sustained in road and 106 in industrial accidents. The "industrial" group included a few patients injured in the course of non-industrial occupations. Of these 200 cases, 47 had gross and unequivocally psychoneurotic complaints.

In 22 other cases a post-concussional or post-contusional syndrome was complicated by psychoneurotic features. In nine further patients a true depressive syndrome of "endogenous" pattern succeeded the injury: and in one instance traumatic delirium following severe brain injury merged imperceptibly into a schizophrenic illness, in a man whose elder brother was already an established schizophrenic. In 34 other cases organic impairment of personality or intellect was encountered: all except three of these patients had suffered prolonged unconsciousness extending over periods varying from several days to many months. The three exceptions comprised an arteriopath of 66 in whom gross dementia followed a closed head injury characterised by only 15 minutes' unconsciousness; and two cases in which severe fractures of the skull had been unassociated with any impairment of consciousness.

Differential incidence of neurosis

Our main concern here is with the 47 cases with indubitably psychoneurotic complaints. Such a development was twice as common after industrial (33%) as after road accidents (16%). It was more than twice as common in men (27%) as in women (12.5%). This difference might at first sight be regarded as partly related to the preponderance of road accidents amongst the female cases. It is true that only six of these resulted from occupational injuries, among which were two cases of gross psychoneurosis. On the other hand, 42 traffic accidents in women yielded only four instances of neurosis whereas 12 were encountered amongst the 52 men similarly involved.

It is a widespread clinical impression that accident neurosis is commoner in older subjects, but no evidence is forthcoming from this material which favours the view that age is of much importance in relation to the syndrome—except that it was not encountered in childhood. Almost exactly half of these patients were over 40. Among these the incidence of neurosis was 24%, as against 21% in the younger group.

Relationship to severity of injury

In whatever way the cases are broken down they demonstrate an inverse relationship of accident neurosis to the severity of the injury. Gross psychoneurosis occurred, for example, in 31% of patients without radiological evidence of skull fracture, in 9% of patients with simple fracture, and in only two out of 25 patients who suffered compound fractures of the skull. In one of those a gross hysterical reaction complicated organic deterioration of personality and intellect following a severe brain injury, and the other patient was already a lifelong hypochondriac. A similarly inverse relationship is shown between the incidence of gross psychoneurosis and the duration of unconsciousness. The incidence of psychoneurosis in patients who were never unconscious was 42%. Amongst all unconscious patients the incidence was 14%. Where the post-traumatic amnesia (PTA) was less than 15 minutes the incidence was 37%, and where it was more than this it was 10%. Of 48 patients with PTA of more than 72 hours only three showed residual psychoneurosis. One was a mental defective, one the lifelong hypochondriac already mentioned, and one a patient with a long history of recurrent psychiatric disability before his accident.

Predisposing factors

The incidence of accident neurosis is related to social status. In the industrial group most of those who developed gross neurotic sequelae were unskilled or semi-skilled workers. Cases from this social group showed an incidence of neurosis of twice the average (47%). Amongst men, labourers, datal mineworkers, and the like furnished the bulk of cases. Amongst women, factory and office cleaners were conspicuous. More than half of the patients with accident neurosis came from the Registrar-General's social classes IV and V (semi-skilled and unskilled

Accident neurosis

workers), as against a 38% representation of these social classes in the 200 cases reviewed, and 34% in the population of Northumberland and Durham as a whole. Among patients above the level of under-foreman or charge-hand, neurotic symptoms or prolonged incapacity subsequent to industrial head injury occurred in only 18% of cases.

The factor of social differential may also be related to the lower incidence of neurosis after road accidents, which cover a wider social range than the industrial group. Even here, however, a disproportionate number of cases occurred in those of lower social status, and the condition was distinctly rare among the professional or managerial patients examined. However, amongst the latter, one intelligent businessman and one professional man frankly admitted to making the most of their symptoms in the hope of turning minor injury to financial advantage.

It has often been suggested that the nature of the accident is a material factor in influencing the subsequent development of neurosis. Some of the accidents in which the patients under discussion were involved were of the most alarming nature, but out of 17 such out-standing instances neurosis developed in only two and indeed many of the most disabling functional sequelae followed trivial blows to the head sustained during the course of some routine occupation quite devoid of special danger. However, the nature of the employment is possibly of some importance. The condition appeared to be more frequent in the employees of large industrial organisations or nationalised industries than in those working in the more intimate *milieu* of small businesses or on farms. The series is not a large one, and allowance must be made for local factors. However, it would appear that under-ground mineworkers and steel erectors, especially in the labouring grades, furnished a higher-than-average proportion of cases: such work is of course dangerous and widely known to be dangerous, while claims for compensation are an everyday matter in the industries concerned.

In relation to personal predisposition, it has been stressed in psychiatric circles that accident neurosis tends to occur especially in patients with a particular type of personality—dependent, insecure, craving sympathy, and at the same time exhibiting well-marked paranoid tendencies. This may be the case, and such features are indeed often conspicuous by the time the patient is seen with the developed syndrome. However, in view of the absence of any valid parameter of personality, and of the fact that assessment of the patient prior to his accident is both subjective and retrospective it can hardly be regarded as more than a clinical impression. Indeed, in response to direct questions few of these patients are prepared to admit to anything other than robust physical and mental health until the very day of the accident, while the collateral evidence of relatives and friends—so valuable in other psychiatric contexts—is often equally unreliable. Assessment of pre-accident personality therefore presents special difficulties, and depends to a greater degree than is usual on information from uncommitted sources such as the family doctor, and on the objective evidence of work and sickness records. Quotation of these often jogs the patient's memory for important events which whether consciously or unwittingly—he had omitted from the most painstakingly elicited history.

With these qualifications, evidence of some significant predisposing factor or factors was found in 20 of those 47 cases in which gross neurosis had followed head injury. Because of the frequent tendency of these patients to conceal positive evidence in their pre-accident histories this figure is more likely to be an underestimate than an overestimate. However, the development of a major psychoneurosis of disabling severity in adult life (barring either a background or organic brain disease or camouflaged psychosis, or else a truly catastrophic emotional situation) usually implies a degree of predisposition hard to disguise even in the most cursory psychiatric history. The absence of any evidence whatever of predisposition to neurosis in more than half of these psychiatrically disabled patients is therefore a very striking feature.

Amongst the predisposing factors encountered in certain cases was below-average intelligence. In these cases, however, emotional stability was more significant: several stable dullards showed no neurotic developments after their head injuries. A past history of evident emotional instability, invalidism, hypochondriasis, or prolonged incapacity after previous minor injuries was an unfavourable feature, as was a shiftless work record. Concurrent menopausal nervous symptoms, coincident hypertension, and arteriosclerosis were occasional factors. Responsibility for the patient's prolonged absence from work was often laid firmly at the door of the doctor—"he won't let me go back"—but in fact convincing evidence of primary iatrogenesis was rare.

Occupational disability

The average duration of absence from work in 31 patients with neurosis who had returned to their employment when they were seen was six months. This figure must be considered in relation to the severity of the head injuries involved. Only four of these 31 patients had sustained fracture of the skull. Sixteen never lost consciousness, and in nine further cases the PTA was measured in minutes; only six patients had been unconscious for an hour or more. This compares with an average period of four months' loss of work in 58 patients who had sustained simple fractures of the skull uncomplicated by neurosis. Forty-six of these patients had been unconscious, 23 for more than five days and only nine for less than an hour.

Accident neurosis

The average of six months' occupational disability with neurosis may be compared also with that in patients who had sustained compound fractures of the skull. Of 22 such cases, five were permanently disabled by epilepsy, hemiplegia, or organic mental change; and two others were away from work for two and a half and four years respectively on this last account. In the remaining 15 cases, however, the average period of absence from work after compound fracture of the skull was a little less than 4.5 months. These encouraging figures for early return to work after severe head injury are very similar to those given by Ritchie Russell (1934) in a survey of consecutive cases drawn from hospital practice. He also convincingly demonstrated the effect of the compensation issue in prolonging incapacity. The present figures demonstrate that, even where this factor is uniformly operative, all but the most severe head injuries cause less occupational disablement than accident neurosis.

Post-concussional syndrome

In 36 of the 47 cases of gross neurosis described above the symptomatology was that of uncomplicated emotional illness, in which symptoms of organic pattern were entirely lacking. In the remaining 11 cases the actual disability at the time of the examination was predominantly and unequivocally neurotic in nature, but persisting post-concussional symptoms were also present. The consistency of the post-concussional syndrome of headache, postural dizziness, irritability, failure of concentration, and intolerance of noise argues a structural or at least a pathophysiological basis. However, such symptoms are by no means invariable, even after material closed head injury, and in most uncomplicated cases the subjective disability is not of long duration. Unless the injury has been of some severity it is uncommon for a patient to be away from work for more than a few weeks after concussion sustained in sporting or other neutral circumstances.

In addition to the 11 cases in which gross neurosis complicated post-concussional symptoms, a post-concussional or post-contusional syndrome was also encountered in 73 other cases of closed head injury in the series, and also in nine of the 22 patients who had suffered compound fractures of the skull. In none of the nine cases of compound fracture was it complicated by neurosis, but in 22 of the 73 other cases there was an admixture of emotional symptoms, such as sleeplessness, self-pity, depression, or frank anxiety, which were interpreted as indicating a neurotic superstructure. This view was usually also supported by the prolonged duration of the syndrome, its failure to improve, and the frequent claims of deterioration in a symptomatology which we know ordinarily tends to spontaneous improvement, and in which there is every logical reason to expect such a development.

106

Again, analysis reveals in these cases an inverse relationship between the severity of the injury and the development of neurotic symptoms. Of 49 patients in this series whose post-concussional syndromes followed head injuries associated with unconsciousness of more than five minutes' duration, only three developed persistent neurotic complications, while these were encountered in no fewer than 19 of the 24 patients in whom post-concussional symptoms of similar "physical" pattern followed head injury without loss of consciousness. In the post-concussional group also, neurotic complications were more than three times as common in the absence of skull fracture as in its presence.

These figures indicate that in this series persistence and psychoneurotic elaboration of the post-concussional syndrome bore an inverse relation to the severity of brain injury similar to that observed in the case of frank neurosis. They suggest that in this context at any rate the psychoneurotic component was an expression of whatever situational factors are responsible for accident neurosis in general, and not a function of structural damage.

In other ways also these 22 patients with psychoneurotically complicated post-concussional syndromes were comparable with the 47 examples of neurosis previously presented. By comparison with the 51 instances in which a post-concussional syndrome was uncomplicated by neurosis there was no difference in age incidence (the averages being 42 and 41.5 respectively) and evidence of neurotic predisposition was again found in less than half. Once more also, the neurotic complications showed a higher incidence in the lower social groups.

Depressive illness following head injury

The nine patients in whom depressive illness followed head injury stand out from the neurotic cases in many ways. In eight the depression was of classical endogenous type and in only one instance did real diagnostic difficulty arise. Seven depressive patients were over 40, the average age being 51. The head injuries were material in all but one instance: one patient had a fractured skull and six had been unconscious. Four patients had a previous history of depressive illness, and three others showed significant predisposing factors in the form of severe hypertension and arteriosclerosis, antecedent menopausal symptoms, and a long history of obsessional neurosis respectively. Two patients were suicidal. Five had been or were subsequently treated with electric convulsion therapy. In each instance improvement followed, even though the compensation issue remained unresolved. These were in fact the only patients in the whole series who exhibited a favourable response of psychiatric symptoms to treatment.

Accident neurosis

This syndrome is one of the most stereotyped in medicine. Sometimes the fright of the accident merges imperceptibly into a continuing complaint of nervous symptoms with an anxiety-depressive cast. More often, and especially where the symptoms have a frankly hysterical flavour, the condition develops after a latent period of weeks or even months. The general symptoms are remarkably constant, and amount to head pains (usually described as "terrible," "terrific," or "agonising") exertional or postural dizziness, irritability, failure of concentration, and restlessness. Sleeplessness is volunteered in rather less than half, but in reply to leading questions the patient will usually claim insomnia of psychoneurotic pattern (difficulty in getting off to sleep), restless sleep, and often nightmares related to his accident. Where there has been physical injury, complaints of intractable pain or other disability in the injured part are common, and these may be associated with motor weakness easily improved on persuasion, or anatomically incongruous sensory loss.

Objective signs of anxiety such as tachycardia, tremor, and axillary hyperhidrosis are, however, relatively uncommon, and have been found in less than 15% of personal cases. Gross dramatisation of symptoms was recorded in more than half. On examination this may be evident in the way the patient shies away from the ophthalmoscope; by the groaning and quivering which ensues when forward spinal flexion is tested; by a flaccid grip easily strengthened by distraction or encouragement; or by the patient's slumping forward with head in hands during the consultation, requesting a glass of water. I had long regarded this last as a pathognomonic sign of accident neurosis, but I understand that it is often seen in women requesting termination of pregnancy on psychiatric grounds.

The behaviour of the patient with accident neurosis at the consultation is characteristic. If he is being examined at the request of the insurance company he frequently arrives late. He is invariably accompanied, often by a member of his family, who does not wait to be invited into the consulting-room, but who resolutely enters with him, and more often than not takes an active part in the consultation, speaking for him, prompting him, and reminding him of symptoms that may for the moment have slipped his memory. The patient's attitude is one of martyred gloom, but he is also very much on the defensive, and exudes hostility especially at any suggestion that his condition may be improving. It is almost impossible to conjure up a smile to relax his appearance of preoccupied tension. His complaint of amnesia is often at variance with the circumstantial detail which invests his account of the events that led up to the accident many months ago. At some stage he will often insist that the cause of this was absolutely outside his control and that it was entirely due to someone else's fault. The "someone else" is rarely specified, but is usually "they"—in some vague way identified with the employing organisation—or the unknown other motorist.

The most consistent clinical feature is the subject's unshakable conviction of unfitness for work, a conviction quite unrelated to overt disability even if his symptomatology is accepted at its face value. At a later stage the patient will declare his fitness for light work, which is often not available. The logic of prescribing light duties rather than his customary employment for the rehabilitation of the neurotic worker may appear obscure, but the reason why such a recommendation is often made by the general practitioner and echoed in consultant reports is clear: light work is better than no work at all, and it is generally appreciated that unless the doctor goes half-way to meet him—and especially if he provokes actual hostility—the patient's complaints will be intensified and disability further prolonged. The equanimity with which these patients will accept the tedium of months or even years of idleness, apparently unmitigated by any pleasurable diversion, is remarkable.

Another cardinal feature is an absolute refusal to admit any degree of symptomatic improvement. With the exception of a few well-defined conditions such as traumatic arthritis and causalgia, there are no physical results of injury the discomforts of which do not in the course of time become somewhat less intense. Far from accepting the suggestion of such improvement, these patients often make the improbable claim that pain at the site of injury has steadily become more severe over a period of months or years.

Equally characteristic is the patient's attitude to medical attention and treatment. In industrial cases periodic attendance on the general practitioner is necessary in order to obtain successive certificates of unfitness for work, but in other instances it is remarkable that the patient will complain bitterly of disabling nervous symptoms lasting for many months—for which she has never once sought medical treatment. In a number of personal cases the aid of the general practitioner was invoked only after searching questions about such treatment had been asked during a consultation for medico-legal purposes.

THE CASE HISTORY

A case history synthesised from several hundred personally recorded would read somewhat as follows. An unskilled labourer, either with an uneventful previous history or who had perhaps suffered earlier accidents in which minor injury was followed by disproportionately long disablement, sustains a bruise when he trips over a piece of wood carelessly left on the factory floor. Although similar occurrences in his

Accident neurosis

home have never been met with anything more than an expletive, he goes straight to the works ambulance-room, where a dressing is applied and the incident duly recorded in the accident book. The injury is trivial. He completes his shift and possibly puts in two or three further days' work. He discusses the incident with his friends, and consults a union official, who encourages him to formulate a claim "just in case the injury should give trouble at a later date." The union official cannot be blamed for such advice. Official posters exhort the workman to report even trivial accidents at once—and in any case a late claim is always suspect.

The man stays away from work to visit his doctor who knows his job is heavy and acquiesces in his suggestion of a week's rest. During this week at home he develops headaches, sleeplessness, nervousness, and loss of appetite: he is irritable and easily startled.

It is easy to feel in retrospect that robust handling by the doctor at this stage might have got the man back to work. Sometimes this is true: everyone knows that for one reason or another some doctors abet scroungers and there are many more who acquiesce in the lay conception that absence from work is in itself a form of medical treatment. But in this connexion the difficulties should not be minimised: there is often another doctor around the corner who may be more compliant.

At any rate, a process has now been initiated which may lead to months or even years of disablement. Some of this time is spent—unfortunately with tacit professional support—in pointless attendance at the physiotherapy department of a local hospital, where his now normal limb is rubbed, heated, and exposed to coloured lights. Such occupation alternates with aimless wandering about the streets, watching television, and sitting moodily in the house. It is punctuated by lengthy periods in an industrial convalescent home in the country—a residential club where he can compare notes with a handful of fellow sufferers.

Throughout this whole period he sees little of his own doctor and a good deal of solicitors, union officials, and medical consultants to whom he is referred for assessment. From his practitioner he merely accepts certificates of unfitness for work; there is by now a tacit understanding between them that no kind of treatment will influence his symptoms at the present juncture. This view is likely to be confirmed by any psychiatrist to whom the patient is referred, and if the doctor does in fact make some well-intentioned attempt to help him by prescribing a sedative or ataractic the patient will tell subsequent inquirers that these were quite useless, and that he has had "no treatment, only some tablets." With repeated examinations and interrogations the familiar syndrome gradually assumes its usual florid form. The case involves an allegation of negligence under common law, and is ultimately put down for hearing at the next assize court; but because the civil list is too full—

mainly of similar proceedings—or for some other reason, it is adjourned, and ultimately comes to trial months later and several years after the accident. In the interim it is clearly against the man's financial interest to return to any kind of work, or to admit the faintest improvement, while a claim of deterioration can react only to his pecuniary benefit.

Finally the case comes to trial. Even at this stage eleventh-hour settlement after hard bargaining is the likeliest outcome. Once in court the issue of negligence may be unproven and the case may collapse, leaving the man without even the solace of financial benefit. More often, however, it is easy to prove a technical breach of a minor regulation, and an award of some kind is made—perhaps a few hundred or even sometimes a few thousand pounds. In the course of the case the counsel for the employer or the insurance company expresses confidence that once it is settled rapid improvement will occur. Counsel for the man enters the caveat that this is not invariable, and that many such patients suffer persisting disablement long after settlement, and sometimes permanently. Neither they nor their expert witnesses, nor the judge who must assess damages, can give a reliable prognosis or even a valid assessment of statistical probablities.

It is remarkable that in a country where industrial accidents cause 800 000 new insurance claims and the loss of 16 000 000 working days annually, where there are more than 250 000 road injuries in a similar period, and where three-quarters of all accidental injuries occur under conditions where compensation is potentially payable, no proper inquiry has ever been conducted into the fate of patients with this well-defined syndrome after they leave court. The barrister's interest ceases the moment judgment is given. The insurance company is licking its wounds and wondering whether it might not have been cheaper to settle—or not to settle. The medical witnesses' interest, already vitiated by the unpredictable dislocation of a busy professional schedule, has evaporated. The only person in a position to know what happens next is the general practitioner—and his part in the case has so far been negligible.

PROGNOSIS OF ACCIDENT NEUROSIS

There are several indications that the prognosis of this condition is more favourable than the apparent severity of symptoms at the time of settlement would suggest. The first is that, amongst a number of patients personally seen in this or some other connexion who had previously suffered from and been compensated for a similar condition, not one has ever admitted to any psychiatric disability remaining from the first accident. The second is that, although the syndrome is a very common one in an industrial area, patients with this disorder in whom the legal issue has been resolved are conspicuously rare amongst the thousands

Accident neurosis

who seek treatment for functional nervous disorders. Thirdly, it is significant that of the many ex-Service men who were drawing pensions for the rather similar condition of war neurosis at the end of the second world war, in the vast majority of cases symptoms cleared up within a few years of demobilisation. In my experience of these ex-Service cases symptoms persisted only in those heavily predisposed to neurosis; inpatients with very inadequate personalities; and in a very small group of patients, apparently previously normal, who had been subjected to prolonged and overwhelming stress, not infrequently occurring in situations which evoked feelings of guilt about the fate of their comrades. Even where psychoneurotic symptoms persisted or persist to the present day, material disablement from the occupational point of view is extremely rare.

The literature of accident neurosis has been reviewed by Pokorny and Moore (1953), but it contains little reliable information on the question of prognosis. Discussion by Purves-Stewart (Buzzard et al., 1928) and by Smith and Solomon (1943) supports the view that it is essentially favourable. Purves-Stewart reported a small group of personal cases, all but one of which promptly recovered and returned to work on settlement. He made two points which are supported by personal experience. These patients are difficult to trace, and the large majority withdraw themselves completely from any form of medical supervision once the case is settled. Secondly, early and complete recovery is as likely to follow the irrevocable rejection as the success of the claim for compensation.

The paucity of reliable figures in this connexion stimulated me to follow up 50 consecutive cases of accident neurosis personally examined between three and four years ago.

FOLLOW-UP STUDY OF 50 CASES OF ACCIDENT NEUROSIS AFTER SETTLEMENT

At the time of the first examination and at the time of settlement of their claims for compensation, each of these 50 patients (41 men and nine women) complained of disabling nervous symptoms occurring after accidents. In 31 the accident had been industrial, in 18 a traffic accident. The ages of the patients ranged from 22 to 70, the average being 42.

Twenty-four of these patients were labourers or unskilled or semi-skilled workers falling into the Registrar-General's social classes IV and V—a proportion again much higher than that found in the population at risk. Fifteen were skilled workmen, three were (untrained) nurses. Other occupations represented were housewife, clerk, shop assistant, university student, haulage contractor, building contractor, and company director.

In three cases there had been no physical injury whatever, while in 35 it had been trivial—head injury without impairment of consciousness

112

(13 cases) or with only momentary concussion (4), general shaking and bruising (10), minor back injury (4), lacerations of face and arm, and bruising of hand (2); in two further cases a finger was fractured. In the remaining 12 patients injuries were more severe—major fractures, multiple general injuries, or head injury with prolonged unconsciousness (30 minutes to four days).

In 36 of the 50 cases the psychiatric picture was typical of "accident neurosis," with conspicuous depression, restless sleep, hypochondriacal invalidism, disgruntlement, and self-pity in varying proportions. In 21 of these 36 cases there were positive physical or psychiatric signs of a hysterical reaction. In another five, phobic symptoms were related to the circumstances of the accident or to the occupation generally.

In four other cases a post-concussional syndrome after trivial head injury was elaborated and prolonged for more than two years, with positive evidence of hysteria. In four patients intractable disabling pain at the site of injury was the main symptom. In all three patients with hand injuries (two with fractured fingers, one merely bruised) a similar complaint was complicated by hysterical contracture of one or more fingers. There were two patients in whom depressive and psychoneurotic features were inextricably mixed, and one unusual instance in which a patient subject to a particularly terrifying experience developed an anxiety state of great severity which rapidly responded to psychiatric treatment—after which he abandoned his claim for compensation.

Personal predisposition to neurosis was evident in the previous histories of only 15 of these 50 cases. Six of the predisposed patients were chronic neurotics, well known to their general practitioners over many years. One was a previous subject of depressive illness. In three other patients the history revealed earlier episodes of neurotic response to stress—for example, invaliding from the Army with intractable headaches which cleared up after discharge. Of the remaining five, four were inadequate or immature personalities with shiftless work records (one being an alcoholic) and one was a dullard.

Of these 50 cases, 42 had been settled by negotiation out of court, and in four the claims had been withdrawn or abandoned. The four remaining cases all came to trial, and in each instance the claim for compensation was rejected. In two instances the complainant failed to prove liability. In one the judge gave it as his opinion that the patient was malingering, and in the other that his chronic neurotic symptoms were not due to the accident. The average delay between accident and settlement was 26 months. Damages negotiated ranged from £20 to nearly £5000, and averaged £454. In some instances, however, this represented an assessment based on the sum of physical and psychiatric disabilities, and in a few it was made on the basis of only partial liability.

Accident neurosis

In a group of cases where physical injury was trivial and residual disability unequivocally psychiatric the average award was only £152 (£181 in men, £83 in women).

The average interval between settlement and re-examination was a little over two years. Only two of the patients had undergone psychiatric treatment for their nervous symptoms (Cases 34 and 36, see below). All but four of the 45 previously employed had returned to their own or similar work. One of the four was in hospital undergoing plastic surgical treatment for his severe general injuries. One was a married woman who had not resumed her part-time occupation because of domestic commitments.

Illustrative cases

Two of the 50 patients were occupationally disabled by psychiatric symptoms at the time of re-examination:

Case 30.—In 1955 a 42-year-old unskilled colliery labourer sustained a minor head injury without loss of consciousness. He was a man of low intelligence with a history of much vague ill-health in the past. After this head injury he worked for a week without interruption, but a few weeks later he developed attacks of weakness of the left side of the body and clouding of consciousness. When seen at this time he presented a difficult diagnostic problem, but exhaustive in-patient investigation was entirely negative, and attacks observed while he was in the ward were grossly hysterical. Apart from these attacks he had no disability whatever. The case was settled out of court by negotiation and he was awarded more than £4000 in damages. It would appear that a diagnosis of traumatic epilepsy was sustained in this negotiation and subsequently accepted by the Ministry of National Insurance, which continued to pay him a pension of £3 16s. 6d. weekly. Since this time he has never returned to work. Re-examination in 1960 again failed to confirm epilepsy and yielded positive evidence of hysteria.

Case 34.—In 1954 a 27-year-old labourer sustained a minor concussion and bruising of his back when he was knocked off his bicycle. Repeated clinical and radiological examinations were negative, but he continued to complain bitterly of pain in the back and down the legs. There was nothing in his past or family history to indicate any predisposition to neurosis, but he continued to complain and did not return to work. He had a great deal of outpatient physiotherapy and rehabilitation and numerous conflicting specialist opinions. When examined two years after the accident there were no abnormal physical signs except those of gross hysteria. The case was settled three years after the accident for more than £2500. However, his hysterical gait continued for 18 months after settlement, finally responding to suggestive psychotherapy in a psychiatric unit. Two years after the accident there was little or no real disability except that he continued to use a stick unnecessarily. He had never returned to work and shows no signs of doing so. He continues to draw a National Insurance pension for industrial injury.

Both these disabled patients were under regular medical treatment from their general practitioners. Of the remaining 48 patients, only five were in receipt of any form of medical treatment. The first of these was the severely injured man previously mentioned, whose marked hypochrondriacal-depressive reaction had cleared up rapidly after a substantial financial settlement for his injuries. The second (heavily predisposed) patient, whose psychoneurotically patterned sequelae of minor head injury have no trouble for two years after he had been compensated to the tune of £400, was suffering from a recurrence of anxiety symptoms in relation to the stress of several months' unemployment because of redundancy. In three others psychoneurotic symptoms had persisted since the accident but were not causing occupational disability.

Case 13.—A 26-year-old labourer returned to work six weeks after a brief concussion sustained by striking his head on a beam at work, but although under no form of medical treatment he was so often late or absent that he was dismissed four months later. During the subsequent three months he held two light jobs for short periods. He then gave up work altogether, and 18 months after the accident he made a claim for several thousand pounds in damages, complaining of constant and steadily worsening headaches and dizziness. By the time the case was settled out of court (for £400) he had been idle for more than two years. After settlement he continued constantly to attend his doctor with headache, backache, insomnia, lassitude, etc., and to draw disablement benefit and hardship allowance under the National Insurance Acts. Finally a medical board terminated his pension, after which he promptly returned to work.

My original notes on this patient commented on his evasive manner and deplorable pre-accident work record, though he had insisted to several examiners on his "perfect health before the accident." His general practitioner's records, however, go back to a decade before his injury and reveal him throughout as "a regular attender at the surgery with a variety of complaints of the same kind as those he brought along after the injury . . . he has been the same ever since he left school."

Case 22.—While handling a piece of light furniture a 49-year-old shop assistant stated she "cricked her back." She did not report the injury, but sent for her doctor the next morning. She was confined to the house for 16 weeks, and, although there were at no time any positive clinical or radiological findings, she remained away from work for two years, during which period she attended the physiotherapy department of the local hospital. On examination at the end of this period she claimed total disablement by continual and steadily increasing pain in the back and down the left leg: and by depression, anxiety and sleeplessness which had begun 14 days after the accident. Total superficial sensory loss of stocking distribution up to the groin on the left side was the only abnormal physical finding; her behaviour was histrionic in the extreme. At this stage the case came to trial, and her claim for damages was dismissed on the grounds of lack of evidence that there had been an accident. She subsequently returned to light work, but continued to attend her doctor with multiple symptoms. He reported that "her condition is the same as it has been for 10 years. She was a neurotic before the accident, and I expect she will remain so."

Case 36.—A housewife aged 39 was treated by her doctor for functional nervous symptoms, and was given a prescription for a capsule of "carbrital" to be taken each night and two codeine tablets to be taken three times a day. Unfortunately the labels were placed on the wrong boxes and the patient took two carbrital capsules on the same morning, with the result that she became drowsy. The error was discovered and caused disproportionate alarm. A phar-

Accident neurosis

macist administered stimulants. The patient's general practitioner advised that she be kept awake, and sent her post-haste to hospital, where her stomach was washed out. Within the course of a few days she was in an extremely emotional state, though she had, of course, recovered completely from the "overdosage." Three months later she claimed gross and disabling psychiatric symptoms which she said had been greatly increased by the experience. Both she and her family attributed her condition entirely to the unfortunate accident and appeared to have forgotten her earlier history. The case was settled by a small payment a few months after it happened. Since then the patient has had a good deal of psychiatric treatment, including brief admission to two psychiatric units for electric convulsion therapy. Review of the case-records indicates that recurrent depressive episodes had begun several years before the incident of the tablets in 1956.

In summary, only two of these 50 unselected patients with accident neurosis were still disabled by their psychiatric symptoms on re-examination two years after settlement. Both instances were characterised by diagnostic confusion, substantial lump-sum payments, and continuing National Insurance pensions for the results of the accident. In three other cases psychiatric symptoms persisted without occupational disablement: in each instance similar symptoms had been present for many years before the accident. Symptomatic recovery in the remaining 45 patients was as complete as their subsequent medical and occupational records indicated. The most they could muster were a few trivial residual symptoms of which "a queer feeling as I turn on the vacuum cleaner" and "some nervousness on overtaking in traffic" are fair examples. Of special interest was the disappearance of contractures in three cases of hand injury; two of these patients claimed some local discomfort in cold weather. Occupational phobias (for work at heights, driving heavy vehicles, and underground work) had also cleared up, and all five of these patients had returned to their previous employment.

Of 15 patients predisposed to neurosis, 11 had recovered after settlement; of 35 without predisposition all but one had recovered completely.

Lecture II

The preceding lecture comprised an account of the incidence, clinical features, and natural history of accident neurosis, based on the records of personal cases. The syndrome is seen to present a unique combination of clinical features, amongst the most remarkable of which are an inverse relation to the severity of the provoking injury; an unexpectedly inconstant correlation with neurotic predisposition; scanty objective signs of emotional disturbance; a differential social incidence; and an absolute failure to respond to therapy until the compensation issue was settled, after which nearly all the cases described recovered completely without treatment. These are observed facts, but a con-

116

sideration of the nature of the syndrome raises more difficult matters of interpretation and speculation.

In subjecting this material to critical scrutiny the first question may well be, how far is there such a thing as accident neurosis? Is this anything more than a convenient label of the kind often employed to spare the investigator further thought about a difficult clinical problem —in this instance the behaviour of a heterogeneous minority of people injured or otherwise involved in accidents? It was with considerable scepticism on this score that I began the present study several years ago. The reader must judge how far the evidence already presented supports my conclusion that, after patients suffering from other definable psychiatric disorders have been excluded, the behaviour of a minority of those involved in accidents is sufficiently characteristic and predictable to justify the acceptance of accident neurosis as a clinical entity. The condition probably affects between a quarter and a third of the victims of accidents which fulfil two conditions. First, the accident must be due to someone else's fault, at any rate in the patient's estimation. Secondly, it must have occurred in circumstances where the payment of financial compensation is potentially involved.

Cursory mention is made in the psychiatric literature of cases in which the syndrome is said to have followed accidents which satisfied the first but not the second of these criteria. Depressive illnesses of endogenous pattern may certainly follow accidents innocent of any financial implications, and very occasionally frank neuroses of anxiety type have been similarly encountered after frightening accidents to predisposed patients limited in duration and responsive to therapy. It is possible that the florid syndrome of accident neurosis outlined above, with its disproportionate disability and absolute resistiveness to treatment, occasionally occurs after accidents occurring under emotionally loaded circumstances in which no question of financial compensation is concerned, but such cases have been personally encountered.

Whatever the cause of accidental neurosis, it is not the result of physical injury. It may develop without any injury at all, it is comparatively uncommon where injury has been severe, and it is characteristically a complication of minor or trivial injury. Indeed, the inverse relationship to the severity of injury clearly evident in the material described above is crucial to its understanding, and makes nonsense of some "explanations" of the condition.

It is difficult to believe, for example, that any form of constitutional difference between those severely and those trivially injured can account for the apparently "protective" effect of severe trauma against the development of neurosis in these patients, most of whose injuries are sustained in similar industrial circumstances, equally subject to whatever emotional loading is implicit in the employee–employer

117

Accident neurosis

relationship in such situations. Another interpretation is that the genuinely injured patient, reasonably confident of justice in the matter of compensation does not need a neurosis, while the grazed or frightened workman develops neurotic symptoms which inflate his trivial or non-existent physical disability to dimensions justifying financial compensation.

But why do only a third of those involved in minor accidents succumb to accident neurosis? The only factual evidence is that such a development is favoured by a low social and occupational status, and that its relationship to a history of psychoneurotic predisposition is surprisingly inconstant—a feature which distinguishes it from almost every other disabling neurosis beginning during adult life, and one which must be regarded as highly significant in any consideration of the nature of the syndrome.

The occurrence of accident neurosis in predisposed subjects is anything but surprising, and the role of predisposition in the persistence of disability after settlement has been demonstrated in the figures already given: of the five patients in whom the condition persisted, four were grossly predisposed to neurosis. However, many patients with accident neurosis have carried on their work for many years before the accident without any trace of psychiatric disability and with little loss of time. Indeed, this feature is often quoted in court to support the genuineness of the patient's complaints. Why do a minority of such patients develop this disabling syndrome? An orthodox psychiatic explanation is that the trivial injury or the concatenation of circumstances surrounding it, implies devastating stress for the individual concerned, because of some hidden constitutional vulnerability. Like many such hypotheses, this view is plausible but unsupported by positive evidence. An alternative interpretation is that accident neurosis represents a unique psychiatric disorder or a very special pattern of behaviour.

The different class incidence of accident neurosis suggests that predisposition to its development might perhaps be conceived in social rather than in formal psychiatric terms. Again, however, this social gradient is open to several interpretations. Some observers endow the economic insecurity of patients in the lower-income groups, with a central role in the aetiology of accident neurosis, which they consider in essence a result of anxiety concerning who will accept liability for the care of the patient's dependants during his disablement—a view which also gains some support from the sex incidence of the condition. However, there is a good deal of evidence against it.

Even in social classes IV and V, accident neurosis is not seen after similar injuries sustained where the question of compensation does not arise, though its occurrence under such circumstances might reasonably be expected if the casual anxiety were primary and without motivation. Secondly, it is hardly compatible with the categorical refusal of many of these patients to return to work—a step which would immediately remedy the allegedly causal economic situation—even when their own doctors have repeatedly urged them to do so and when they are palpably fit for employment by any but their own standards. Thirdly, acceptance of liability for the accident at an early stage in negotiation is rarely if ever followed by recovery, though it reduces the outstanding issue to a simple one of "how much?" Finally, a flood of common-law claims continues despite the basic security afforded by the industrial injury provisions of universal National Insurance.

An alternative explanation of the class gradient relates to the question of social responsibility. It encounters the initial difficulty that little reliable information is available about the social attitudes of these patients before their accidents, and it relies chiefly on the suggestion that the attitude of patients with the established syndrome to work and society is so abnormal that it seems more likely to represent an inherent orientation than merely the symptom of an acquired neurosis. It must be admitted that an egocentric denial of social obligations is not unknown in other forms of chronic psychoneurosis.

The relation of accident neurosis to a lack of social responsibility is supported by its infrequency in workers who take pride in an important job, and its predilection for those human cogs in the industrial machine whose employments afford little opportunity for any kind of satisfaction or self-fulfilment.

Clearly recognisable malingering is rare, but the condition is still more rarely diagnosed. Many of those intimately concerned with compensation work—and I refer here to trade union and insurance officials as well as to judges, barristers, and solicitors—are convinced that it is far from uncommon in these cases, and deplore the inability of doctors to recognise the condition or their hesitancy in expressing an opinion in this connexion to which they will freely admit in private conversation. Except in connexion with criminal offences or in the presence of outspoken psychopathy, accident neurosis is the only context in which frank simulation has been personally encountered on more than a few occasions. It was seen in three of the head injury cases described in the first lecture—a "hysterical" gait which disappeared as soon as the patient left the consulting-room; tell-tale nicotine stains on the fingers of a limb allegedly the site of flaccid paralysis; and a puzzling aphasia after a trivial blow on the head, correctly diagnosed only by the private detective who heard the patient's clarion call for "tea and muffins" ring out across a crowded tearoom within half an hour of an inconclusive consultation. Such instances encourage little confidence in one's ability to recognise similarly motivated simulation in the large majority of cases where the symptomatology is entirely subjective.

Whatever the true position in the case of malingering, gross exaggeration of disability is a common feature of accident neurosis.

Whether such exaggeration is conscious or unconscious is a question often debated between lawyers and psychiatrists in court. To many psychiatrists it presents no problems, and they authenticate the complainant's unawareness of motivation with a confidence that seems impressive—until one reflects that differentiation between conscious and unconscious purpose is quite insusceptible to any form of scientific inquiry, and that it depends on nothing more infallible than one man's assessment of what is probably going on in another man's mind. To me the question is unanswerable in general and answerable only by guesswork in the individual patient. Its implication is, of course, that the unconsciousness or subconsciousness of the mental processes involved is a touchstone of "genuineness' and therefore of compensability. But does this uncertain and arbitrary differentiation merit the central place accorded to it in medico-legal thinking ? Whether exaggeration and simulation are "conscious" or "unconscious", their only purpose is to make the observer believe that the disability is greater than it really is. To compensate a man financially because he is stated to be deceiving himself as well as trying to deceive others is strange equity and stranger logic.

NATURE OF ACCIDENT NEUROSIS

It may be because accident neurosis is more commonly dealt with by orthopaedic surgeons and solicitors than by psychiatrists that it has been the subject of so little systematic psychiatric study; for example, only seven of the 50 cases followed up here were ever seen by a psychiatrist. It is in textbook contributions rather than in original papers that formal psychiatric appraisals of the disorder must be sought, and with a few outstanding exceptions such a search reveals little that is enlightening or realistic. The studies of neurologists have been more numerous but equally fragmentary.

Most writers accept the consistent relationship of the syndrome to the compensation issue, the hopelessness of treatment, and its usual tendency to recover after settlement—though in the last connexion many psychiatrists make more of the occasional exceptions. In general, neurologists have approached the problem pragmatically, attributing a central aetiological role to the inescapable factor of compensation, and regarding the syndrome as motivated by a hope of financial gain which few of them are prepared to accept as exclusively unconscious. Most psychiatrists have considered such an interpretation too unsubtle, and the relations between neurosis and compensation as obscure if not actually questionable. Such views lean heavily on the distinction between conscious and unconscious motivation, the difficulties of which have been mentioned.

One such psychiatric interpretation allows a secondary contribution of compensation to the causation of accident neurosis, in that it is supposed to furnish the patient with the leisure and opportunity to "play out" his pre-existing latent emotional conflicts in the form of a nervous illness. This view almost certainly originated under the circumstances of the old Workmen's Compensation Acts, where continuing payments were often made throughout disablement, and it seems less even credible under current conditions, where present financial sacrifice is apparently sustained by nothing more than the hope of ultimate financial redress. Nor is it compatible with the relationship demonstrated between severity of the injury and incidence of neurosis; severer injury would surely afford a more sustained opportunity for the emotional indulgence postulated.

Other psychiatrists stress the aetiological contributions of immature behaviour-patterns, previously suppressed longings for sympathy and attention, or masochistic desires to experience pain and misery. It is difficult to feel that such facile verbalisations do more than describe the patient's symptomatology in terms of the observer's articles of belief. Physicians of the psychoanalytic persuasion, always alive to the emotional significance of money, have accorded it a more important part in the present context, regarding financial compensation as perpetuating disability by the mechanism of "secondary gain." In this way it is allotted a subordinate aetiological role, the primary cause of this as of other neurosis being "avoidance of the Oedipus situation . . . activating one's infantile sado-masochism or one's castration-anxiety, or both" (Fenichel, 1932). Until the victim of accident neurosis struck his head a smart blow on a low beam in the mine he was presumably coping with these knotty problems, at any rate to his own satisfaction.

Some psychiatric conjectures about accident neurosis seem indeed to signify little more than a refusal to concede a connexion between the nervous disorder and the prospect of compensation which is implicit in the facts of the case. Such an attitude may owe something to that addiction to obliquity of thought which is an occupational risk of the psychiatrist's calling, but probably more to a natural reluctance of the mind trained in recognising deeper motives to the acceptance of a psychopathology so superficial and so banal, however cogently sustained by the natural history of the syndrome.

My formulation of the problem, conceived within the framework of the clinical facts outlined above, is necessarily tentative, and begins indeed with a reservation. For what it is worth as a clinical entity, accident neurosis represents what is left of the nervous sequelae of

Accident neurosis

accidents when other organic complications such as intellectual and personality change and occasional frank psychoses—especially though not exclusively depressive—have been excluded. I would also feel bound to exclude a small but important group of outspoken anxiety states, accompanied by appropriate somatic and autonomic signs, which sometimes follow a terrifying experience. Such syndromes usually affect predisposed subjects, and the general flavour of the case as well as the presence of objective signs and the absence of hysterical features bespeaks an acute psychiatric illness of real severity. Like most such illnesses these usually show a prompt response to treatment.

It will be seen that the diagnosis of accident neurosis is not always as easy as may have been suggested above. There is indeed a further complication. In this clinical situation the prognosis of organic deficit, depressive illness, or authentic anxiety state is less predictable than when similar illnesses occur under other conditions such syndromes may be unduly prolonged and elaborated by the mechanisms which are responsible for accident neurosis itself.

If the clinical findings described above are fairly representative of the problem as a whole—and there is no dearth of clinical material available to confirm or refute them—then it seems clear that accident neurosis is not a function of the accident itself, but of the setting in which this occurred. In my opinion it is not a result of the accident but a concomitant of the compensation situation and a manifestation of the hope of financial gain. The condition is not encountered where this hope does not exist or where it has been finally satisfied or dissipated. There is no feature in the natural history of the disorder which is incompatible with this view and there are many which can hardly be accounted for by any other. Nevertheless—and despite the rather stereotyped symptomatology of the syndrome, which can reasonably be described as representing the layman's idea of a "nervous breakdown"—accident neurosis is not an entirely homogeneous syndrome, but presents a spectrum ranging from gross conversion hysteria at one end of the scale to frank malingering at the other.

To accept these cases uncritically as instances of hysteria is to concede a general unconsciousness of motivation which strains my credulity. Indeed, what "evidence" is available on this issue points rather in the opposite direction. If the question of financial compensation is tactfully discussed with the subject of accident neurosis its significance is in most instances freely admitted: quite often, indeed, it is revealed as an all-absorbing obsession. Intriguing variants of this common reaction are represented by the patient who begins the consultation with an unsolicited protestation of his utter disinterest in the compensation issue; and by the occasional claimant who avows entire ignorance of the reason for his examination and expresses surprise at its connexion with a claim for damages which had entirely slipped his memory.

LEGAL ASPECTS

The legal issues, both of principle and of expediency, involved in a consideration of accident neurosis have been summarised by MacMillan (Buzzard *et al.*, 1928) and more extensively presented in a well-documented review from the United States by Smith and Soloman (1943).

The first and crucial legal question is: Can accident neurosis (or traumatic, compensation, or litigation neurosis, which, as Smith and Solomon point out, are all alternative terms used to describe the same familiar clinical syndrome) reasonably be regarded in law as directly resulting from the accident? From the purely judicial point of view there is nothing special about this question. Such issues of causation are of course "the daily business of the judge . . . to discriminate between those things which were and those things which were not, the direct consequence of a wrong or tort" (MacMillan). Judges are, of course, equally familiar with the common tendency of litigants to exaggerate the wrong done to them, to introduce illegitimate items of claim, and to extend the hypothesis of causation beyond what is probable and reasonable.

In deciding such issues, two legal principles are often invoked. First, the question of remoteness. The damages claimed as the direct result of an accident must be in respect of the "natural and probable consequences" of the occurrence—an apparently simple concept, but one often difficult of application. If the sequel claimed is too indirect, too remote in time or in the chain of causality, damages may be disallowed. Secondly, the directness of the relationship between occurrence and sequel may be interrupted by what is known in law as a *novus actus inter veniens*—the intervention of a new cause operating to produce the end-result: for instance, a motorist liable for fracturing the plaintiff's arm will probably not be held legally responsible for permanent disability which subsequently results from negligent surgery; this amounts to a *novus actus*.

Several arguments of principle have been adduced in favour of regarding accident neurosis as a result of the accident to be accepted and compensated at its face value as relevant cause of disablement. First, it is impossible to maintain that the plaintiff would be in his present condition if there had never been an accident, and therefore, however trivial the physical or mental trauma involved may appear to the observer, it must be accepted as having wreaked disproportionate havoc in this special instance. Secondly, since courts of law, at any rate in Great Britain and the United States, have gradually come to accept as axiomatic the current view that mental suffering is every bit as real and distressing as that which results from physical injury, such suffering is surely equally worthy of financial compensation. Thirdly, whatever predisposition or undue vulnerability of the personality to neurosis may be postulated retrospectively, the employer took his employee, or the bus company its passenger, as it found him, and if this particular employee or passenger develops disabling neurosis after a trivial accident the employer or the company cannot at this late stage evade responsibility by pleading psychoneurotic predisposition in mitigation of damages, any more than by pleading the pre-existence of a thin skull in the case of a fracture.

The legal arguments which have been put forward against the eligibility of the condition for financial compensation have centred chiefly round the question of how far the neurosis can be regarded as a "natural and probable consequence" of the accident. Since such a sequel ensues in only a minority of otherwise similar accidents, and since it usually follows minor injury, it is argued that some other causal factor must be operative, probably some form of constitutional vulnerability. The analogy of the "cracked vase" has been used, in which a previously invisible fault begins to leak water after an insignificant impact, and it is suggested that, since the accident can be held only partly responsible for such a sequel, the condition cannot logically or equitably be regarded as compensable in its entirety, and that the defendant should only be held responsible for such disability as a normal person might be expected to suffer as a result of a similar occurrence. Where previous neurotic disability or evidence of significant predisposition can be proved such a view seems often to be tacitly accepted in court; but we have seen that no such evidence is found in more than half the cases under consideration, and the courts show a natural reluctance to accept a "crack in the vase" which is merely inferential.

There is, however, another serious practical difficulty involved in compensating neurosis, which is unrelated to the more theoretical questions of aetiology. In assessing the nature and severity of such a disability the assessor—whether medical or judicial—is almost entirely dependent on the patient's own description of his subjective sufferings, and even in the last resort on his own assessment of their severity. Minimisation of symptoms is by no means unknown after serious injury—for example, to the brain—but it is rare in any form of psychoneurosis, and its presence has certainly never been described as a feature of the condition under discussion. Indeed, in these cases, where the patient is engaged in making out a case for proportionate financial redress, some degree of exaggeration of disability might be regarded as no more than an anticipated human failing. That such a plaintiff is also the main witness regarding the degree of disability is clearly paradoxical;

it precludes any objective basis for judicial assessment, and renders this almost entirely dependent on subjective considerations.

Since these disproportionate results of trivial injury are not seen except where financial compensation is in question, since they are often claimed by subjects in whom there is no evidence of special psychiatric vulnerability, and since there has often been an appreciable latent period between the accident and the onset of nervous symptoms, it is perhaps surprising that the doctrines of remoteness and of the *novus actus interveniens* (in this instance the hope of compensation) have not more often been invoked in trial of such cases.

In general, however, the law favours the plaintiff. Most cases are settled, and no claim is too ludicrous to lack a certain nuisance value in cash. Once in court the judicial assessment sometimes seems to be based on little more than the axiom that but for the accident the man would not have been in his present condition—a statement unexceptionable in itself, but a convenient oversimplification of a complicated relationship. Its acceptance implies that subsequent absence from work must also be regarded as fully attributable to the accident—though to the doctor it may clearly be disinclination rather than incapacity which automatically pushes up the "special damages" by a thousand pounds.

But this is only one of many discrepancies between the approaches of the doctor and of the lawyer in this common field. In the matter of aetiology, for example, the doctor is unwilling to commit himself categorically without objective evidence, and even then his answer can rarely be couched in the "either-or" terms inevitably demanded as the basis of a clear-cut judicial decision: on the other hand, the more realistic concept of multiple causation is difficult to translate into terms of legal settlement. Again, doctor and lawyer are sometimes at cross-purposes over the question of settlement, the lawyer insisting that there should be no settlement without clinical finality, the doctor that there can be no clinical finality without settlement.

PREVENTION

That the situation outlined above is unsatisfactory goes without saying. Despite the millions of words that have been written on the subject, the nature of psychoneurosis remains obscure, but in a general sense there would be wide agreement that hysteria at any rate represents some form of biological protection against stress or danger—an escape from or a protection against reality. Without prejudice to the vexed issue of conscious or unconscious motivation, it must be conceded that to endow such a condition with the added attraction of secondary financial gain is to ask for its persistence for as long as it yields benefit—which in my view is exactly what happens in the syndrome under consideration. That a disability motivated by the hope of financial

125

Accident neurosis

gain is regularly thus rewarded can hardly be considered desirable from any point of view. Nevertheless it is much easier to see what is wrong than how to remedy it.

The function of the trade union official is to pursue what he regards as his member's interest; that of the solicitor to press his client's case, such as it is, to the best of his ability. It would be unrealistic to hope that either will discourage compensation claims for neurosis, all but the most outrageous of which will end in some degree of pecuniary benefit to the party he represents. The conscientious doctor who tries to keep his patient at work despite his minor injury is pitting himself single-handed against powerful social and economic forces all of which press in the opposite direction. It seems certain that effective prevention would demand far-reaching social readjustments rather than purely medical measures.

It is said, for example, that some large business concerns in the United States have successfully employed a system of rehabilitation through work rather than compensation, the injured worker being provided with first-class medical treatment and drawing his pre-accident earnings while he is nursed back through an early return to light duties and gradually to his old job. A somewhat similar approach characterises the management of industrial injuries in Communist countries, and it clearly has much to recommend it. In Britain and elsewhere, however, it encounters the immediate difficulty that the widespread application of the insurance principle absolves the employer from his direct responsibility for the injured workman, and that he is under little obligation to find any interim employment for a man who is now the insurance company's liability. There seems to be little doubt that in certain industries this shifting of responsibility militates similarly against the general adoption of effective but expensive measures for the prevention of accidents.

From a purely medical point of view a strong case can be made out for regarding neurosis as a non-compensable disability. For practical purposes this appears to be the position in France, but, however justifiable such a step might appear from the point of view of social prophylaxis, the chances of its legal acceptance in Great Britain seem slender. Not only would it make compensation crucially dependent on a diagnostic differentiation between psychoneurosis and psychosis—a field in which not even the most expert would claim infallibility; it would also imply the unconditional rejection of a number of claims which would be fairly generally regarded as perfectly genuine.

Mention must be made of the marked improvement in the situation with regard to industrial injury which has followed the supersession of the old Workman's Compensation Acts by the industrial injuries provisions of the National Insurance Act of 1946. Under the new Act, medical assessment has been vested in medical boards (composed of experienced doctors usually also engaged in independent practice) and, on appeal, in medical appeal tribunals (constituted by senior consultant surgeons and physicians sitting under the chairmanship of an experienced lawyer). In difficult cases either body can request examination by an independent specialist. This arrangement has greatly reduced the delay and expense inseparable from the more formal legal proceedings by which such cases used to be dealt with in the county courts, and it appears to be reasonably satisfactory to all parties concerned.

The fact that disablement caused by industrial injury is compensated at a higher rate than that resulting from illness is a relic of the old Act which seems hardly logical under present circumstances, and this is probably the main cause of a large number of pettifogging claims for trivial injuries which are also encouraged by the ease and informality of procedure. Such claims are, however, easily disposed of. The inclusion of psychiatric with physical sequelae of injury in the assessment of disability is specifically allowed for under the Act. However, a procedure in which doctors rather than lawyers play a major part in assessing disability had led to a reduction both in the number and in the monetary value of awards for functional nervous disorders. Indeed, it is my experience that severe diability from accident neurosis is hardly ever encountered in these instances unless there is a concurrent claim at Common Law.

Why can this efficient and economical arrangement not be extended to cover the minority of industrial injury claims which are still sent to the courts to be dealt with under Common Law, because of an allegation of negligence or failure to observe a statutory obligation? The first reason for this is that the medical aspect of such cases is often overshadowed by other features which may involve complex technical and legal problems quite beyond the competence of a medical tribunal. Secondly, damages in Common Law are final and irrevocable lump-sum settlements, which cannot subsequently be revised in relation to the patient's condition, as can pensions paid under the National Insurance Scheme. Such damages must take account of social and domestic factors independent of the purely clinical issue of disability— to say nothing of the financial evaluation of pain and suffering. Finally, while it may be questionable how far the average plaintiff himself would resent being deprived of the full panoply of trial by an assize judge, it is unlikely that the legal profession would willingly relinquish more of its traditional responsibility to yet another administrative body.

The frequently made recommendation that the judge in such cases should sit with a medical assessor to advise him also has obvious attractions, but it is open to similar criticism. Most medical experts would certainly prefer to be called as witnesses by the court, instead

Accident neurosis

of on behalf of the plaintiff or the defendant. On the other hand, few would relish a situation which arbitrarily elevated one of their number to a quasi-judicial capacity. There is no certainty in medicine, and with all its faults the judge's weighing of evidence brought out by cross-examination of two experts, often of somewhat different outlooks, is less likely to leave relevant medical considerations undisclosed and argument unheard than a statement of opinion by a single expert, however authoritative.

There is, however, one measure which I would strongly urge as certain to affect an appreciable reduction in the human and economic wastage inherent in the present situation, and one which would almost certainly be widely acceptable. There can be little doubt that the law's delays are a potent factor in increasing the total sum of disablement caused by accident neurosis, and that a separate trial of the issue of liability within six months of the accident would minimise its effects, at any rate in those cases where liability is not proved. Equally the medical issues involved should be similarly decided once and for all at the end of a rather longer but fixed interval of time. From a medical point of view the patient's interests are certainly better served by an early settlement than by one that is delayed, even though delay may imply some degree of financial advantage.

What the doctor himself can do is limited. It is clearly incumbent on him to encourage a robust attitude to minor injury. Although accident neurosis is a motivated illness, its occurrence is far from invariable even where the motivational background is consistent, and there can be no doubt that the "tough" person is less likely to claim. This may be in part because he does not develop the minor neurotic nucleus around which the predisposed subject builds his edifice of disability, but we have seen that predisposition is far from invariable, and the influence of social attitudes is almost certainly more potent.

There are many middle-class patients who sustain real physical injuries under conditions which would thoroughly justify claims for compensation, but who flatly refuse to claim. They may press most vigorously for restitution of damage to their cars, and may indeed exhibit a remarkable lack of scruple in describing the condition of the vehicle before the accident—but they feel that to make a fuss of minor personal disability or to attempt to turn it to financial advantage represents a socially unacceptable standard of behaviour.

It has been argued that the "toughness" of the injured steeplechaser, in contrast to the "tenderness" (in the Jamesian sense) of the injured workman, is innate. This deterministic view can hardly be wholly applicable in a fluid society. Genetic or early influences no doubt play a part in determining such patterns of behaviour, but these are pre-dominantly cultural, and vastly affected by environment and example, as, for instance, of school or regiment. I have been struck by a group of patients, not predisposed to neurosis, who had survived the hazards of operational war service psychiatrically unscathed, but who broke down with gross hysterical disability after minor injuries sustained under industrial conditions where serious risk was remote. Why had these patients not succumbed with a hysterical reaction to the infinitely more stressful circumstances of aircrew, tank, or submarine service? Age and the acquisition of family responsibilities may have played a part, but it is also true that while such breakdown under Service conditions would have achieved its primary purpose of ensuring the withdrawal of its victim from danger, it was socially unacceptable, and implied rejection from the group of which he was a member. Incidentally it would also have involved financial sacrifice rather than the possibility of financial gain. Neither disadvantage obtains under current industrial conditions.

CONCLUSIONS

Like its causation, the prevention of accident neurosis can be realistically conceived only in social terms. Consideration of its epidemiology and clinical features allows little doubt that the condition could be prevented, and its prevention would certainly make a significant contribution to the national economy. But the minor measures discussed above would hardly do more than scratch the surface of a problem which is more properly the concern of politics than of medicine. A Milroy lecturer need make no apology—and may perhaps even be excused the customary invocation of Virchow—if he seeks in conclusion to outline his own tentative view of the aetiological background of the syndrome in political terms.

To say that our society is in a state of transition is to utter a platitude. All societies have always been in states of transition. That the conflicts between different concepts of social organisation seem especially acute in our own day may be due to nothing more than the fact that they are close at hand. In any case, however, they constitute powerful determinants of human behaviour, and in my view their operation is clearly evident in the clinical situation under discussion.

In practically every civilised country the past half-century has witnessed the socialisation of considerable sections of economic and public activity. The process has been uneven. In some countries this development has occurred explosively and more or less completely in others piecemeal. Among countries not formally committed to Socialism, Britain lies to the left of centre in a spectrum which has the United States at one end and some of the Scandinavian countries at the other. In Britain large sections of public activity are fully socialised. Side by side with such developments, however, the institutions and many of the attitudes of capitalism persist—to say nothing of those archaic but virile remnants of feudalism which intrigue many foreign visitors to our country.

Our present fluid social compromise of welfare capitalism includes a comprehensive scheme of insurance which afford the sick or injured workman and his family a degree of financial security comparable with that which obtains in most Socialist countries. What our society has signally failed to provide are the industrial discipline which is inherent in Socialism, or the industrial morale to which it aspires. The average industrial worker—and here I literally mean the average worker and not a member of the politically sophisticated minority—either turns a deaf ear to the perennial pleas of politicians and leader writers for "a sense of partnership in industry," or for "co-operation in management," or regards them with frank and sometimes even ribald cynicism. Unconvinced that a wider distribution of consumer goods has changed the basic structure of society, he continues to nourish a strong awareness of the antithesis between "us" and "them," between worker and employer (with whom salaried management above a certain level is tacitly equated). It is fashionable to deprecate the role of such class antagonisms in contemporary society, but a glance at the recent history of labour relations in several of our more prosperous industries lends little support to such complacency.

This, then, is the social setting in which accident neurosis flourishes. The exploitation of his injury represents one of the few weapons available to the unskilled worker to acquire a larger share—or indeed a share of any kind—in the national capital. Its possible yield may not bear comparison with the weekly recurring fantasy of a win in the pools, but it is more clearly within his grasp, and it may yet endow him with a capital sum such as he could never have saved during a lifetime of unremitting labour. The employer or his representative, the insurance company, is fair game. To question the moral issues of the situation would seem hardly more relevant to the claimant than to argue the ethics of unearned income, capital appreciation, or the take-over bid—phenomena which manifest the operation of similar motives at other levels of what he accepts without question as a ruthlessly acquisitive society.

How far has the socialisation of large sectors of our economy influenced this situation and these attitudes? It can be said with some confidence, for example, that nationalisation of the industry had radically affected the orientation of the coal-miner to his employing organisation. The hatred of the miner for the coal-owner had its roots deep in history, and was felt with a passion unknown in other fields of industry. The miner of today grumbles with his fellows about bureaucracy, but he will defend the Coal Board vehemently against outside criticism. I think it would be an exaggeration to claim that he feels a close sense of identification with it. The chain of command is still too indirect for such identification to permeate the lowest levels of the industry. Nevertheless, the miner of today feels that in general the Board's interests are his own and that in the last resort their collaboration is vital to the survival of the industry and of the curiously individual pattern of society which it sustains.

The conception of accident neurosis outlined in these lectures would be strengthened if it were possible to claim that the incidence of the condition had been reduced by this change of ownership and attitude in the coal industry. No figures are available in this connexion, but the attitudes of the injured miner in the matter of claims for compensation do not appear to differ in any obvious way from those of workers employed by the larger private firms. Like other nationalised industries the Coal Board runs its own insurance scheme, generously administered and continuing a long tradition of settling nearly ever case round the conference table, It is my impression that this scheme works better than where the responsibility has been handed over to an insurance company. Within the limitations of the industry, management makes great efforts to furnish light employment as soon as practicable, medical referees are often asked to adjudicate on conflicting medical reports, and the inevitable delays of litigation are avoided. But the successful operation of the scheme owes more to the responsibility of the men's representatives than to that of the claimants themselves. The best of these are men of the highest calibre and integrity who have spent a lifetime in the industry and who have too great a sense of social responsibility to have any patience with dishonesty or exaggeration.

If such information were available a third lecture could be written on the epidemiology of accident neurosis and its differential incidence in countries with different forms of political, judicial, and administrative organisation. Personal experience suggests, for example, that it is probably a less conspicuous and ubiquitous problem in Eastern than in Western Europe. But he would be a bold man who ascribed any such apparent reduction in incidence to a change in ethos, rather than to the deliberate formulation of administrative policies which have rendered the disorder unprofitable and therefore without purpose.

I thank the patients, solicitors, and insurance companies who so generously gave of their time and trouble to ensure the completion of the clinical data; and my friends of the Bench and the Bar who have—I hope—purged my contribution of legal solecisms.

BIBLIOGRAPHY

Bleuler, E (1924). *Textbook of Psychiatry*. Macmillan, New York.
Brain, W R (1942). *Proc. roy. Soc. Med.*, **35**, 302.

Accident neurosis

Buzzard, Sir Farquhar, MacMillan, H P, Purves-Stewart, J, Sharpe, S, Brend, W A, Russell, R, and Wilcox, W (1928). **21,** 353.
Collie, Sir John (1932). *Fraud in Medico-Legal Practice*, Arnold, London.
Denker, P G (1939). *NY St J Med*, **39,** 238.
Eichhorn, O, and Moschik de Reya, N (1951), *Mschr. Psychiat. Neurol*, **121,** 51.
Fenichel, O (1932). *Psychoanal Quart*, **1,** 157, 572.
Freud, S (1922). *Introductory Lectures on Psycho-analysis*. Allen and Unwin, London.
Neuhaus, G (1934). *Neb St med J*, **19,** 248.
Oppenheim, H (1889). *Die Traumatischen Neurosen*. Hirschwald, Berlin.
Pokorny, A D, and More, F J (1953). *Arch industr Hyg*, **8,** 547.
Ross, T A, (1936). *An Enquiry into the Prognosis in the Neurosis*. Cambridge University Press, London.
Russell, W R (1934). *Trans med-chir Soc Edinb.*, **48,** 129.
Smith, H W, and Solomon, H C (1943). *Virginia Law Rev*, **30,** 87.
Walshe, Sir Francis (1958). *Med Press*, **239,** 493.

Fifty years after Flexner

HENRY MILLER MD Durh, FRCP

Professor of Neurology and Dean of Medicine, University of Newcastle
upon Tyne

It is an inherent peculiarity of the Englishman that he loves to brood
over his institutions, and to examine and criticise the bodies they serve
is a favourite pursuit of many concerned with the teaching of medicine
in hospitals and universities. Often such examination and analysis is
obsessively preoccupied with the individual predicament of the critic.
However, it is useful occasionally to take a fresh look at a situation
which we who are busily occupied in its day-to-day activities are often
inclined to regard as immutable. In fact, of course, the present situation
represents nothing more than a stage in an untidy historical process to
which each generation must make its contribution, and effective change
depends on continuing examination and criticism.

The present evolution of British medical education is in essence
based on the views propounded half a century ago by Abraham Flexner,
and it is interesting to examine the current balance-sheet of profit and
loss which has followed the almost unquestioning academic acceptance
—and tardy implementation—of the recommendations which he made
between 1910 and 1912. Recent public controversy concerning medical
education, apart from present discussions as to its total quantity, is
devoted to questions of detail. It is concerned with reorganisation of the
curriculum (an occupational disease of deans), the allotment of time
between its various parts, the relation between its traditionally preclinical and clinical phases, and the place of the specialties in the educational pattern. The system can only be understood in its historical
context, and here the publications of Flexner are a vital source of
first-hand material. What in fact did he recommend? How did he
envisage the future of medicine? How far have his hopes been realised?
How far have they been disappointed in the event? Our present pattern
of medical education is only one of several that are operating more or
less successfully at the present time: good medicine can be taught and
practised under widely varied conditions—within the framework of
almost unrestricted private practice that still obtains in some European
countries, and also under the auspices of those monolithic Governmental agencies, dissociated from the universities, that are responsible
for medical education and research in many parts of Eastern Europe.

133

Fifty years after Flexner

Abraham Flexner was born in Kentucky in 1867, the sixth of nine children of a Jewish immigrant from Bohemia. His brother Simon, the bacteriologist, subsequently became director of the Rockefeller Institute. Abraham graduated in arts at Johns Hopkins and became a schoolmaster. Within a few years his dissatisfaction with orthodox educational methods led to the establishment of his own school at Louisville, and he soon acquired a national reputation as a successful liberal educationalist of energy and originality.

After more than a decade of schoolmastering his first essay into larger fields came with his unheralded appointment by the Carnegie Foundation to investigate medical education in the United States and Canada. He travelled widely and observed percipiently. Although his visits to each school lasted no more than a day or two, he had little difficulty in confirming suspicions, already widely held, that the general position was profoundly unsatisfactory. In many instances it was frankly scandalous, the medical schools being nothing more than highly profitable commercial enterprises in the hands of cliques of local practitioners, innocent of laboratory accommodation or equipment and often only tenuously connected with a hospital. Published in 1910 as the famous *Bulletin Number Four* of the Foundation, his survey had an immediate and dramatic effect on medical education in North America. Institutions and individuals were indicted frankly and by name. It is a remarkable tribute to the adaptability of American institutions that within a year or two many medical schools close their doors for ever, and that others were radically reorganised on lines greatly influenced by the enlightened example of the Johns Hopkins University recently established in Baltimore. The American vocabulary does not admit the category of the impossible, and our American colleagues are always stimulated by obstacles which we in Britain are only too ready to accept as mercifully absolving us from further effort.

In 1912 Flexner was commissioned to make a similar but more selective survey of medical education in Europe. This was intended less as a critical essay or an encouragement to reform than as an attempt to seek out what was good in European training that could be applied in America. He found much to criticise in Europe; and, while his observations were apparently ignored elsewhere, they made an immediate impact on British medicine, and continue to exercise a potent influence in determining our unevenly evolving pattern of medical education. He was enormously impressed by the character and efficiency of the German university medical schools, which at that time led the world in scientific medicine. He admired the bedside teaching and the free access to hospital patients of the English system of medical education, but disliked its amateurism. Teaching in England was a secondary occupation of doctors chiefly concerned with extra-mural practice: he favoured the antithesis. Of organised clinical research there was practically none. The basic sciences were completely dissociated from clinical practice; their teachers lacked prestige and were inadequately remunerated. The continued existence of hospital schools without preclinical and scientific institutes he regarded as already an anachronism, and it is a sobering thought that this outdated pattern is still with us. University College was the one hopeful English medical school, and even here teaching and research occupied little of the time of a staff busily engaged elsewhere. No doubt because of its similarity to the Continental pattern with its formalised pedagogy, he had an *a priori* prejudice in favour of Edinburgh, but after inspection he regarded these virtues as dissipated by rigid traditionalism. Inbreeding he found everywhere. Although the universities were formally responsible for medical education, they had little control over the appointment of their clinical teachers but were saddled with instructors chosen by hospital staffs. Flexner regarded teaching and research

Fifty years after Flexner

as the equally important functions of the university and was convinced that the time had come for medicine to take its place *as a science* among the other scientific disciplines. This implied the creation of university hospitals under the direct control of the faculty, staffed by men whose prime concern was teaching and research. He denied responsibility for the full-time principle, which he attributed to Ludwig and Mall, but it was implicit in his view. Furthermore the academic clinical unit was not to be an extra grafted on to the existing hospital pattern, but was to take over the institution as a whole. In later years he was critical of the British compromise whereby the hospital, often with palpable reluctance, developed academic units as excrescences on its existing structure.

Flexner's views were naturally castigated by members of an intensely conservative profession, always sensitive to criticism, whose prestige and pocket were threatened. Eminent physicians were not lacking to point out that Flexner was neither a physician not a surgeon, that he had no scientific training or qualifications, and that besides being a schoolmaster he laboured under the additional handicap of being an American. However, among those primarily concerned with education his observations received serious consideration. He found a receptive listener in Haldane, already commissioned to undertake an official study of professional education in England. To him Flexner's insistence on professionalism in teaching, on the importance of research, and on the virtues of the German university system was especially welcome. But the outbreak of the 1914–18 war brought early developments in the direction envisaged in Flexner's report to an end, and it was not until 1918 that his ideas began to bear fruit.

His autobiography (*I Remember*, published in 1940) reveals a man highly intelligent, immensely industrious, with a strong sense of dedication, perhaps rather humourless. His ideas show a remarkable consistency. Fascinated by the problems of administration, he was a subtle and skilful negotiator. He retained a sense of wonder that an obscure second-generation American could find opportunity to do so much, and a simple delight in the distinguished company amongst which his great talents led him.

How far major historical developments spring from the qualities of particular individuals and how far from general movements of thought is a perennial subject of speculation, but it is difficult to escape the conclusion that the development of academic medicine in Britain during the past half-century has owed much to the facts that Flexner was by culture a German and by profession a schoolmaster.

THE PRESENT

The slow and half-hearted application of Flexner's ideas to the institutions of British medicine was as typical of our society as was their almost immediate implementation in the United States. The years since the 1939–45 war have seen a sharp acceleration of the process here, and although one or two Metropolitan outposts have been slow to fall there is now no clinical school which has not made a gesture in the direction of full-time academic units in the major subjects of the medical curriculum. The rate of this development has varied. The process is most advanced in the provincial schools, which are more closely integrated with their universities than are those in the capital. Three stages can be distinguished: first, the reluctant acceptance by the hospital and its staff of the academic super-structure; second, a period of growing influence of the academic *cadre* within the hospital organisation; and, third, an increasing though tacit measure of control in the staffing and organisation of the institution by university representatives which bids fair to implement Flexner's idea of the university hospital. In some centres this position has almost been reached. In a few, and especially in London, there remains a sense of strain and sometimes open conflict between hospital and university, but in others the fusion of academic interests and staff is virtually complete. The historical process is evident for all to see; and, difficult though this may be for some of our Metropolitan colleagues to appreciate, the battle is over except for "scattered mopping-up operations".

The kind of man who occupies the full-time clinical chair has changed with the years. Among the first were a number of idealistic and academically minded individuals who cheerfully accepted the derisory salaries then offered in exchange for liberation from what they regarded as the thrall of private practice and for the freedom to pursue their special professional interests. In a few instances a newly established chair was occupied by a junior clinician chiefly distinguished by his failure to establish himself in the rough-and-tumble of consultant practice. This no longer happens. The academic departments have attracted most of the outstanding graduates of the post-war years, and their steady growth has led to an embarrassing choice of candidates for the occasional clinical professorship that becomes vacant. This is certainly the position in medicine, where the rewards of private practice have always been less seductive than in some other fields, and where an increasing number of men unlikely to reach professorial status decline to take advantage of permissive indulgence to undertake private practice and prefer to devote time unoccupied in routine clinical duties to research projects. At present there are more appropriate applicants than available senior posts. The establishment of the system has produced the men, and it has been justified more by second than by initial appointments.

The gains yielded by this development are obvious. The budgets of most of our clinical departments are ridiculously small by American standards, but the men appointed are free to spend some time in medical research. Indeed, considering their small numbers, the members of the full-time units already make a disproportionate contribution to our medical literature. The system has also established teaching as a central and not merely a peripheral interest of a considerable part of the hospital staff. There is in fact some danger that preoccupation with the machinery and logistics of medical education may come to be regarded as a substitute for its application.

Those too young to recall the time when the senior physician and surgeon of the hospital fulfilled the responsibilities and often carried the titles of professors of medicine and surgery need look no further than the special departments of their teaching hospitals to appreciate the benefits of genuine academic affiliation and support. The development of academic departments in ophthalmology, orthopaedics, otology, neurology, and radiology has hardly begun, and in this we are already far behind the more advanced countries of Western Europe as well as the United States. Even in the best of our teaching hospitals under-graduate and postgraduate education in these important specialties is in the hands of clinicians grossly overloaded with routine clinical commitments, distracted by outside practice, working in departments that are usually without any staff contribution from the university and without laboratory facilities.

In neurology there is only one real full-time academic unit, recently established, in chronic financial difficulties, and largely dependent on short-term support scraped up from a variety of sources. The generation of neurologists recently retired from hospital practice included a number of physicians of international stature, well able to stand comparison with their great predecessors of the nineteenth century. To this small band of men we owe the present reputation of British clinical neurology. In the intervals of exacting hospital work, under-graduate and postgraduate teaching, and busy private practice, they made major contributions to the study of the nervous system and nervous diseases. To these outstanding individuals the *milieu* in which they worked was a stimulating one, and it is improbable that any would willingly have abandoned it to become full-time academic physicians. Nevertheless, their conditions of work imposed limitations on the contributions they were able to make. Most were in the form of occasional papers or reports of small series of cases, or speculative or reflective essays, rather than the long-term organised studies of disease that are essential if the scattered knowledge of the subject is to be systematised. What is especially significant is that today these men are convinced without exception that the establishment in the medical schools of academic units in clinical neurology, closely integrated with internal medicine and with the laboratory departments, is an urgent need unless this branch of medicine is to be left behind by current developments in more farsighted and realistic countries: the potent contemporary resurgence of Parisian neurology at the Salpêtière is only one straw in the wind. I choose this field of medicine because I know it intimately, but the problem affects every specialty, and the country's leaders in ophthalmic and orthopaedic surgery find themselves in situa-tions which are if anything even more unsatisfactory and frustrating.

THE INADEQUATE IMPLEMENTATION OF FLEXNER'S RECOMMENDATIONS

It has been said of Christianity that we do not know whether it works or not, because it has never been tried. In the same way most of the disappointments of Flexnerisation in Britain spring from the simple fact that money has never been made available to implement it. The universities have never been given the resources to establish the academic clinical units which Flexner envisaged as setting standards both in patient-care and in investigative medicine. This failure remains evident in the hospital environment, in the provision of personnel, and in the support of research. Given adequate finance, most of our problems could be solved. Without it we are beating the air.

THE HOSPITALS

It would be hard to find a more telling example of public squalor in an affluent society than the appalling physical conditions under which distinguished physicians and surgeons are expected to teach and practise twentieth-century medicine in some of London's most famous hospitals. It bespeaks an extraordinary sense of priorities that such conditions are tolerated in a city dwarfed by an orgy of commercial building, and in a country where interminable homilies on impending national insolvency go hand in hand with the maintenance of expensive military establishments from Berlin to Borneo. It is paradoxical that the two decades that have witnessed the greatest scientific advance in the history of medicine have also seen a decline in British hospital building unparalleled during the preceding century. Meanwhile our spirits have been sustained on a diet of grandiose plans for hospital reconstruction—which those responsible for them now blandly declare to have been quite unrealistic. The present Government was elected to the accompaniment of brave sounds about the modernisation of Britain and the social application of science, and undoubtedly began its work with considerable reserves of professional and academic goodwill. So far, however, it appears to be actually slowing the tempo of university development, and in the matter of hospital rebuilding its very tentative proposals for the future would not meet even the urgent needs of the present. We have only a handful of centres for modern cardiac surgery, organ transplantation, and the treatment of renal disease: we are lagging in these investigative fields. Nor can we offer our patients the benefits that have already accrued from the United States' vast investment in clinical research in these rapidly developing areas of medicine.

It would be naïve to express surprise at the equanimity with which successive Governments have regarded the deteriorating hospital service, since it is in the nature of governments to ignore inconvenient situations until they become scandalous enough to excite powerful public pressure. Nor, perhaps, should one expect patients to be more demanding: their uncomplaining stoicism springs from ignorance and fear rather than from fortitude; they are mostly grateful for what they receive and do not know how far it falls short of what is possible. It is less easy to forgive ourselves. The cynical disillusion freely expressed at the hospital or university luncheon table is rarely followed up by political pressure, and it has been left to figures on the fringe of medicine to inform and agitate public opinion about the appalling implications of present neglect. Perhaps it is too much to expect presidents of Royal Colleges to stump the country addressing public meetings on the impossibility of operating twentieth-century medicine with nineteenth-century plant. Indeed election as president of a college, a vice-chancellor, or a member of the University Grants Committee usually spells an inevitable preoccupation with the politically practicable, and insidious identification with central authority, and a change of role from informed critic to uncomfortable apologist. However, discretion is not always the better part of valour, and too dedicated a sense of responsibility in making an inferior and out-of-date machine work in some sort of way may actually impede radical improvement. We have accepted our present conditions as inescapable for so long that it is a shock to visit countries that do *not* expect their hospitals to last for a century or more, and which not only recognise that new techniques demand new buildings but have actually taken action accordingly. The rapidly and efficient organisation of the Emergency Medical Service hospitals in 1939 shows what can be done when the will is there: fifteen years of obsessive planning and replanning at a cost of thousands of frustrating man-hours is *not* an inescapable prelude to not even starting to extend a hospital.

STAFFING

The position vis-à-vis personnel is not much more satisfactory. Indeed the complacency of the Ministry of Health in relation to the continuing dependence of its hospitals on a precarious flow of junior medical officers from India and Pakistan is an astonishing feature of British post-war medicine. Badly needed in their own countries, these young doctors come here ostensibly for training, but are often employed as pairs of hands in hospitals ill-equipped and inappropriately staffed for postgraduate education. This is hardly surprising when we consider that many of our own younger graduates holding what are optimistically designated as training posts are still so fully occupied in the hard grind of clinical routine that they have difficulty in obtaining release even for the part-time postgraduate courses that are a hopeful development of the past few years. The term "registrar", borrowed from the teaching hospitals, has always been quite inappropriate to describe peripheral appointments of this kind. The almost fortuitous development of large-scale medical immigration has had two further effects—it has softened the impact of massive medical emigration, and it has also enabled us continually to postpone the creation of a realistic staffing structure in the peripheral hospitals. No great grasp of statistics is needed to demonstrate that most of the necessarily large number of junior doctors in these institutions have little hope of finally achieving the independent charge of patients that goes with consultant status, and they have so far had little opportunity of a satisfying career at a more modest level.

Conditions in the hospitals of the United States are notoriously uneven, but in the good and the best the training of the next generation of consultants and specialists is approached very much more seriously and more professionally than in Britain. There are now, for example, more postgraduate than undergraduate medical students in the United States, and the posts their trainees hold over a planned period of several years are training-posts first and foremost with a secondary service contribution. Indeed its comprehensive and widely-publicised programme for specialists in training represents one of the major activities and attractions of every important American medical centre. Our system of miscellaneous and often virtually unplanned succession of junior appointments has some advantages. It is in keeping with our national character, its competitive and democratic nature does not easily lend itself to nepotism, and it avoids excessive standardisation of the final product. However, to combine it with a disproportionate veneration for the wholesale ingestion and regurgitation of factual information that passes for higher knowledge and advanced training in medicine and surgery is less admirable: our American colleagues pay more attention to the training and less to the results of examinations which can dog the British aspirant to a career in hospital medicine into middle life. It is evidently possible for a country to lead the world in medicine without a galaxy of Royal Colleges and a plethora of post-graduate diplomas, and it is significant that enthusiasm for this latter system shines most brightly in the less developed countries of Asia.

Since the teaching hospitals remain within the Health Service and are certain to become still more closely integrated with the regions in the near future, and since there is a good deal of coming and going between academic and regional units, these general considerations have their repercussions on academic staffing. This is necessarily at a rather more generous level than in the regions, but where it is realistically scaled to its purpose it invariably depends on the energies of the head of department in obtaining extra funds. In the best professorial units more than half the staff are paid from outside sources. In all departments financial considerations dictate a crippling inflexibility of establishment: it is exceptional for any British professor to be able to create a new established appointment for an outstanding man in the way that is customary in the United States. The knowledge that his parent department is run on a shoestring is one of the most powerful stimuli to the emigration of the energetic and ambitious young medical scientist. Until a few years ago, for example, the annual departmental grant to the department of medicine of one British university was £100, and such grants are still entirely unrealistic in relation to the financing of the research programmes that are supposed to be an integral function of any active university department. If it were not that in my own hospital an enlightened board of governors subsidises research to the tune of £25 000 a year from its endowment fund, the academic clinical staff might as well spend its afternoons playing golf. But not all hospitals have enlightened boards of governors or endowment funds, and in any case these funds will not last for ever.

RESEARCH

Effective prosecution of the research activities which Flexner regarded as an integral part of the academic unit presents difficulties just as real, if not so publicly conspicuous, as those entailed by obsolete accommodation and equipment. In this connection the line has been held only by a progressive increase in Governmental support of the Medical Research Council. This, is however, a holding measure only, and contributes little to solving the long-term problem that the budgets of university departments remain entirely unrealistic for the functions they are expected to perform. Within the limits of its budget—which amounts to about a penny a week for each man, woman, and child in Britain, or about a twentieth of what it costs each of us to maintain a military presence East of Suez—the MRC does such a splendid job that one can almost forgive the anodyne statements of its parliamentary apologists that all is for the best in the best of all possible worlds and that money is available for all worth-while projects. Since what is considered worth while in this context depends on what money is available, the tautology defies contradiction.

If the Council likes a project it will probably be financed on a three-year to five-year basis. This may be all it deserves, but from the beginning it renders the temporary engagement of professional and especially technical staff very difficult. It at the outset or on the expiry of a temporary grant of this kind the applicant envisages anything on a longer-term basis he is likely to be referred back to his university where his request—probably a large one if it is realistic—is in competition with every other university activity for a slice of cake that is always too small. What happens? Some applicants throw up the sponge or are too discouraged by the prevailing financial climate even to begin. Many hesitate to ask the university for financial support which they know can be given only by depriving their colleagues, both medical and non-medical, of more modest requirements. The most determined seek financial support from other than public funds. Even where such

Fifty years after Flexner

funds are obtainable they often remain unclaimed; progress may be critically delayed because of a legalistic insistence that the lease of Crown land for the erection of elaborate and expensive research laboratories should be restricted to a term of 20 years—or even because of a reluctance to accept responsibility for the cleaning of premises provided and equipped for the public benefit, on public land, and at no public expense. At a time of little confidence in future Governmental intentions the universities also fear and sometimes have to decline gifts that carry with them even possible obligations for the future. Nor is growing irritation on the part of private Foundations unexpected when they are continually solicited for the erection of buildings which should clearly be the responsibility of any adequately financed university or hospital authority.

Considering its ultimate dependence on medical education and research, the Health Service has signally failed to make the contribution in this connection that might reasonably have been expected. It has not developed research activities on its own account—not even the operational research necessary for its own efficient organisation—nor has it furnished the physical facilities within which medical research can be prosecuted in its hospitals. Hospital budgets and grants for capital expenditure are such that even today research is unbelievably regarded as something of a luxury. Meanwhile the Medical Research Council, no doubt driven to desperation by the continuing inability of universities and teaching hospitals to afford adequate facilities for the dispersed research which is an essential part of a vital educational system, is about to establish a central hospital for clinical research—a development that is certain to bleed still further the universities' slender contingent of clinical researchers.

Whatever may be the case with other classes of medical emigrant, the cause of the one-way flow of medical scientists across the Atlantic is related less to income than to facilities. The real income of the medical academic in the United States is not vastly different from that of his British counterpart. The expensively trained emigrant of this kind represents a valuable national investment. He goes to the United States usually reluctantly, and not only because his present facilities are inadequate, but because the bitter experience of the past decade has gone far to convince him that adequate facilities are unlikely to be made available within his working life. He goes to the United States to escape the tedium of duplicating applications for essential equipment, and even for physical accommodation, to a succession of charitable Foundations, and with the well-founded conviction that if his new university cannot itself give him the tools to do the job these will be forthcoming from one or other agency of the US Public Health Service—an organisation which, unlike its British counterpart, has always accepted the prosecution of research as a built-in part of its function. Like many of my colleagues I no longer try to dissuade my juniors from leaving to work in the United States. Medicine is more important than nationalism and will outlive the indifference of Governments: it is better that a good man should work where he can make the best contribution to the advance of medicine than that he should stay to be frustrated by a society too myopic to appreciate his potential.

NATIONAL PARSIMONY

In brief, then, the failures of Flexner's concepts as they have been applied in Britain spring mainly from a national parsimony, evident in affluent as well as difficult times, and from a complacent acceptance of the amateurish and second-best. It is tempting but not entirely fair to attribute all our present difficulties to the succession of politicians nominally responsible for Health and Education during the past two critical decades. It is easy to forget that we owe the initiation of the Health Service to a politician of genius—and that the medical profession's contribution at that stage presented a classical combination of the obstructive and the ineffective: it is ironical that today the profession champions the Service against the politicians' neglect. It is unthinkable, however, that Aneurin Bevan's political heirs will bring themselves to supervise the dismemberment of their party's greatest achievement. Nor is it possible to believe that the melancholy procession of mostly unmemorable incumbents who passed through the Ministry of Health during 13 years of Conservative Government were all as ineffectual as the present state of the service might suggest. It is now clear that the advisers on whom they had to rely were inaccurate in their estimates of the inevitably rising cost of an increasingly technological service and of the number of doctors required to man it—as well as in the ingenuous misconception that it would reduce the incidence of illness. The pattern of sickness in a community depends on complex factors, and it is of course materially altered by the quantity and quality of medical care available. But neither the gradual improvement in the public health that is clearly discernible nor the more dramatic conquest of specific diseases can be expected to reduce the load on medical services. A dead patient presents no economic problem, but one rescued by modern treatment remains susceptible to other illnesses that bring with them fresh demands on our resources.

Despite the seriousness of the present situation I am sustained by a conviction that the financial problems of medicine in our society will be overcome. Except for an eccentric fringe, the profession and the public are committed to the splendid conception of a comprehensive public medical service and are more inclined to meet its cost than in the case of many more dubious Governmental actvities. The misconception

143

that private practice can make any serious contribution to the provision of modern medical care is too pathetic to merit serious discussion: it may furnish consolation to the sufferer from a minor ailment but has little to offer in renal failure or ventricular fibrillation. When the public becomes fully aware of the disparity between the medical service that is available and that which is possible, some Government will find the money, even if by some form of personal taxation specifically earmarked for the purpose. When we say we cannot afford properly equipped universities or a truly comprehensive Health Service, all we are really saying is that we prefer to spend our money in other ways.

Meanwhile our tardiness has given us one advantage. We can observe the impact of the Flexner pattern on American medicine over half a century, and assess its limitations as well as its great contribution to the advance of medicine and medical education. These problems will remain to be faced even when the situation is no longer bedevilled by inadequate finance.

INHERENT DEFECTS IN THE FLEXNER CONCEPT

The florid overgrowth of so-called "dynamic" psychiatry is one price America has had to pay for Flexner's sadly premature categorisation of medicine among the "hard" sciences. Today even Central Europe has largely outgrown the psychological determinism of the 1890s, and it is in the United States alone that psychoanalysis dominates clinical psychiatry and unbelievably aspires to the status of a science. However, this need not surprise us: after 50 years of passionate concentration on laboratory medicine, the psychiatrist is often the only person who can spare the time to take the patient's history.

Fifty years ago Flexner's optimism that medicine was about to take its place beside the basic objective sciences of chemistry and physics was understandable, and indeed we owe the triumphs of the current scientific revolution in medicine almost entirely to the laboratory. But, as we travel the road, the goal of parity with the basic sciences seems to recede. The platitude that medicine is an art as well as a science is enough to raise the hackles of any self-respecting materialist, but it is the sober truth. The fact is that medicine consists of a few well-lit islands of scientific certitude, surrounded by a boundless ocean of shadowy uncertainty and ignorance. Flexner's ideal clinical professor would withhold action where data were inadequate or their meaning dubious, or the variables too numerous to be manageable. Not for him a diagnosis based on intelligent guess-work, on the tentative interpretation of fragmentary information, or on the evaluation of conversational nuances or states of mind; still less acceptable an improvised therapy consisting of little more than persuasion sustained only by the physician's authority and personality. Needless to say, if such an ideally scientific physician were ever to exist he would rapidly and deservedly lose his patient to the nearest quack.

It is a very limited concept of medicine that strives to understand disease but not the needs of sick people, and its limitations are evident not only to patients but to the many aspirants to a medical career who are activated by a genuine concern for man. No-one can doubt the need for the intensive study of clinical phenomena, or that some medical scientists should spend the whole or the major part of their time in studies of this kind. It is, however, open to serious question whether prowess in this field, sometimes apparently quite irrespective of clinical or teaching skills, should determine a professional appointment the essential function of which is the education of the next generation of doctors.

THE FULL-TIME PRINCIPLE

The separation of academic medical scientist from working clinician is of course far from absolute. There are physicians and surgeons who fill both roles with distinction; the quality of the younger men and the postgraduate opportunities now open to the more energetic and imaginative amongst them should ensure more in the future. Nevertheless the barrier persists, maintained by a rigid insistence on the "full-time" principle of academic employment—a tacit feature of Flexnerism. When professorial units were an innovation this separation of sheep from goats may have served a useful purpose, but the results of creating this élite have not been entirely favourable. Medicine is by definition a clinical study, and the professor of medicine or surgery who is in reality an applied physiologist without personal responsibility for the care of patients is evading an intrinsic function of his appointment.

Disease and illness are not limited by the walls of the hospital but are community matters at both the individual and the collective levels: it seems hardly logical to entrust the professional education of men who may never practise medicine in an institution exclusively to those who never work outside it. Today also the academic is adjured to come down from the university's red-brick tower and throw himself into the life and work of the community, refreshing it with his wisdom and expertise. Our professors of architecture design buildings and our engineers machinery, while our chemists lend their skills to industry. There is no reason to doubt their view that the busy practice as well as the teaching of their subjects informs their instruction with an actuality it might otherwise lack. Whatever the initial value of the academic doctor's aloofness from the world it is now a shibboleth, bringing in its train troubles worse than those it set out to cure. There have been instances, both in Britain and in the Commonwealth, where a chair has been occupied by an inferior man simply because the best candidate declined to sacrifice his freedom to do a small amount of private practice. This rigid system has outlived its usefulness. Again we can profit by American experience: "Harvard full-time" is approximately equivalent to "nine-elevenths" in the Health Service, and its operation has not strikingly jeopardised the quality or the output of the Harvard clinical professors by comparison with our own. There is no reason why the professor or reader in a clinical subject should not have a choice between being full-time or "nine-elevenths", and it is to be hoped that some at any rate would opt for limited outside work. This improves the quantity and quality of clinical material coming to a department, establishes it firmly in the community and amongst the outside doctors whom the staff may otherwise never meet face to face, and ensures that the important field of domiciliary consultation does not become a prerogative of the second-rate. Fortunately there are moves in this direction. The Scottish schools have a long tradition of personal chairs for distinguished part-timers, and several provincial English schools are now steadily moving towards a situation where sheep and goats can fraternise and freely share such pastures as are available. In some universities there is no contractual obligation for the full-time professor to eschew private practice so long as it does not interfere with his university duties; the fact that those who treat private patients arrange for fees to be paid to the university for departmental use may be attributed to tradition, chivalry, or quixotism—or to a reluctance to contribute still further to the inland revenue account—rather than to any stipulation in this connection.

There is no evidence that the few American medical schools with a full-time faculty have benefited from this development, and most British teachers of medicine consider that a combination of full-time and part-time teachers brings colour and variety as well as realism to what might otherwise tend to become an inward-looking educational routine. The entirely institutional doctor has a continual struggle to escape being cast by his juniors as the ultimate authority whose sole function is to pronounce a final clinical decision based on a sheaf of data collected by them. Their solicitude in trying to shield him from the patient and still more from the patient's relatives is well meant, since such interviews often represent the most taxing part of medical practice, but the professor who does not sometimes teach his juniors the technique of consultation is teaching less than half his subject.

THE DEPARTMENTAL INCUBUS

The English teacher of medicine must also ask critically whether the teutonically inspired professorial department so dear to Flexner really furnishes the best environment for medicine to flourish. It is of course questionable whether a pyramidal hierarchy of this type is favourable to *any* kind of intellectual enterprise; and in recent years it has been attacked from many sides, especially as it operates in the red-brick universities. A lecturer of 20 years' standing is not entirely consoled by the reflection that "lecturer" is a career grade, or by an almost invariable conviction that he is professionally superior to his chief—which may of course even be true. In Oxford and Cambridge the harshness of this situation is mitigated by the existence of an alternative ladder of promotion within the colleges. Everywhere the departmental incubus lies much less heavily on the clinician than on his paraclinical and especially his preclinical colleagues. For this there are historical reasons. The first is that the existence of a large number of senior part-time teaching appointments greatly dilutes clinical professorial authority. The practice of clinical medicine is a highly personal occupation, and, although the traditional organisation of the British teaching hospital into a constellation of competitive "firms" of equal status may carry with it the untidiness and inefficiency inherent in any democratic arrangement, it has undoubted advantages. It stimulates individual effort and avoids the unhealthy predicament evident in many monolithic departments where the professorial advancement of a junior may depend entirely on the patronage of the mandarin at the top of the pyramid.

There has always been the occasional clinical department where the professor has retained direct personal charge of all the available beds, but these are few and far between. It would be difficult to sustain that the greater latitude allowed to their juniors by the clinical professors is entirely due to a higher standard of civilisation and innate generosity than obtains in the laboratory departments. There is a simpler reason. The clinician able enough to secure a highly competitive appointment in a clinical professorial unit, who then discovers that he is denied the opportunity of individual professional expression and responsibility, can easily escape. He will either seize the first available opportunity of transferring his allegiance to the hospital staff and setting up in competition along the corridor, or, if chronology is unfavourable, he can leave the institution altogether to build up his own individual empire in a regional centre.

At a time when microbiologists, cytologists, clinical pathologists, and medical biochemists are all at a premium very much the same applies in the main paraclinical fields, where transfer from a university department to a regional hospital may yield increased professional opportunity further sweetened by financial advantage. There are still a few paraclinical departments where professorial dictation is reflected in a continually changing staff, but in the end this situation becomes so transparent that the departmental head is usually driven to concede some degree of personal autonomy to his juniors.

Fifty years after Flexner

THE PRECLINICAL DILEMMA

In the preclinical field the situation is regrettably different, and makes a further contribution to the depressed morale in these departments noticed by Flexner half a century ago. These departments are almost invariably inadequately housed and equipped and traditionally are loaded with heavy teaching responsibilities. The academic clinician has his own patients and his own defined sphere of activity within a department: if these are not forthcoming he seeks his opportunity elsewhere. The anatomist or physiologist, on the other hand, works elbow to elbow with his colleagues sharing the same facilities and equipment—a situation that encourages the unattractive expression of those fine nuances of status so dear to the Englishman. Furthermore the anatomist or physiologist, after the first few years at any rate, has nowhere else to go. If he possesses the higher qualifications that would ensure appropriate employment in clinical medicine, he has often entered the preclinical field because of a temperamental reluctance to exploit them outside it. All he can do is to move to another department of anatomy or physiology; and in so small a field this may present real difficulties, especially for the nonconformist.

Taxed with this gloomy picture some preclinical professors will explain that their departments require so much administration and employ so many ancillary staff that a managerial system of organisation is imperative, and that the problem they are working on is of such intrinsic interest and importance that its needs must occupy the entire attentions of those rebellious members of the junior staff who would incomprehensibly prefer to pursue their own interests. The clinical professor will frequently try to balance his team by appointing as reader a man with a different research activity, but preclinical departments are often wholly devoted to a particular body-system. The idea that such departments should contain three or four professors each with separate interests and with a rotating chairmanship is a healthy development of current American university organisation that is greeted with apathy or hostility in British circles, where the prospect of even a second chair tends to be regarded as a potential menace to departmental autarchy rather than a graceful tribute to the importance of the subject.

The traditional preclinical departments of the medical schools are clearly at risk today, and it seems likely that they will be reoriented to furnish a less departmental introduction to human biology. Many young physiological investigators tire of studies restricted to the cat or frog, and prefer the excitement of working directly with the human subject in centres for cardiac or cerebral surgery, organ transplantation, or the modern management of renal disease. The general physiologist may retain his role in the teaching of the general principles of physio-

148

logy to medical and science students. The professional anatomist's understandable predilection for pursuits other than that of anatomy is traditional, but he will probably continue to play a similar part in the undergraduate teaching of his subject as well as in its more detailed presentation to intending surgeons. However, the historical truth must not be forgotten that human physiology and anatomy are secondary derivatives of clinical medicine—and not the reverse. In many fields the modern clinical specialist is better informed as to the normal structure and function of the system with which he is concerned than any general physiologist or anatomist can ever hope to be. The expert ophthalmic surgeon who spends every day operating on the human eye may know less about the eye of the iguana than his academic colleague, but what he knows is acutely relevant to man. The clinical team that uses elaborate physiological measurements in man as the basis for modern cardiac surgery will obtain little joy from academic studies of the conducting mechanism of the equine heart, but could surely be appropriately entrusted with student education in cardiovascular function and structure.

The tendency to bring back the clinician into preclinical education is accentuated by what can only be described as an obstinate sectarianism on the part of some anatomists and physiologists who give the impression of positively taking pains to ensure that the possible clinical relevance of their instruction is reduced to a minimum. It is surely a dangerous fallacy for a medical school to imply that the techniques of objective observation, measurement, and experiment can be inculcated only in the animal laboratory and not in a relevant clinical context.

The increasing adoption of the integrated medical curriculum widely favoured at the present time is likely to achieve a progressive improvement in this situation. The participation of clinicians at all stages of the course and in all professional examinations is breaking down the traditional but arbitrary and outdated division between the clinical and preclinical phases of undergraduate medical education and between physiologist and physician. It will also in the end ensure that, wherever possible, the illustration of general physiological principles by clinical example does something to preserve the philanthropic enthusiasm that fires so many young recruits to medicine and is so easily extinguished by forced feeding with anatomist's anatomy and physiologist's physiology.

THE FUTURE

The harvest of modern scientific medicine reaped during the past two decades has included the conquest of bacterial infections, such as tuberculosis, and of poliomyelitis; the virtual clearance of depressive illness from the chronic wards of the mental hospitals; and, probably more important still, the effective freeing of millions of people from pain, discomfort, and distress which remains the central function of medicine. But a community that wishes to enjoy such benefits must be prepared to pay for them and to accord a very different degree of priority to medical education and research and to medicine in general than they have received in the past. Our medical students represent neither better nor worse material than those of the United States—or, for that matter, of Greece or Nigeria. What they are able ultimately to achieve and contribute depends almost entirely on the relative importance attached to medicine and medical care in the milieu in which they will work, and this is one important measure of any community's civilisation.

It does not require the deliberations of a Royal Commission to appreciate that, even if wholesale emigration can be checked, the technological development of modern medicine requires an increase *now* of at least 50%, and almost certainly more, in our annual output of medical graduates. Something of this order would be necessary to furnish generally even the not-extravagant standards of patient care now achieved in a handful of the best hospitals. It would demand a 50% increase in student intake in 1967 to every medical school that could achieve this with an urgent programme of temporary building, together with the immediate creation of not less than six new schools. This is proportionately much less ambitious than the programme of medical-school expansion already vigorously under way in the United States— a country not even committed to a comprehensive medical service. The need for action on such lines if the National Health Service is to survive is already widely accepted as a matter of the utmost urgency. The continuing failure of Government to implement it exerts a deplorable effect on professional morale, and is widely cited in favour of a pessimistic view, now honestly held by an appreciable minority of doctors, that the service is officially regarded as expendable.

If this is not to be, our first priority must be an immediate, radical, and inevitably expensive improvement in the often scandalous physical conditions in which an increasingly disillusioned and suspicious profession wrestles with the problems of teaching and practising medicine. The little that has been achieved in this connection since the bright morning of the Health Service 18 years ago is a terrible commentary on a miserable succession of impotent Ministries and uninterested administrations.

To speak of the impending disintegration of the hospital service is to invite the accusation of alarmism, but it would be foolhardy to ignore some serious omens that clearly point in this direction. I will mention only two. There are fewer and fewer applicants for consultant appointments in such exacting specialties as neurosurgery, ophthalmology, otology, and radiology. The protracted training required in these and some other highly technical branches of medicine and surgery renders them an especially sensitive barometer of professional confidence, and it is alarming that there has recently been not a single applicant for a number of consultant appointments of this kind which by British standards at any rate have been regarded as first-class. Within recent months this has applied even in general medicine—a new and sinister development. Secondly the number of final-year medical students who request permission to undertake their preregistration appointments abroad is increasing annually by leaps and bounds. Practically always they opt for North America, where excellent appointments under good modern conditions are theirs for the asking, and where they soon encounter exciting professional opportunities of every kind that make return here improbable.

The profession must make clear to Government and public the grim and sober truth that without a very large increase in national expenditure on the hospitals, here and now—and far beyond anything so far envisaged even on paper and for an indefinitely receding future—they will progressively run down and the present second-rate service will shortly give place to one that is fourth or fifth rate. If as a profession we make this grave situation crystal-clear to a Government and public that at present seem deaf to such considered warnings, there is little more we can do. The expansion, development, and revitalisation of British medicine that is urgently needed will be an exacting and exhausting exercise for everybody engaged in it; and if, after due consideration of priorities, the nation is unwilling to provide the necessary resources there will be many who will return with clear consciences to the comfortable cultivation of their professional gardens. After all, the practice of medicine is still a fascinating pursuit even in a declining civilisation.

If Government deprives us of recourse to such individual salvation and envinces a genuine determination to measure up to the needs—what then?

The radical improvement in the physical environment of medicine that has already been stated as our highest priority must be accompanied firstly, by a strengthening and expansion of existing professorial units. These must become central and not peripheral to the major divisions of the parent hospital, breaking down the wall between full and part time staff and providing academic encouragement, opportunity, and facilities equally to both. This fusion has already been achieved in occasional departments and has a powerful effect both on morale and on output. Secondly, workers in the basic sciences must take an active part in every aspect of a clinically centred curriculum. Thirdly, academic units must be established in the specialties where the calibre of the present departmental head justifies such a development or when his retirement permits an appropriate appointment. The extent to which such developments will depend on laboratory support implies also the necessity for an energetic and comprehensive programme of training for medical biochemists, immunologists, virologists, and experimental pathologists some medically qualified, probably more with training in science. Facilities for training such essential workers are already in existence, and their full employment and expansion are held up only by financial stringency. The breaking down of stultifying departmentalism in both clinical and preclinical spheres is a domestic matter, but it is none the less indispensable.

With all this must come an ever-increasing use of regional-hospital facilities for undergraduate as well as postgraduate clinical education. The fears of dilution that often obstruct academic promotion in other connections must not be allowed to operate here. It is only by pressing every potentially good and interested teacher of medicine into service that we can achieve the necessary increase in the annual rate of medical graduation that is vital unless we are to become a medically third-class nation. If this means bringing the university hospital under the administrative umbrella of the regional hospital board, there will be many who will consider that the undoubted advantages of such a merger in quantity and flexibility of resources outweigh its calculated risks to teaching-hospital standards of excellence.

Psychiatry—medicine or magic?

PROFESSOR HENRY MILLER

Vice-Chancellor of the University of Newcastle upon Tyne

I must begin my remarks with a qualification introduced by any speaker about to attack a persecuted minority. *Many of my best friends are psychiatrists.* This statement is more than formality in the present context, because as a clinical neurologist I have had the good fortune to work with and learn from a team of eclectic and realistic psychiatrists of outstanding calibre. They are the sort of psychiatrists who send the patient back to me with the polite suggestion that I have another look for the cerebral tumour—and they have an infuriating habit of being right. This is certainly one of his most important functions, and the psychiatrist whose knowledge and experience of the pleomorphism of organic disease is too insecurely based for its exercise is a danger to the patient.

A few years ago a senior psychiatric colleague and I founded the Society for the Abolition of Psychiatrists. Before I am overwhelmed with applications to join—and they have already come from some of Britain's most eminent psychiatrists, as well as from a number of patients—I must point out that the society has not yet received its charter, and does no more than epitomise our firm conviction that *the psychiatrist must be first and foremost and all the time a physician,* expert certainly in unravelling the complexities of mental symptomatology, but also at least as adept in general medicine as his cardiological or neurological colleagues. In fact psychiatry is neurology without physical signs, and calls for diagnostic virtuosity of the highest order. In view of the considerable mortality and serious morbidity with which the psychiatrist is concerned it is truly alarming that his is the only one of its branches that can be practised at a responsible level without a thorough training in internal medicine—without such a background of general clinical experience as even our dermatological colleagues demand. And regrettably this position seems likely to be both perpetuated and consolidated by a College of Psychiatrists. I hold no particular brief for Royal Colleges or examinations, but when one considers the disguises in which liver failure, encephalitis and lung cancer may present themselves to the psychiatrist he is perhaps the best of all possible excuses for the con-

An address given at the World Psychiatric Association London Symposium, 17 November, 1969.

tinued existence of the MRCP. The present move towards psychiatric autarchy is likely to sacrifice the slow but clearly perceptible improvement in psychiatric standards that has resulted from Health Service opportunities and pressures for closer embodiment in the mainstream of medicine.

I hope I have already made it clear that I have a high respect for psychiatry and that I regard it beyond doubt as the most important, the most fascinating and much the most difficult branch of medicine. Unfortunately it is also the most abused, and it is little consolation to reflect that much of the abuse of psychiatry is self-abuse; many psychiatrists lend it their whole-hearted collaboration.

In a nutshell, most of the abuses of the psychiatrist arise from his reluctance to restrict his activities to the field in which he is genuinely qualified to operate. The Oxford Dictionary's definition of a psychiatrist is "one who treats mental illness'. Not, you will observe, one who prevents wars, cures anti-semitism, offers to transform the normally abrasive relations between men into a tedium of stultifying harmony, is the ultimate authority on bringing up children or selecting managing directors—or misuses his jargon to confuse any and every topical issue in an incessant series of television appearances.

DEFINING MENTAL DISEASE

If we look again at the dictionary definition we must consider the term "mental disease". What does it mean ? In my submission it means *disease with mental symptoms*. Mental disease is no more exclusively a disease of the mind than rheumatoid disease is exclusively a disease of the joints: it is just that both are conveniently categorised on the basis of their most conspicuous symptomatology. To the lay public, mental illness used to mean and perhaps to some extent still means insanity, a social rather than a medical categorisation, suspect because of its spurious definitiveness, but on reflection perhaps less blurred than the contemporary term "mental illness", which is used to cover everything from shoplifting to frontal tumour. What mental illness means to the physician of course is illness with mental symptoms, illness that presents as a psychological disturbance. To many laymen and to a mercifully shrinking band of metaphysical psychiatrists this means illness due to emotional causes. But the experienced physician knows that illness with mental symptoms often results from physical causes, and indeed that what we know with certainty about the aetiology and pathogenesis of mental disease has been gleaned almost entirely from investigation at this level: it is necessary to mention only the spirochaete, the porphyrins, and the catecholamines. We know that models of some types of mental disease can be induced with reasonable predictability by the use of certain drugs. We know also that both

Psychiatry—medicine or magic ?

general and neurological illnesses may lead to characteristic psychiatric syndromes that clear when the illness is relieved. We know that certain drugs have a quite specific effect on certain psychiatric symptoms such as sleeplessness, tension and depression. As a matter of fact this is really about all we know.

Since the flight into so-called dynamic psychiatry with its speculative and entirely affirmative basis in psychological determinism, psychiatry has suffered from a surfeit of complicated and improbable theory and a dearth of simple testable hypotheses. Not unnaturally the psychiatrist who believes that the phenomena of mental illness can be explained on the basis of a universal theory, and not be verifying fragmentary pieces of hard information one by one to build a growing structure of certain knowledge, finds little difficulty in inflating his theory to explain not only mental disease but also normal human behaviour, interpersonal relations, and ultimately world affairs. The results of these exercises are not impressive. Such energies would be better directed to mastering and investigating the clinical pharmacology of the powerful and effective drugs at the psychiatrist's disposal so that their employment can be more critical and more discriminating.

THE PSYCHIATRIST'S IMAGE

The psychiatrist is of course encouraged in his universal pontification by the inexplicable veneration with which his views are regarded by many who ought to know better. Socially I suppose this springs in part from the priest's loss of prestige and from the collapse of religious values. Certainly the highly wrought and arcane structure of psycho-analysis betrays its man-made origin as transparently as does that of any highly organised religion. Nor is it fanciful to note the similarity that obtains in the internecine strife so full-bloodedly enjoyed by adherents of competing faiths whether religious or psychiatric.

But at a simpler level the popular endowment of the psychiatrist with universal omniscience also arises from a basic lay fallacy that few psychiatrists make any attempt to dispel. There are many quite well-educated people who believe that psychiatrists have special and mysterious methods of finding out what is going on in their patient's minds that are denied to the rest of the profession and to the rest of humanity. Such people do not appreciate—because they have never been told—the simple fact that *a psychiatrist is a physician who takes a proper history at the first consultation.* He spends longer over it, and sees fewer patients. Does the psychiatrist know more about the roots of normal human behaviour than anyone else? His claim to do so arises from the fact that he studies the caricatures of normal human behaviour that present as psychoses or neuroses. He can certainly theorise about normal behaviour, but when he moves outside a professional relation-

155

Psychiatry—medicine or magic ?

ship it seems doubtful whether his views are more interesting or his conclusions any more reliable than those of the rest of us. They are certainly less illuminating than those of the poet, dramatist or novelist.

Incidentally, one curious phenomenon concerns insight. This is the subject of so much discussion in psychiatric circles, in clinical formulations, and especially among those psychiatrists who lay great store on introspective data, that one might imagine it would be a quality carefully cultivated as well as highly valued by psychiatrists themselves. I have no hesitation in saying quite categorically that this is not so. My careful personal observations confirm the rather unexpected finding that the practice of psychiatry in any of its forms does not necessarily confer any insight whatever. Whether mechanist or psychoanalyst, there are many psychiatrists who manifest that insightless insensitivity to audience reaction that is the hallmark of the bore.

THE PSYCHIATRIST AT LAW

I have emphasised the psychiatrist's eagerness to account for psychological phenomena on the basis of some universal theory as evidence of his rejection of the methods of science, and indeed lack of objectivity is probably the main reason for the reluctance with which the typical psychiatrist is accepted into the scientific community. I was staggered at a recent meeting to hear an eminent British professor of psychiatry explain to an audience of lawyers, judges, and doctors that since the taking of a psychiatric history and the making of a psychiatric formulation involve the psychiatrist so intimately with the patient at an emotional level it was entirely impossible for him to act as an objective expert witness in a court of law. He must always, according to this professor, be "on the side of" the person examined—a sort of perpetual prisoner's friend. Needless to say this remark was greeted with alarm by one group of lawyers and with hilarious relief by others, who felt it fully confirmed everything they had long felt about psychiatric evidence in court. I do not believe this view would be sustained by most psychiatrists, and I know that it is perfectly possible for a psychiatrist with some expertise in forensic work to give an excellent and indeed invaluable clinical opinion in a court of law. However, one must admit that there is a tendency for the psychiatrist to regard as a patient any individual whose history he takes under whatever circumstances.

The word malingering does not figure in the index of several standard textbooks on psychiatry, and we all know of appalling instances where the lying statements of criminals were given spurious authenticity by being incorporated in the text of a psychiatrist's report as though they were indeed matters of fact. In these circumstances it is hardly surprising that the judge in court has so often to point out that the psychiatric assessment is based on what the person examined told the

156

psychiatrist, and that if the subject of the examination is endeavouring to escape from the consequences of a criminal act, to avoid an unpalatable social responsibility, or even to elicit sympathy, it would be as stupid to regard his statements about himself and his feelings as necessary valid evidence as it would be to accept without question a criminal's uncorroborated account of his crime.

I have also observed that even outside a medicolegal situation quite sophisticated psychiatrists in search of psychopathogenesis will cheerfully accept the patient's or the family's (usually creditable) account of the cause of his illness, even though the same doctor would contemptuously brush aside the patient's equally insupportable theories as to the origin of his gallstones or cerebral thrombosis. Unless one accepts that psychogenesis is a game for amateurs the two situations seem to be not absolutely different.

A further vexed issue concerns how far the psychiatrist should permit his subject to be used, loosely and sometimes cynically, to ensure the smooth working of society. The term "psychopathic personality" lost its meaning in the Hitler war because it was used as a medical label for ridding the armed forces of incompetent or uncontrollable soldiers. Whether we lost much thereby is another matter. The term shares with some other psychiatric categories all the vices of a circular definition: irresponsible behaviour is caused by psychopathy, a diagnosis based on the subject's irresponsible behaviour. In this context I don't think any great harm was done. It was more important to ensure the survival of civilisation than to worry about terminology. However, in peace-time the psychiatrist should perhaps be less ready to act as a garbage-can for the problems of society and the law in connection with antisocial behaviour. If the shoplifter is genuinely suffering from an agitated depression by all means advise treatment rather than prison but do not speculatively attribute all stealing and swindling to mental disease. What society does of course is to make the most convenient commonsense disposal of such cases if any particular theory were shown to yield a better pragmatic result it would no doubt become the basis of forensic practice, but so far there are no signs of such a development.

Nevertheless the psychiatrist's willingness to regard as a patient anyone from whom he takes a history leads to considerable abuse. His appearance in court to give evidence in a case of divorce or marital conflict after having talked to only one member of the marriage deprives his opinion of any conceivable value. It is probably of little value anyway. The fact that two people decide that they do wish to spend more time together does not prove that they are mad or even ill in the mildest way. But any psychiatrist who gives an opinion in such a case without seeing both partners brings ridicule on his subject. He has in any case nothing to offer in this situation unless mental illness is present.

Psychiatry—medicine or magic ?

I would draw special attention to three current fashions in psychiatry that may contribute to its abuse. The present tendency to explain every phenomenon of internal medicine on the basis of autoimmunity is the most recent illustration of the general vulnerability of medical science to fashion, and there can be no doubt that psychiatry is at least as liable to this danger as any other branch of medicine.

I would draw attention first to the concept of *social psychiatry*, to the vogue it enjoys here at some cost to the clinical approach, and to the way in which with characteristic American thoroughness it is tending to displace the rather tarnished image of psychoanalysis as the mascot of the American academic psychiatrist.

I would be the last person to discourage epidemiological research, to which I have devoted many years of personal effort. There can be no doubt that properly organised this can display trends in differential prevalence and incidence, it can reveal broadly operative contributory aetiological factors, and it can pin-point sensitive areas suitable for more intensive and definitive investigation either in the clinic or the laboratory. Occasionally, also epidemiological serendipity will unveil a truly significant rather than a merely contributory aetiological agent. Furthermore epidemiological studies sharpen precision in diagnosis, and encourage the formulation of those operational classifications that are needed to establish real differences and similarities between clinical categories. However, it must be kept clearly in mind that epidemiological study can be carried out only where there is a firm and widely agreed basis of clinical diagnosis and classification, and that while it yields useful information it is naïve to expect it often to yield final answers. To shift the basis of psychiatry from medicine to sociology is to move from the well-lit contours of hard knowledge and clear definition into the half-light of a subject that is in its infancy, that is imprecise, that is still desperately short of basic data, and that is itself still groping for its first principles and for a clearly defined role in the scientific galaxy. In the hands of a lunatic fringe of psychiatrists the social element in psychiatry can also be invoked to absolve the psychiatrist from the exhausting personal exercise of actually treating the mentally ill.

The second equally dangerous trend is the deliberate inflation of the field of psychiatry from its preoccupation with the study and treatment of mental illness to what has been euphemistically termed the *science of behaviour*. I have already voiced my doubts as to the extent to which the psychiatrist's experience of the abnormal can reasonably be used as a guide to general behaviour, and airily to describe psychiatry as comprising "the science of behaviour" strikes me as a piece of arrogance that can only bring discredit on the practitioner of a subject that is already quite difficult enough. Of course all human behaviour can be

158

described in the psychiatrist's terminology. Equally it can be described in the terms and concepts of the anthropologist, the historian, the sociologist, the economist, or psychologist—or even the practical politician. I can see no conceivable reason why the psychiatrist's monarchy of the kingdom of the abnormal should endow his particular synthesis with any particular virtue. Indeed, rather the reverse.

The latest fashion in psychiatry—or it might be safer to say the penultimate fashion, since fashions succeed one another so rapidly that I am probably already out of date—is to divorce the subject entirely from medicine and to regard mental illness as a matter exclusively of the individual personality and his *interpersonal relationships*. This view light-heartedly begs the question of psychogenesis, and accepts disturbed interpersonal relations as the cause of mental illness on the basis of affirmation alone and without troubling to adduce the kind of evidence that would be demanded in any other field of medicine.

It also comfortingly absolves the investigator from the hard exercise of diagnostic classification, and the search for other aetiological agents. It converts therapy into a miasma of well-motivated and mostly bumbling interference with complex relationships subjectively assessed by a mind with no verifiable basis of authentic professionalism. Attributing everything to psychogenesis it ignores the enzyme, the inclusion body and the toxic chemical, or any of the other agents by which mental disturbances can be predictably provoked. If the rest of medicine has restricted its aetiological hypotheses to those based on interpersonal relationships it could also have built a precarious edifice of similar causation for gallstones, piles and baldness. It would be characterised by a vast sprawling, and inconsequential literature and it would never have discovered the sleeping tablet, to say nothing of the antibody or the antibiotic.

On thinking over these remarks you will observe that the real issue concerns the use of the term *mental illness*. As in the case of physical illness the definition has a social as well as a semantic importance. All of us have physical and mental disabilities and for all of us they increase with advancing years. All of us occasionally magnify disabilities of both kinds to obtain our own ends. Such exaggerations range from fabricating a sick headache or pleading normal fatigue to avoid an unattractive social engagement to simulating more serious disability for more serious purposes—madness to escape imprisonment. The practitioner of internal medicine or neurology is fallible, but probably more sparing than the psychiatrist in bestowing the accolade of illness with its consequent privileges. This, I believe, is where he is most abused.

It is a platitude to say that the depressive patient should not be told to pull himself together and get on with the job. However, there are many circumstances when the patient with less serious psychiatric

Psychiatry—medicine or magic ?

symptoms needs to be told very firmly that they are no more important than the low back pains that trouble so many of his contemporaries, or the piles or bunions that worry the rest. I am fortunate that the psychiatrists with whom I have worked have been prepared to say this, and to make the rarest of all psychiatric diagnosis—that there is nothing seriously wrong with the patient and nothing requiring psychiatric treatment. If such self-denying stringency were more widely cultivated, abuse of the psychiatrist at every level of medicine and of society would be less conspicuous.

Bibliography of H G Miller

This list, which is not comprehensive, has been compiled with the help of the Department of Neurology, Royal Victoria Infirmary, Newcastle upon Tyne.

Miller, H G, Comparison of physical standards in two groups of children. *British Medical Journal*, 1938, **2**, 718–9.

Miller, H G, Spontaneous subarachnoid haemorrhage in children; clinical study of five cases. *Archives of Disease in Childhood*, 1938, **13**, 258–63.

Miller, H G, and Crombie, O M R, Complete freedom from dental caries; comparative study of 25 children. *Lancet*, 1939, **2**, 131–3.

Miller H G, Granulocytopenia and anaemia following medication with sulphanilamide. *Newcastle Medical Journal*, 1940, **20**, 49–54.

Miller H G, Myasthenia gravis and the thymus. *Archives of Pathology*, 1940, **29**, 212–9.

Herbert, F K, Miller, H G, and Richardson, G O, Chronic renal disease, secondary parathyroid hyperplasia, decalcification of bone and metastatic calcification. *Journal of Pathology and Bacteriology*, 1941, **53**, 161–82.

Miller, H G, and Studdert, T C, Pernicious anaemia of pregnancy; study of 23 cases. *Lancet*, 1942, **2**, 332–4.

Miller, H G, Neurological disorders in relation to pregnancy. *Postgraduate Medical Journal*, 1944, **20**, 158–63.

Ballard, S I, and Miller, H G, Sequelae of cerebrospinal meningitis; analysis of 60 cases. *Lancet*, 1945, **2**, 273–5.

Miller, H G, and Ballard, S J, Psychiatric casualties in women's service. *British Medical Journal*, 1945, **1**, 293–5.

Miller, H G, and Nelson, M G, Polyarteritis nodosa developing during antisyphilitic treatment. *Lancet*, 1945, **2**, 200–2.

Ballard, S I, and Miller, H G, Secuelas de las meningitis cerebrospinal; un analisis de sesenta casos. *Dia Medico (Buenos Aires)*, 1946, **18**, 495–500.

Miller, H G, and Daley, R, Angina pectoris with associated left paroxysmal ptosis. *British Heart Journal*, 1946, **8**, 29–32.

Miller, H G, and Daley, R, Clinical aspects of polyarteritis nodosa. *Quarterly Journal of Medicine*, 1946, **15**, 255–83.

Miller, H G, The recognition of neurotic illness. *Practitioner*, 1947, **159**, 128–35.

Daley, R, and Miller, H, Ed, *Progress in Clinical Medicine*. London, Churchill, 1948.

Miller, H G, Discussion on periarteritis nodosa. *Proceedings of the Royal Society of Medicine*, 1949, **42**, 497–506.

Miller, H G, Discussion on speech defects in children. *Proceedings of the Royal Society of Medicine*, 1950, **43**, 579–88.

Miller, H G, Clinical considerations of cerebrovascular disorders occurring during the course of general diseases of an inflammatory or allergic nature. *Proceedings of the Royal Society of Medicine*, 1951, **44**, 852–5.

Daley, R, and Miller, H, *Progress in Clinical Medicine*, 2nd edn. London, Churchill, 1952.

Miller, H G, Acute disseminated encephalomyelitis treated with ACTH. *British Medical Journal*, 1953, **1**, 177.

Miller, H G, Parkinsonism and its management. *Practitioner*, 1953, **171**, 15–20.

Miller, H, Prognosis of neurologic illness following vaccination against smallpox. *Archives of Neurology and Psychiatry*, 1953, **69**, 695-706.

Bibliography of H G Miller

Miller, H, and Evans, M J, Prognosis in acute disseminated encephalomyelitis: with a note on neuromyelitis optica. *Quarterly Journal of Medicine*, 1953, **22**, 348–79.

Miller, H G, and Gibbons, J L, Acute disseminated encephalomyelitis and acute disseminated sclerosis. *British Medical Journal*, 1953, **2**, 1345–8.

Stanton, J B, Gibbons, J L, and Miller H G, Considerations sur quelques syndromes encephalomyelitiques et radiculoevritiques. *Revue Neurologique*, 1953, **89**, 46–50.

Miller, H, Allergic disorders of nervous system. *Medicine Illustrated*, 1954, **8**, 216–20.

Miller, H, The muscular dystrophies. *Medical Press*, 1954, **231**, 218–301.

Miller, H G, Polyarteritis nodosa. *Practitioner*, 1954, **173**, 133–9.

Miller, H, Treatment of Parkinsonism [contribution to sectional meeting at BMA Annual Meeting, Glasgow]. *British Medical Journal*, 1954, **2**, 158.

Gibbons, J L, and Miller H, Familial recurrent encephalomyelitis. *Annals of Internal Medicine*, 1954, **40**, 755–64.

Miller, H, and Stanton, J B, Neurological sequelae of prophylactic inoculation. *Quarterly Journal of Medicine*, 1954, **23**, 1–27.

Miller, H, and Stanton, J B, Significance of neurological complications in serum sickness: Report on a case treated with cortisone [in Germany]. *Nervenartz*, 1954, **25**, 118–21.

Morley, D, Court, D, and Miller, H, Developmental dysarthria. *British Medical Journal*, 1954, **1**, 8–10.

Miller, H, British experiences with anticoagulant therapy in cerebrovascular disease. *Kulonlenyomat*, 1955.

Miller, H, Management of multiple sclerosis. *Medical World*, 1955, **83**, 426–8.

Miller, H, Migraine. *Medical Press*, 1955, **232**, 315–7.

Morley, M, Court, D, Miller, H, and Garside, R F, Delayed speech and developmental aphasia. *British Medical Journal*, 1955, **2**, 463–7.

Miller, H, Discussion on cervical spondylosis. *Proceedings of the Royal Society of Medicine*, 1956, **49**, 197–208.

Miller, H, The neurological complications of the acute specific fevers. *Proceedings of the Royal Society of Medicine*, 1956, **49**, 139–46.

Miller, H, and Daley, R, *Progress in Clinical Medicine*, 3rd edn. London, Churchill, 1956.

Miller, H, Stanton, J B, and Gibbons, J L, Para-infectious encephalomyelitis and related syndromes. *Quarterly Journal of Medicine*, 1956, **25**, 427–505.

Jackson, R H, Miller, H, and Schapira, K, Polyradiculitis (Landry-Guillain-Barré syndrome). *British Medical Journal*, 1957, **1**, 480–4.

Miller, H, Clinical manifestations of tissue reaction in the nervous system. *Modern Trends in Neurology*, 1957, **2**, 164–76.

Miller, H, Neurological complications of the acute specific fevers. *Practitioner*, 1957, **178**, 331–6.

Miller, H G, Stanton, J B, and Gibbons, J L, Acute disseminated encephalomyelitis and related syndromes. *British Medical Journal*, 1957, **1**, 668–72.

Miller, H, Epilepsy—the epileptic clinic. *Newcastle Medical Journal*, 1958, **25**, No 3.

Miller, H, Neurological complications of pregnancy. *Newcastle Medical Journal*, 1958, **25**, No 6.

Miller, H, Neurology in *British Encyclopaedia of Medical Practice: Medical Progress*, pp 170–83. London, Butterworth, 1958.

Miller, H, Neurology in the general hospital. *British Medical Journal*, 1958, **1**, 477–80.

Miller, H, Allergy and the nervous system [contribution to the section meetings at BMA Joint Annual Meeting with the Canadian Medical Association]. *British Medical Journal*, 1959, **2**, 489.

Miller, H, Anticoagulants in neurology [contribution to symposium on anti-coagulations, BMA Annual Clinical Meeting]. *British Medical Journal*, 1959, **2**. 879.

Miller, H, Ed, *Early Diagnosis*. Edinburgh and London, Livingstone, 1959.

Bibliography of H G Miller

Miller, H, and Schapira, K, Aetiological aspects of multiple sclerosis. *British Medical Journal*, 1959, **1**, 737-40.

Daley, R, and Miller, H, *Progress in Clinical Medicine*, 4th edn. London, Churchill, 1961.

Miller, H, Anticoagulant therapy in cerebrovascular disease. *Newcastle Medical Journal*, 1960, **26**, No 3.

Miller, H, The management of Parkinsonism. *Practitioner*, 1960, **184**, 170-4.

Miller, H, Ridley, A, and Schapira, K, Multiple sclerosis—a note on social incidence. *British Medical Journal*, 1960, **2**, 343-5.

Miller, H, and Smith, M, The cost of drug treatment. *Lancet*, 1960, **1**, 45-7.

Field, E J, and Miller H, Studies in the inhibition of experimental allergic encephalomyelitis. *Archives of International Pharmacology*. 1961, **34**, 1-2.

Foster, J B, Miller, H, Newell, D J, and Kinlen, L J, Multiple sclerosis—a trial of treatment with tolbutamide. *Lancet*, 1961, **1**, 915-7.

Miller, H, Accident neurosis. *British Medical Journal*, 1961, **1**, 919-25 and 922-8.

Miller, H, Aetiological factors in disseminated sclerosis. *Proceedings of the Royal Society of Medicine*, 1961, **54**, 7-9.

Miller, H, The background of contemporary neurology in Great Britain. *World Neurology (Minneapolis)*, 1961, **2**, 322-7.

Miller, H, Clinical applications of steroid therapy in neurology. *Proceedings of the Royal Society of Medicine*, 1961, **54**, 571-4.

Miller, H, Newell, D J, and Ridley, A, Multiple sclerosis—trial of maintenance treatment with prednisolone and soluble aspirin. *Lancet*, 1961, **1**, 127-9.

Miller, H, Newell, D J, and Ridley, A, Multiple sclerosis—treatment of acute exacerbations with corticotrophin (ACTH). *Lancet*, 1961, **2**, 1120-2.

Miller, H, Newell, D J, Ridley, A, and Schapira, K, Therapeutic trials in multiple sclerosis: Preliminary report of effects of intrathecal injections of tuberculin (PPD). *Journal of Neurology, Neurosurgery and Psychiatry*, 1961, **24**, 118-20.

Miller, H, Chemotherapy of infections of the nervous system. *Practitioner*, 1962, **188**, 17-21.

Miller, H, Ed, *Modern Medical Treatment*. Edinburgh, Livingstone, 1962.

Miller, H G, Newell, D J, Ridley, A R, and Schapira, K, Therapeutic trials in multiple sclerosis—final report on the effects of intrathecal injection of tuberculin. *British Medical Journal*, 1962, **1**, 1726-8.

Johnson, R T, and Miller, H, Dermal sensitivity tests in multiple sclerosis. *Journal of Neurology, Neurosurgery, and Psychiatry*, 1963, **26**, 151-3.

Miller, H, Apoplexy, in *Compendium of Emergencies*, ed H Gardiner-Hill. London, Butterworth, 1963.

Miller, H G, Foster, J B, Newell, D J, Barwick, D D, and Brewis, R A L, Multiple sclerosis: Therapeutic trials of chloroquine, soluble aspirin and gammaglobulin. *British Medical Journal*, 1963, **2**, 1436-9.

Poskanzer, D C, Schapira, K, and Miller, H, Epidemiology of multiple sclerosis in the counties of Northumberland and Durham. *Journal of Neurology Neurosurgery and Psychiatry*, 1963, **26**, 368-76.

Poskanzer, D C, Schapira, K, and Miller, H, Multiple sclerosis and poliomyelitis. *Lancet*, 1963, **2**, 1436-9.

Schapira, K, Poskanzer, D C, and Miller H, Familial and conjugal multiple sclerosis, *Brain*, 1963, **86**, 315-32.

Miller, H, Litigation and accident neurosis. *Proceedings of the Medico-Legal Society of New South Wales*, 1963-4.

Miller, H, Headache. *Transactions of the Ophthalmological Societies of the United Kingdom*, 1964, **84**, 627-36.

Miller, H, Some neurological complictions of surgical treatment. *Proceedings of the Royal Society of Medicine*, 1964, **57**, 143-6.

Miller, H, Trauma and multiple sclerosis. *Lancet*, 1964, **1**, 848-50.

Miller, H, The treatment of epilepsy. *Clinical Trials Journal*, (London) 1964 **1**, 47-51.

Bibliography of H G Miller

Miller, H, The treatment of multiple sclerosis. *Practitioner*, 1964, **192**, 62–70.

Miller, H, Schapira, K, Rafalowska, J, and Warecka, K, Multiple sclerosis in Poland and in Northern England. *Neurology (Minneapolis)*, 1964, **14**, 779–84.

Miller, H, The British National Health Service. *Trephine*, pp 23–6. Moorooka, Australia, Co-op Press Ltd, 1965.

Miller, H, Epidemiological studies in multiple sclerosis. *Journal of the Medical Women's Federation*, 1965, **47**, 35–8.

Miller, H, Late sequelae of head injuries, in *Proceedings of the 8th International Congress of Neurology, Vienna*. Verlag der Wiener medizinischen Akademie, 1965.

Miller, H, Neurological emergencies—apoplexy, in *Compendium of Emergencies*, 2nd edn, ed H Gardiner-Hill. London, Butterworth, 1965.

Miller, H, Pain in the arm, *South East Scotland Faculty Journal*, 1965, **5**, 2.

Miller, H, The painful arm. *Transactions of the Medical Society of London*, 1965, **81**, 28–38.

Miller, H, Textbooks for pleasure. *Journal of the American Medical Association*, 1965, **192**, 145–8.

Miller, H, The treatment of migraine. *Prescriber's Journal*, 1965, **5**, 5.

Miller, H, Simpson, C A, and Yeates, W K, Bladder dysfunction in multiple sclerosis. *British Medical Journal*, 1965, **1**, 1265–9.

Miller, H, and Stern, G, The long-term prognosis in severe head injury. *Lancet*, 1965, **1**, 225–9.

Poskanzer, D C, Schapira, K, Brack, R A, and Miller, H, Studies of blood groups, genetic linkage, trait association, and chromosomal pattern in multiple sclerosis. *Journal of Neurology, Neurosurgery and Psychiatry*, 1965, **28**, 218–22,

Simpson, C A, Newell, D J, and Miller, H, The treatment of multiple sclerosis with massive doses of hydroxocobalmin. *Neurology (Minneapolis)*, 1965, **15**, 599–603.

Simpson, C A, Vejjajiva, A, Caspary, E A, and Miller, H, ABO blood groups in multiple sclerosis. *Lancet*, 1965, **1**, 1366–7.

Simpson, C A, Vejjajiva, A, and Miller, H, Treatment of multiple sclerosis with tranylcypromine. *Lancet*, 1965, **1**, 817.

Vejjajiva, A, Foster, J B, and Miller, H, ABO blood groups in motor neurone disease. *Lancet*, 1965, **1**, 87–8.

Daley, R, and Miller, H, *Progress in Clinical Medicine*, 5th edn. London, Churchill, 1966.

Brewis, Mary, Poskanzer, D C, Rolland, C, and Miller, H, Neurological diseases in an English city. *Acta Neurologica Scandinavica*, 1966, **42**, supp. 24.

Miller, H, Advances in neurology. *Practitioner*, 1966, **197**, 447–54.

Miller, H, Fifty years after Flexner. *Lancet*, 1966, **2**, 647–54.

Miller, H, Mental after-effects of head injury. *Proceedings of the Royal Society of Medicine*, 1966, **59**, 257–61.

Miller, H, Multiple sclerosis, in *Medical Annual*, 1966, pp 26–32. London, Churchill Livingstone, 1966.

Miller, H, A new look at medicine and politics [book review]. *British Medicial Journal*, 1966, **2**, 1315–9.

Miller, H, Polyneuritis. *British Medical Journal*, 1966, **2**, 1219–25.

Miller, H G, Treatment of epilepsy, in *Second Symposium on Advanced Medicine*, ed J R Trounce. London, Pitman Medical, 1966.

Prineas, J, Teasdale, G, Latner, A L, and Miller, H, Spinal fluid gamma-globulin and multiple sclerosis. *British Medical Journal*, 1966, **2**, 922–4.

Schapira, K, Poskanzer, D C, Newell, D J, and Miller, H, Marriage, pregnancy and multiple sclerosis. *Brain*, 1966, **89**, 419–28.

Wright, B M, and Miller, H, Is a regular medical check-up desirable? [transcript of BBC broadcast]. *Listener*, 4 August, 1966.

Miller, H, Neurological manifestations of collagen-vascular disease. *Journal of the Royal College of Physicians of London*, 1966–7, **1**, 15–19.

Miller, H, Depression. *British Medical Journal*, 1967, **1**, 257–62.

Bibliography of H G Miller

Miller, H, Economic and ethical considerations [contribution to Royal Society of Medicine symposium on the cost of life]. *Proceedings of the Royal Society of Medicine*, 1967, **11**.

Miller, H, Facial paralysis. *British Medical Journal*, 1967, **3**, 815–9.

Miller, H, Medicolegal aspects of head injury. *Current Medicine and Drugs*, 1967, **7**, 3–9.

Miller, H, Political medicine man. *Encounter*, 1967, **28**, (No 1) 67–70.

Miller, H, In sickness and in health. *Encounter*, 1967, **28**, (No 4).

Miller, H, Three great neurologists. *Proceedings of the Royal Society of Medicine*, 1967, **60**, 399–405.

Miller, H, Cendrowski, W, and Schapira, K, Multiple sclerosis and vaccination. *British Medical Journal*, 1967, **2**, 210–3.

Powell, E, and Miller, H, Medicine and politics [transcript of BBC broadcast]. *British Medical Journal*, 1967, **1**, 555–9.

Prineas, J, Simpson, C A, and Miller, H, A therapeutic trial of Atromid in multiple sclerosis. *Neurology*, 1967, **17**, 1185.

Teasdale, G M, Smith, P A, Wilkinson, R, Latner, A L, and Miller, H, Endocrine activity in multiple sclerosis. *Lancet*, 1967, **1**, 64–8.

Vejjajiva, A, Foster, J B, and Miller, H, Motor neurone disease. *Journal of the Neurological Society*, 1967, **4**, 299–314.

Miller, H, Epidemiological aspects of multiple sclerosis. *Proceedings of the Royal Society of Medicine*, 1968, **61**, 937–40.

Miller, H, Medical aspects of head injury, in *Traumatic Medicine and Surgery for the Attorney*. New York, Bender and Co, 1968.

Miller, H, The modern concepts of polyneuritis. *Kulolenyomat az Ideggyogyaszati Szemle*, 1968.

Miller, H, Neurology [a personal book list]. *Lancet*, 1968, **1**, 971–3.

Miller, H, The organisation of neurological services and neurological training. *Proceedings of the Royal Society of Medicine*, 1968, **61**, 1004–10.

Miller, H, Pain in the face. *British Medical Journal*, 1968, **2**, 577–80.

Miller, H, Post-traumatic headache, in *Headaches and Cranial Neuralgias: Handbook of Clinical Neurology*, Vol. 5, ed. P J Vinken and G W Bruyn. New York, Wiley, 1968.

Miller, H, The clinical contribution to multiple sclerosis research. *Transactions of the American Neurological Association*, 1969, **94**, 114–25.

Miller, H, New doctors' dilemmas. *Encounter*, 1969, **30**, (No 3), 25–34.

Miller, H, Real goals for medicine. *Science Journal*, October, 1969.

Miller, H, The abuse of psychiatry. *Encounter*, 1970, **31**, (No 5), 24–31.

Miller, H, The decade ahead. *Community Health*, 1970, **2**, 148–52.

Miller, H, Psychiatry—medicine or magic. *British Journal of Hospital Medicine*, 1970, **3**, 122–6.

Daley, R, and Miller, H, *Progress in Clinical Medicine*, 6th edn. Edinburgh and London, Churchill Livingstone, 1971.

Miller, H, Medical education and medical research, *Lancet*, 1971, **1**, 1–6.

Miller, H, and Cartlidge, N, Simulation and malingering in relation to injuries of the brain and spinal cord, in *First South African International Symposium on Forensic Medicine*, 1971.

Miller, H, and Hudgson, P, Neurological emergencies, in *Compendium of Emergencies*, 3rd edn, ed H Gardiner-Hill. London, Butterworth, 1971.

Miller, H, Foreword to *Patient, Doctor, Society*, London, Oxford University Press, 1972.

Miller, H, Keeping people alive. Foreword to *Future of Man*, pp 127–33 London, Academic Press, 1972.

Miller, H, Ministering to need. *World Medicine*, 1972, **7**, (15), 31–47.

Miller, H, Psychosurgery and Dr Breggin. *New Scientist*, 1972, **55**, 188–90.

Miller, H, Reflections in a hospital—then and now. *Encounter*, 1972.

Miller, H, Then and now. *World Medicine*, April 1972.

Miller, H G, *Medicine and Society*. London, Oxford University Press, 1973.

Miller, H, Neurological complications of general surgery, in *Proceedings of the 10th International Congress of Neurology*, Amsterdam, Excerpta Medica, 1973.

Bibliography of H G Miller

Miller, H, The politics of medical research in the US. *Minerva*, 1973, **11**, (No 4), 642–7.

Miller, H, Priorities in medicine. *Royal Society of Arts Journal*, 1973, **121**, 157–166.

Miller, H, Two great contemporaries. *World Medicine*, 1974, **9**, (27), 15–20.

Miller, H, Viewpoint—the charm of neurology. *British Clinical Journal*, 1974, 435–7.

Miller, H, Half century of medical research. *Minerva*, 1975, **13**, 1.

Miller, H, and Hall, R Ed, *Modern Medical Treatment*, 2nd edn. Oxford, Blackwell, 1975.

In addition to the above, Henry Miller wrote regularly for the
Listener and *Encounter*.

'Medicine and Society' a monograph.